St. Louis Community College

Library

5801 Wilson Avenue
St. Louis, Missouri 63110

Legacy of
Fear

Recent Titles in
Grass Roots Perspectives in American History
Series Editor: David P. Thelen

Soldiers and Society: The Effects of Military Service and War on American Life
Peter Karsten

Grass Roots Politics: Parties, Issues, and Voters, 1854-1983
Richard J. Jensen

Chains of Fear: American Race Relations Since Reconstruction
Michael J. Cassity

Legacy of Fear

AMERICAN RACE RELATIONS TO 1900

Michael J. Cassity

Grass Roots Perspectives in American History, Number 4

GREENWOOD PRESS
WESTPORT, CONNECTICUT • LONDON, ENGLAND

Library of Congress Cataloging in Publication Data

Cassity, Michael J.
  Legacy of fear.

  (Grass roots perspectives in American history,
ISSN 0148-771X ; no. 4)
  Includes index.
    1. United States—Race relations.   2. Afro-Americans—
History.   I. Title.   II. Series.
E185.C374   1985   305.8′96073   84-8981
ISBN 0-313-24553-3 (lib. bdg.)

Library of Congress Catalog Card Number: 84-8981
ISBN: 0-313-24553-3
ISSN: 0148-771X

First published in 1985

Greenwood Press
A division of Congressional Information Service, Inc.
88 Post Road West
Westport, Connecticut 06881

Printed in the United States of America

10 9 8 7 6 5 4 3 2 1

Material in Chapter 39 appeared in Michael J. Cassity, "Slaves, Families, and 'Living
Space': A Note on Evidence and Historical Context," *Southern Studies*, 17 (Summer 1978),
and is reprinted with permission of the editor.

For Rebecca Rose Cassity
and Jessica Mariah Cassity

Contents

Acknowledgments

As is altogether appropriate upon the completion of a project such as this, one feels small. The influence, the assistance, the encouragement and support, and the direction provided by so many others, directly and indirectly, has come so generously that perhaps all that remains of my own contribution lies in the errors of fact and judgment. This, and a little of what is good in these pages, I claim as my own.

David P. Thelen provided his usual incisive and penetrating criticism and pointed commentary on the specific documents and arguments I presented; he also demonstrated a persistent attitude of encouragement and indulgence at the right times. I am grateful that he is a friend as well as a critic. Numan V. Bartley also read through the entire manuscript, found much to disagree with, and, like Thelen, tried to save me from the error of my ways in style and substance. His numerous suggestions and questions provided me significant opportunity to improve my work. This is not the first time that I have benefited from these two individuals. I hope to continue to do so.

I am happy to acknowledge other debts as well. Lynn Questel provided enormous assistance in the seemingly endless task of locating and gathering important source materials. The late John C. Rainbolt, some time back now, taught me by his own example ways to extract the maximum meaning from any particular bit of evidence by seeking a broader historical context. Danney G. Goble, as true a friend as could ever be hoped for, inspired some of my interpretations of specific documents and events although he will be quick to deny this.

Gilbert C. Fite, Paul C. Nagel, and Lester D. Stephens in their successive terms as department head in the University of Georgia not only tolerated but also actively encouraged my efforts in this study through the supportive allocation of resources and time. The secretaries in the history department who shared the burden of typing the manuscript proved each one to be efficient and good humored in the performance of their task. I also want to thank that large group of individuals who allowed me to use material that they had written or that they control and whom I have acknowledged at the appropriate points in the collection of documents and those many people on the staffs of various libraries and research collections who provided so much help in my quest for source material.

My parents, Ralph O. Cassity and Elizabeth L. Cassity, and my brother Joe Cassity, all understand the debt I owe them; they also understand that it is a debt that can never be repayed. I hope that the scars left by my work on this project in the growth of my daughters Rebecca Rose and Jessica Mariah can in sufficient time heal. As always, my wife Constance helped me gain perspective not only on the past but on the present. I hope I have kept that perspective and that I will not lose it. That is, after all, what it is all about.

Introduction

The beginning point for this inquiry into the origins of modern American race relations is a plain question: Why have Americans often feared that greater freedom for others necessarily implies a loss for themselves? At its broadest this is obviously not a question confined to relations between black and white Americans, or between rich and poor, or between male and female. It is a question that reaches into a variety of relationships of authority, public policy, and popular sentiment. Yet it is a question of particular relevance to the study of American race relations since the rationale for racial subjugation has often involved an answer, however crudely put, to precisely this question, and since alternative visions of society seeking the realization of justice, equality, and freedom, and the elimination of racial discrimination must confront that dilemma. It is also a question that requires more than a consideration of the words of particular spokesmen, whether self-appointed or proclaimed by "society," and more than a consideration of the problem of justice framed in the terms of modern jurisprudence. Thus stated, the problem involves two particular factors: (1) a perception of the American people, black and white, as agents of history often independent of the courses urged upon them by their leaders in the shaping of American race relations; and (2) a historical awareness in which the opportunities, limitations, aspirations, frustrations, and hopes and fears of the American people are continually transformed and are not assumed to be themselves unchanging phenomena through the centuries. Put quite another way, this is an effort to explore the social and historical context of particular events in the lives of the American people that either shaped the course of development of American race relations or that reveal the subtle forces at work and how people managed to cope with them on their own terms.

Any effort to explore American race relations faces a variety of problems of focus, theory, evidence, and perspective that can each serve to illuminate the issue at hand or to make the interpretations that much more tentative. One particular obstacle is the tendency to separate race relations from other social relationships with the consequence being all too often a distortion of focus and a neglect of active forces shaping those relationships. By integrating the pattern of race relations into the larger structure of life that gives them their particular forms and logic, however, it is possible to avoid some of the isolation of the issue into a narrow struggle between the races, between racial subordination and equality—the kind of framework that lends itself more to moralizing than to understanding. A major goal of this study is to suggest some ways in which American race relations emerged from certain patterns of life and social organization and how those patterns are related to the larger society.

If this quest for social context is to be useful, it must be something more than a colorful backdrop against which can be seen significant developments. In this study that social context is sought in the effort to locate the material social environment and the particular traditions and legacies of the past which together inform and restrict the behavior of individuals. In concrete terms this effort to locate actions in their appropriate contexts usually involves the examination of experiences of identifiable people in the circumstances in which they were lived by those people. People—black and white—are placed in circumstances which they have not always chosen, are confronted by forces not of their own making, and are faced with the day-to-day demands of everyday life, demands that are themselves intimately related to the larger society. It is an effort to understand the material forces shaping the choices available to people and the ever growing and changing relationships of race and class and community—indeed, of love and deference and freedom.[1]

By considering the changing pattern of social organization, that social context also becomes a historical context. Of special importance in the effort below to identify this historical context is the concept of the market as a set of changing social relationships. It is the market that permits a focus on the kinds of relationships that gravitate around a scarcity consciousness and competitiveness that loom large in the consideration of loss and gain in questions of equality and subordination. What is so valuable about this notion, though, is not its application to the question as an economic formula in the production and distribution of goods but its larger implications as a framework and reference point for the organization of society. Medieval society and even to some extent early American society tended to restrict the acquisitive passions of man through devices such as the just wage, just price, and usury laws, and also through paternalistic provision for community needs through some of the same mercantilist arrangements. The erosion of those controls and the consequent liberation of individual energy through the contract, the corporation, and individualistic conceptions of rights, especially in the nineteenth century, unleashed or propelled into society exactly those same acquisitive passions.[2] The reverberations of the change were enormous as the structure of society altered from the proclaimed object of protection of the commonwealth to that of individual freedom. The organizing principles of society were revolutionized and in this change the whole realm of social relations was transformed. Race relations was but one of many mores caught up in the transformation of a pre-market society to a society dominated by the market and industrial patterns of organization. The implications in terms of work processes, the distribution of rewards, the materialistic domination of values and priorities, individual relationships, the fate of pre-market cultures, the competition for pride, dignity, and self-respect, dominate the relationships between the races as well as challenge whole ways of life.

Despite this emphasis on social context in the search for meanings of particular events or actions and despite the emphasis on the market as a historical force shaping that social context there is no intention here of ascribing the course of race relations in America to a deterministic, inevitable pattern of change. Indeed, one basic theme of this presentation is exactly the opposite: people, in active relationship with their environments, have made conscious decisions, consequences with which we now live. Just as those decisions were made by men and women, so too can men and women move the relationships of their society today in the directions they most want. To view the problem otherwise is to accept a view of man as a powerless captive of external forces, not to attribute to him the ability of free-will in transcending the forces shaping his society. In 1943, Francis Downing explored the problem of racial violence in Detroit and confronted exactly that dilemma of origins and also the way in which authorities continually sidestepped the question of origins and responsibility. In that assessment Downing offered this reminder: "Despite some of our alleged philosophers, there are still causes for things. And results are still their fruits." And that is exactly the issue involved in the search for the origins of American race relations.

The origins of slavery and black subjugation in America lie in the social revolution transforming Europe in the sixteenth and seventeenth centuries. As revolutions go, it was a slow one. But by the sixteenth century it was clear that European states were becoming national, expansionistic entities embarking on competitive courses at once religious, commercial, and political. Within one of these countries, England, that revolution had produced specific social tensions that would have far reaching results. The very fabric of society in England was being questioned and even altered at significant points. In a process that might reasonably be equated with the larger rise of liberal individualism that would become especially vivid in the seventeenth and eighteenth centuries, England's economy was making the adjustment from a medieval organization to a market-dominated, even industrial orientation.[3] Markets and commerce dictated the rise of urban areas, the shifts in population, alterations in transportation, the rise of independent power bases for a business community and a commercial view of the proper orientation of the state, and in some degree transformed the individual from a political subject to a citizen and from a laborer on the manor and user of the village common to a man competing for the right to survive. The tension emerged at each point of change. As R. H. Tawney observed nearly a half-century ago, the mercantilism of the time was changed in the 1640s from government impositions on business to business policies imposed on the government. Where mercantilism had served to protect the commonwealth, the market economy operated to assist those already with power in the plundering of the commonwealth. With the creation of a market in wool the village common was enclosed and the villagers forced off. With the beheading of a king came the increased power of the merchant class in Parliament. Individualism instead of the community governing the conduct of commerce may have had a liberating effect; it also generated enormous tensions in society. To some the fate of a society beset by those tensions and changes punctuated by revolution in political structure appeared most uncertain and could even hinge on the necessity of expansion, an expansion that could minimize the pains of change and even export the social problems of England.

When ships from England reached Africa as part of the expansionist impulse, the voyagers beheld a people whose fate would ultimately be directed by these problems. The black man in Africa represented a new sort of phenomenon for those pale and pristine English travelers.[4] The very color of these people seemed to be a self-fulfilling prophecy. In England color had traditionally held certain values and connotations with white being the pinnacle in a chain of color symbolism. On the other hand black lay at the bottom of the same chain. Black signified, as the *Oxford English Dictionary* notes (in Document 1), "having dark or deadly purposes, malignant; pertaining to or involving death, deadly; baneful, disastrous, sinister. . . . Foul, iniquitous, atrocious, horribly wicked. . . ." In sharp contrast with this was the color of white which connoted "morally or spiritually pure or stainless; spotless, innocent. . . . Free from malignity or evil intent; innocent, harmless, esp. as opp. to something characterized as '*black.*' " The stigma of color enlarged as some attempted to explain the dark pigmentation of the Africans by reference to the vague but symbolically potent scriptural account of the curse of Ham by his father Noah when the son looked upon his father's nakedness. While the curse was to be a "servant of servants," the name

Ham, which was only later supplied to the text, meant "dark" and "hot." Regardless of the perspective, most of the English explanations of the pigmentation implied a fated inferiority, baseness, or servility for these black people.

As if those conceptions were not sufficient to mark the black man as a different and lesser being, the qualities that most impressed the English who came into early contact with Africans seemed to confirm the judgment of inferiority: given the strange environment in which they were encountered, they sometimes appeared to be beasts, or odd linkages between humanity and the other creatures of the jungle. Such a view, of course, could have dominated characterizations of black culture from only the most jaundiced perspective. With some elaborate hierarchically organized societies, the African nations often even resembled European monarchies. No matter that the large nations and small tribes had their own social organizations, their own religions, and their own histories, they were sufficiently different that Europeans could justify the shift in their trade from pepper, gold, and ivory to slaves. Africans did not follow the path of Christianity, their association with the wild animals of the jungle implied a bestiality or savagery, the climate and apparent anatomical differences suggested a libidinous creature far from civilized, they sometimes practiced polygyny, and some of these nations themselves practiced slavery—if of a dramatically different kind than that which would grow in the New World in the next two centuries—all this facilitated the beginnings of the slave trade.

As England expanded to permanent colonies in America in the seventeenth century, the forces of labor demand and labor supply joined in the Atlantic. Labor need was complex and did not in itself require African slavery for a solution. Given the erosion of traditional deference and obedience of servants toward their masters in the social revolution of the seventeenth century, the enslavement of black people became a significant alternative to other forms of labor. And given the persistence of traditional work habits and economic views among those sent to turn a profit in the colonies through disciplined productivity, the tension between servants and masters and the consequent social unrest made African slavery that much more attractive to those seeking productive labor *and* social stability.

The problem was evident as early as the initial settlements at Jamestown. The labor shortage at Jamestown, as Edmund Morgan has shown, was not a shortage of people to do the work there.[5] The shortage was of the labor those people were willing to expend. As dismal as the consequences of the refusal to work were—catastrophic and fatal starvation being but the most dramatic reward—the new settlers abidingly refused to make the necessary sacrifices. As Morgan explained, the new settlers were English to the marrow; they carried with them across the

Atlantic the attitudes toward, and habits of, work characteristic of England in the sixteenth and seventeenth centuries. The productive discipline of modern industrial society, or even of the devoted Puritan zealots to the north, simply was not there and all the logic of famine and starvation could not alter the premium placed on leisure and slow paced work. If ever a scarcity consciousness might appear to be a natural assumption it was in Virginia in the seventeenth century. But the opposing qualities were understandable enough. The structure of work and society that characterized pre-market societies for centuries represented barriers to production that would have to be overcome, despite the pain involved and the cultural sacrifices required, for the investment to produce a profit. That sacrifice of culture for economic growth would remain one of the central factors shaping American race relations for more than three and a half centuries.

The immediate solution to the labor shortage was indentured servitude. The terms of the indenture emphasized servitude more than limited duration. The prime requisite of the indenture proved to be obedience for the servant rather than the customary obligations of the master of a craft, whose obligations to instruct and attend to the needs of his servant shaped traditional articles of indenture. Indeed, indentured servitude created as many problems as it solved. It remained inefficient because of work habits and because of the period necessary to train a worker which often proved to dominate a sizable portion of the indenture. After his liberation from the terms of servitude the freeman would most likely work for himself rather than for another, a factor which could even create an additional demand and competition for servants. Many indentured servants, moreover, came as convicts sent to the colonies as an alternative to the gallows or were captured and "spirited" away from England and often proved to be less than model workers (Documents 3, 4, and 5). In fact, just as the term servant was broadly applied to mean anyone who worked for an employer for wages, so too did most servants in England tend to be increasingly "unruly" and suspicious of authority (see the admonitions against this independence of mind in Document 2).[6] This general framework for the supply of labor to the colonies held serious limitations.

The initial cultivation of tobacco as a promising marketable crop between 1612 and 1614 only emphasized the need for a reliable source of manageable labor. The first Africans that arrived in 1619 fit this labor need within the general labor framework already established. It was only through a vague and clouded process that their treatment and status became distinct from those of white servants. But the changes came nonetheless. Indentures were sometimes made for longer terms than for whites, apparently because of the racial distinctions; life servitude became a possibility for black servants; and the servant status was increasingly one to be passed on to succeeding generations of blacks (Document 6).

By the middle of the seventeenth century the labor force consisted of people from a wide variety of backgrounds. The general common denominator, however, was a dissatisfaction with their circumstances. Some who found themselves caught up in a system of what may in fact have been white slavery, especially those who had been kidnapped from their homes in England, experienced a voyage and treatment upon reaching Virginia that bore a marked similarity to the experiences of blacks. The blacks themselves came in utter subjection to force with severities of treatment tempered only by consideration for their value as investments as seasoned labor. Even the willing immigrants came less than voluntarily since often, as Christopher Hill has suggested, they were the victims of the enclosures, prepared to risk what little they had for the hope of free land.[7] In any event the conditions of indenture were closely calculated to benefit the employer rather than the servant and to get maximum work before the termination of the contract. Even freemen found disappointment and aggravation at every hand. Prime land had already been occupied and the dire circumstances of life in Virginia contrasted dramatically with the promotional claims for the land as a cornucopia. Discontent was abroad in the land.[8]

In addition to the onerous terms of labor, those fundamental forces at work reshaping English society and relationships, at home and in the colonies, made the questioning of traditional paternalistic and servile relationships legitimate and proper. If a people might behead their king, might also a worker question his master? In the discontent and protest and questioning that ensued in the colonies those groups of people viewed by the gentry as the "giddy multitude" found common cause. Timothy Breen, the closest student of that discontent, has observed that this commonality and mutual support does not necessarily demonstrate the absence of racial animosity or hostility among the working segment of the population, but it does show at a minimum the ability of the social (or economic) issue to transcend or overpower that racial separation. In case after case of blacks and whites running away from their masters together the potential of the tumultuous laborers appeared as a threat. Breen has chronicled other cases from the early 1660s of conspiracies among indentured laborers to overthrow their masters and secure their freedom, conspiracies that generated deep fears amongst the ruling elite of Virginia. The threat of insurrection by these workers culminated in the partially successful revolt led by Nathaniel Bacon in 1676 in which blacks and whites joined together in challenging the established authorities (Document 13). The interracial cooperation evident in this movement and in preceding efforts indicates the essential importance of some notion of class cooperation as opposed to racial competition.

Equally important was the pervasive fear among Virginia's elite that such a coalition of slaves, servants, and others could topple the proper authorities, a fear which did not fade until appropriate measures had been taken to change the circumstances of labor in the colony and to divide along racial lines those most disposed to threaten the power structure.

The tension and social hostility between classes began to ebb after the last of the disruptions around 1682. With an improvement in tobacco prices, the poor freemen found better circumstances than they had seen since arriving in Virginia and were even able to expand their operations in some instances. The availability of credit and the removal of Indians from western land permitted expansion and better times. The indentured servants changed in their nature after 1682, coming much less frequently under duress, and not as punishment, and at any rate in declining numbers. The black population, however, increased as England began to ship blacks directly from Africa instead of to the colonies by way of the Barbados, a trip that significantly altered the composition of the black population. Not having the exposure of "seasoning" to acquaint them with the English system, arriving after a brush with death that claimed many of their fellow captives in the trip across the Atlantic, unable to speak a word of English, it is not surprising, as Timothy Breen has phrased it, that "no white servant in this period, no matter how poor, how bitter or badly treated, could identify with these frightened Africans." Their circumstances of origin, of culture, of transportation, and finally of work now made them completely alien to Virginia's white servants and masters and color provided the central identifying characteristic. Increasingly the social distinction of color replaced that of work.[9] The southern colonies entered a new period of stability that was both caused by and reflective of this change in society. That stability came at the expense of black people, a phenomenon that would last for centuries.

In reflecting on the developments of the seventeenth century that culminated in the creation of the institution of slavery, a curious pattern appears. In a process that could well be taken to be that of the liberation of the individual from ancient restraints and the presentation of new opportunities, the traditional or status oriented society (to use C. B. Macpherson's conceptualization) eroded under the weight of a new individualist orientation. Where status and reward and role in society had all been traditionally ordained by society's rules emphasizing heredity and lineage, the promise increasingly was that status, reward, and role would be determined by an individual's talent and ability and effort. The irony that provides perspective on this development is that it could come to the limited extent that it did (for the liberation could even at best be considered to be the narrow one of freedom from traditional protections as well as restraints and too often a liberation to the market as a commodity as in the case of those villagers who moved to town or to the New World because of the enclosures) only with the subjugation of an entire group of people on the basis of their color. There is yet a further irony though: this rise of liberal individualism and the rise of the market had the effect of creating a society in Virginia and the other Southern colonies that strikingly resembled a feudal pattern of organization, where work, reward, and hopes followed the lines of birth and where obligations of one to another were defined by born position. The alternative to this form of social organization can be found in the testimony of action presented by those at the bottom of society in the years before 1682. To create another kind of system that did not know slavery would have required the established authorities to respond to need instead of power and to recognize other values than economic productivity as paramount.

The economic dimensions of the institution of slavery were obvious. Just as slavery originated in part to meet a specific economic need, its importance as the central component of a system of production would continue until its demise. In many ways it could be regarded as a distinctive system of production in a larger market set of economic arrangements. But that sort of focus, even with its capacity for capturing some of the elements of exploitation in economic terms, remains perhaps too narrow to capture effectively the social contours of the institution of slavery and to permit an appreciation of the tensions and patterns of life it overshadowed. Despite its economic significance slavery also had definite social origins and would bear important social consequences for the duration of the institution and after.

Slavery's social importance begins with its pivotal role in what amounted to a pre-market set of social relationships. As carefully developed by C. B. Macpherson, the notion of such a pre-market or status society revolves around the relationship between work and authority.[10] In slavery, as in the traditional or status society, a group of people perform work because they are so fated at birth; they are simply born into the class of workers. They do not enter the work relationship through any kind of bargaining process nor are they able to bargain with their employers over their rewards or conditions of work. As Macpherson notes, "There may be a market in slaves, but a market in slaves comprises only an exchange relation between masters, not between slave and master, and is therefore not a market relation between all the persons concerned." The absence of a market as a device for determining rewards or social role means that that function is assumed in an authoritarian way by custom, society, or the ruling class. Compared with the operation of the market in other and later societies as a liberating force for the individual in determining the allocation of work responsibilities and rewards, the authoritative nature of the pre-market, slave society is underscored. By the same token the allocation of status and responsibility falls also on the ruling elite. While the slave in such a society has the obligation to obey the master and to attend to him, so too does the master hold certain paternalistic obligations toward his wards which date back into feudal times. And it is that quality of mutual obligation that would be the defining and distinguishing element of this form of social organization: the assumed relations between one and another would tend much more closely to be those of obligation rather than right or acquisitiveness. The parallel with feudal organization would never be exact and there would always be major shortcomings. Yet the institution could not exist without those feudal pretenses sufficiently internalized to make them believable to others.

The structure of authority in the slave South may not have been that of an aristocracy revived from feudal times, but often it appeared to be next of kin.[11] In terms of privileges and power it was a system that revered certain families in the life of the community, bestowed upon them honor, and exacted from them obligations in terms of government and economy. In a decentralized form of government where the county loomed as the most relevant political unit, an oligarchy of planters usually prevailed for long periods both in the administrative matters of the county and in the dispensation of justice. In such instances economic power fused with political power and social ranking to create the aura of aristocracy and oligarchy, to whom the lesser whites might turn for largesse or vengeance and to whom blacks owed fealty. This system, moreover, penetrated all social relations with private and privileged systems of education that reinforced the training of the gentry with attitudes of noblesse oblige and proper values, with the practice of the code duello stressing honor and pride above all else, with the restriction of womanhood to a narrow, sheltered, and confined sphere in keeping with a closed society, with the popularization of romantic literature harking back to more gallant times of feudal England and indeed with the effort in the 1850s to emulate those feudal practices. In many ways this was all a matter of pretense rather than reality and perhaps in the case of the jousting tournaments a consciously devised pretense mobilized to justify a closed society and to accentuate the qualities distinguishing that society from alternative forms. It would distort the picture to include the aristocracy of eighteenth century Virginia, the days of Jefferson and Washington, in the same society that Clement Eaton described as a closed society in the period shortly before the Civil War. Part of the difference obviously lies in the physical distinction between a tidewater aristocracy and a cotton and slavery based society. But perhaps equal significance should be attached to the historical developments that propelled Southerners before the Civil War to emphasize the importance of slavery to a larger way of life that they conceived to be almost aristocratic in its values and ethos.

At the core of those developments that altered the nature of American society lay the emergence of the market. As in England, so too in the colonies in the eighteenth century: the notion of the market as a system for the determination of rewards and work reached further and further into economic and social arrangements. It did so not without resistance. Periodic bread riots protested the price of bread climbing in response to fluctuating harvests and markets in support of traditional concepts of just prices and just wages to the activities of revolutionary committees attempted to thwart profiteering through taking advantage of wartime scarcities. Opposed or accepted, market economics were spreading through the colonies. Indeed, the revolution with its commitment to the rights of man gave the notion a boost in a major way that could not help but reshape social arrangements. To observe either the Declaration of Independence or the Bill of Rights is to be reminded of the highly individualistic logic of the revolutionaries, even if that logic included profound assumptions and objectives about the community of man and the natural harmony of social relations in a free society. But the rights of man became not just a slogan for unity; the idea of individual liberty became to some degree the organizing principle of a nation. As such it could conform in a general manner with the idea of the market as a liberating force. Indeed, Adam Smith's 1776 tract, *The Wealth of Nations*, neatly fused the idea of such a market with the protection of the public through competition. The determination of an individual's just desserts and fate in society, the logic ran, should derive from that person's ability and resources. What Bernard Bailyn has termed the contagious effect of this revolutionary rhetoric can easily be seen in the area of race relations.[12] The enslavement of men by other men proved anathema to the revolutionary spirit. In some instances this denial of opportunity and liberty was actually removed in the name of the revolution. Perhaps in more instances those who prospered from the toil of their slaves dredged deeper into Lockean forms of casuistry to justify the historical oppression of their minions or escalated their racial theories the better to correspond with slavery. Only one thing was certain. As early as the revolution it was obvious that the freedom of man, regardless of how conceived, would be a major issue for the new nation.

At its most literal the debate began, continued, and remained in the province of the elites of the nation. In the halls of Congress and in the national press, not to mention the less public expressions emanating from Southern social centers, the leaders of the country and its regions posed what they figured to be the central questions regarding the institution of slavery and its alternative. That discussion of the issue managed to intensify in a counterproductive fashion the significance of slavery in the eyes of both defenders and abolitionists, making it for Southern spokesmen the central and honorable institution of a different way of life and for Northern abolitionists the central flaw of the republic. At the same time it revealed assumptions about the nature of the institution and alternative perspectives about the proper organization of society. The pre-eminent pattern of social change in the North, with its expanding internal improvements, commercial growth, and legal innovations in market relationships through the contract, the corporation, and the commoditization of land can be aptly characterized by James Willard Hurst's notion of "The Release of Energy."[13] The emergent order associated with the marketplace rested on an assumption that human nature is basically creative and to be fulfilled must have the broadest possible opportunity for the release of that creative energy. Indeed, the incentives of the market, profit and poverty, seemed especially appropriate to elicit from each individual his fullest endeavor. And slavery, in the eyes of both its opponents and adherents, denied exactly that liberty and those incentives. Thus "the conviction that slavery had proved to be a system which did not fulfill the proper property function of generating a constantly expanding reach of human creative power,"[14] not only brought some to an abolitionist perspective but even helped justify the confiscation of property in slaves, property in other respects being virtually sacred.

Such denial of liberty seemed to others the justifying quality of slavery. George Fitzhugh, perhaps the most articulate of these spokesmen, turned his defense of slavery into an attack on the freedom of the marketplace arguing that its chief advantage was to free those who benefited from the system as owners from their responsibility toward those who labored in it. By reducing those responsibilities between worker and employer to the cash nexus of the market, to be determined by the forces of competition in the market, the social responsibilities of slave and master to each other had been eliminated.[15] Somewhere in such a narrowed debate the dignity of man and the real breadth of human potential and freedom became lost or pushed aside as the choice offered up was essentially a choice of masters and repressive systems.

The repressive nature of the market, seen by blacks later upon emancipation, was already evident in the urgings made upon freedmen by their abolitionist friends to restrain themselves once that they were free, and in fact to repudiate in the name of productivity and as a credit to the race central elements of the culture that blacks had perpetuated. Moreover it was already abundantly clear that that freedom, its market conceptualization aside, was to be sharply circumscribed by segregation.

The repression generated by slavery, at first obvious, quickly becomes more subtle. A litany of terrors associated with human bondage stands at the forefront in the consideration. Those terrors remain, as they were then, the most visible forms of repression in slavery. But curiously, and in a way that seems to confirm the possible counterproductivity of all social forces, the cultural forms of repression seem to have been most effective in the white population. Restraining slaves was one thing; restraining masters was quite another.

In the cultural relations between the white and black worlds under slavery, various forms of antagonism and reciprocity emerge that produce a complex and ambiguous picture of the social relations fostered by slavery. To begin with, as Eugene Genovese has eloquently noted, even under the most systematic efforts at paternalism, the slaves managed to retain for themselves an ample "living space" wherein they determined and expressed values and relationships of their own making, of their own heritage, at their own initiative. Evidence of this can be seen in the slaves' strikingly different religious beliefs and practices (Documents 40-45) and coherent family structure through generations. The preservation of family legacies and names was much more common (see Documents 35-37) than suggested by slaveholding elites and abolitionists who informed the world that slaves were either not permitted to maintain families or were unable or not inclined to do so. Slavery limited the breadth of this "living space," but it never managed to remove it. Apart from the collective manifestations of religion and family, various black responses to masters that might be characterized as obsequious, dull, or uninspired often proved to be a charade behind which marched calculating militance and resistance. With the conflicting demands of humanity and subservience slavery could not be anything but ambiguous. One thing, however, remains clear: black autonomy and initiative remained alive, flexible, and proud.[16]

In striking contrast to that black autonomy and freedom of action within the confines of the slaves' "living space," however, is the vast dependence of many whites upon blacks for their own dignity and cultural definition. The promulgation of racism, a set of attitudes and stereotypes that attributed to blacks qualities opposite those presumably possessed by whites, can in part be traced to the collective fears, yearnings, and need for justification of the system by white owners. The "licensed" nature of black culture in slavery suggests this. One white view of black people revolved around their uncivilized habits, habits that marked them as inferior to the more civilized white race. They were considered notoriously lazy, promiscuous, heathenish and superstitious in religion, irresponsible, completely immoral, and anything else that suggested a lack of discipline. These accusations occasionally had a germ of truth, though one far different from that assumed when applied as a pejorative. Most workers were utilized in an agricultural system of production where the rhythms of season and sun dictated the work pace and the distribution of the tasks during periods of time; the consequent work pace would be irregular. The slaves might slack on a dull, plodding task or conversely take substantial enthusiasm to a challenging and fulfilling obligation (as in Document 22). What W.E.B. Du Bois would term, after considering the cultural legacies employed, a Black Work Ethic, would appear from a perspective that valued discipline most of all as laziness. Perhaps the real point of comparison lay not so much with the white counterparts of those blacks in bondage but in the industrializing centers of the Northeast where the discipline of the clock began to do more than measure the time spent; it actually paced the work itself.[17]

That slaves might be sexually promiscuous was much discussed and much contemplated. Indeed it seems to have had a certain appeal to white observers. The appeal could even be so great that the slaves could often be clothed in the scantiest costumes in the field or in the big house without so much as a blush from the most genteel members of the established white society. Or it could even be so great that white masters would be attracted to their black slaves in covertly or overtly sexual ways. At the very minimum, as Dr. Francis Le Jau expressed it in 1708, black promiscuity was "tollerated or at least Connived at by us under a pretence of Impossibility" to alter (see Documents 24, 27-31). Indeed, Berquin-Duvallon a century later in New Orleans found the mulatto women there to be more faithful to their husbands than the white men who savored their caresses were to their wives (Document 25). The preoccupation with the sexuality of this "uncivilized" people reflects more of a yearning than a serious disgust.[18]

Perhaps what was ultimately involved in the generation of these racist views more than anything else was the projection onto black people of the yearnings and desires repressed by white society. The hate that accompanied those views stemmed from the fear that the masters were just like those they held in bondage—which of course they were. Thus whites might pursue several courses: one was an overweening artificiality and incredible restraint exercised in even the most informal of social functions (Document 30), provoking comment by "civilized" Northerners. The ultimate product of that effort to create a civilization that would be a counterpoint to the culture of the blacks was the grace and style and pretension romanticized time and again for future generations as the civilization of ante-bellum life that took its noble stand. Another course, both in the North and the South, would be the tolerance or encouragement of slave behavior that conflicted so stridently with their own vaunted code precisely because it offered such a contrast. The paradox glares: this system of social control served mainly to restrain white people and to contribute to the development of a separate black culture by assuming and hoping that blacks would never completely assimilate the values and disciplines that separated the races. In the North some freedmen were learning that even as much as they might imbibe those values, the barrier of segregation emerged. The question for the future would involve not just the location of power in society when this system of social control collapsed but the very nature of society and the nature of freedom. The irony is that the emancipation of the slaves liberated white Americans from restraints. The tragedy is that an opportunity for a genuine freedom for white and black alike would pass by unfulfilled.

The emancipation of the slaves did not automatically mean the end of oppression. Social and racial tensions persisted though often greatly altered in form. The institutional and cultural manifestations of the new forms of bondage and subjugation had been anticipated earlier by friends and antagonists of slavery both, who predicted: The new freedom to be experienced would be essentially a market-bound conception that valued not the creative potential or free individualistic nature of man but instead stressed the individual's responsibility for his own fate. This notion of self-reliance in other contexts could be benign; it could even be noble if carried logically forward to complete independence. But in the context of a society where individuals were free to sell their labor as a commodity and in which access to land was limited to those who had sufficient resources that they did not need to sell their labor as a commodity, freedmen would be dependent first on a market for their labor and second on those who had land. This could mean, as one planter put it, the bleak freedom to starve (Document 58).

Even before the end of the Civil War the military authorities and the friends of the freedmen in areas dominated by Union forces anticipated the contours of the social and economic revolution about to proceed. With the necessity of the wage stimulus, the sanctity of the contract, the obligation to work for survival (indeed the notion that idleness is a crime), and the government as the supervising and enforcing agent of the new work relationships all in mind, it was then obvious that freedom, the freedom of the marketplace, came not as a vast release from oppression but as an alternative system of restraints and that in fact the new work relationship was to be reduced to that of a wage relationship instead of part of a broader traditional social system of obligations and responsibilities.[19]

At the same time that this new society based upon the market system of relations was emerging, it also became obvious that many of the social implications of slavery would be in doubt with the demise of that core institution. Under slavery, even if a black be among those who were free, there could be no doubt about his social position since caste and race had long ago merged to form permanent barriers and privileges. Perhaps what was so alarming to many whites in this transition was not that they would now be competing with blacks for limited economic rewards, but that the market pattern of relationships itself threatened old verities. The central assumed truth was the superiority of white people to blacks. Thus, as in Document 56, when racial violence erupted it would often be as a pogrom to prove this point, possibly to the blacks but more likely to the whites themselves. In this sense, what was being suppressed was not so much the black population of Memphis and other communities who happened to be the convenient and unfortunate victims of it all, but the assumptions, hopes, and theoretical promises of the market.[20]

The promises of this market-conceived freedom demanded for their fulfillment, paradoxically, the repudiation of other forms of freedom and the acceptance of the social and psychological restraints appropriate to the development of a self-discipline and calculating acquisitiveness. Hence the freedmen were urged by their friends not to be "too free" (Document 57), to produce for the market instead of for subsistence, to cultivate habits of sobriety and productivity and the values of possessive individualism, and to forsake their own culture (or, as it appeared to the well-meaning Northern missionaries to the freedmen, their *lack* of culture, so different was it from their own) for something more civilized and reserved.[21] The impact of this proselytizing is difficult to calculate. Some would say, in an effort to bolster their racial views, that it had no impact and that the black population remained uncivilized and perhaps proved the difficulty (or, again, the impossibility) of improving the race. Others, like the missionaries themselves, while experiencing frustrations remained optimistic. As for the blacks themselves, the impact came mainly in the form of a tension between two cultures, one having its origins in the relationships of the market, the other its origins in pre-market habits and relations, dating back to Africa. The tension was compounded by the fact that whatever cultural patterns blacks adopted white people on one side or the other might interpret as confirming hidden fears about the nature of the Negro or about themselves. At a minimum, the acculturation effort seems to have succeeded largely in forcing black culture into less outward and visible forms, even to the point of denied existence (as in Document 61).

This would be the future for blacks: caught between the grinding and opposing forces in the market and the resistance to that market. In economics the market reshaped the institutions of the South. The supply of black labor and the demand for that labor by landowning planters created a system of sharecropping which amounted to a form of wage labor with the wage being paid in this capital-scarce region in the form of a share of the crop at the end of the year, and then a system of tenancy dominated by the crop lien, a system more individualized but with the same effect in terms of bondage to the land.[22] In both systems continual indebtedness replaced the chains of slavery. But with the crop-lien system of tenancy even the landlord found his power slipping away, not to his tenants, but to his source of capital, usually a local merchant or banker with the ultimate source resting in the Northern banks and industries. As power and status waned, resistance increased. In the by now characteristic pattern of American race relations, that problem would seldom be challenged directly in political and economic terms. The penetration of the market with its blessings going to those with the greatest resources spurred negative reactions against the most visible beneficiaries of this system—those black people who no longer bore the chains of slavery and who, during Reconstruction at least, attempted to participate in the political process. Thus the disfranchisement of blacks by violence (as in Document 66), by intimidation (as in Document 67), and a more general subjugation of blacks who only sought to vote or even merely sought to get by in normal ways during the course of a day or who encountered whites seeking a victim proceeded sometimes under the guise of the Ku Klux Klan or other clandestine organizations and sometimes without formal direction. The combination of economic pressures and social coercion meant, of course, the complete return to a caste system—a return to a pre-market social arrangement without in the process dividing along class lines, a prospect that would have meant poor white and black against the white planter class or, increasingly, against the merchant and business class. This development stifled people who shared the same problems and who were equally resistant to the ravages of the market. A form of stability arose at the expense of those black and white people who were already the victims of the system.

The impulse toward segregation could obviously fit into this pattern of resistance to the potentially atomizing and individualizing force of the market. Indeed, such often appears to have been the case in the early instances of segregation in the free North during the days of slavery. The social chasm during slavery could be universally assumed despite the closest contact between masters and slaves, even to the extent of slave and mistress sharing the same sleeping quarters (as in Document 48), but in a society where that chasm could not be assumed it had to be created to avoid the possibility of assumptions of equality becoming too widespread. These impulses surfaced in the South on an irregular and uneven basis in private policy and practice and gradually by law as well.

Two perspectives are especially revealing in this growth of Jim Crow society. One involves the flexibility of the system, a flexibility that sometimes made it possible for blacks to cross the white barrier (as in Document 74) when the rules prohibited interracial contact and that made it possible for officially open doors for both races to be subverted (as in Document 73). How universal the effort to secure Jim Crow proved to be is one question that remains to be answered; how universally those practices were observed is another. By the same token the lack of formal strictures should not be taken to be evidence of openness.

The other perspective on the problem of segregation moves to another level. Inasmuch as segregation could be a device geared for the suppression of the black population it appears as an irony that the same system could serve contrary purposes. Yet just as close contact of the races during slavery served as an instrument of social control, so too could separation of the races mean a blow for autonomy and against domination. One potentially powerful agent of control lay in religion. With enormous energy ministers mined the preachings of the Apostle Paul to declare the sanctity and duty of obedience of slave to master throughout the centuries. They never tired of it. Upon emancipation one of the quickest moves for independence, cultural and physical, came in the emigration of blacks from those churches where they had been captive congregations. One church history noted that the blacks left the church and when the churchmen offered them the gospel again, "they declined it as coming from us" (Document 71). In its place came the African Methodist Episcopal Church. But even there when the leadership seemed to be aiming more at acculturation than at traditional forms of salvation, the independent spirit reigned in the local congregations unchecked by hierarchical pressure (Document 71).[23]

Perhaps the most dramatic withdrawal of blacks from white society and torment can be found in the migration of thousands of "Exodusters" from the Mississippi valley to the free lands of Kansas in 1879. To many, including prominent black leaders, this phenomenon seemed an act of desperation, an act of flight and escape instead of something positive. While this perspective holds a certain truth, it also neglects the important act of will and the enormous risk involved in the physical uprooting of thousands of people and the defiance of systematic pressures and controls in their home states. Moreover, while this was clearly a form of black separatism, there was evident in this effort more than a rejection of white culture and institutions. Some would call the internalization of hopes and faith and aspirations an example of self-help; others later in a more self-conscious spirit would term it black nationalism. The independence sought often could be delineated in individual terms—a search for individual landholdings, an escape from the plantation credit system, or simply new hope for individual and family—but the larger significance of that independence is probably a cultural one. Given the necessity and generosity of cooperation by blacks along the journey to Kansas and the black autonomy evident in the various communities once established, incipient black nationalism becomes clearer. So too do the creative and positive elements of this flight from oppression.

Aside from massive exodus from the South, itself a possibility that carried no promises of true freedom, the options available to secure equality seemed limited. Some leaders of the commercially alert "New South" like Lewis H. Blair insisted that only two choices could be made: either promote market forms of relationships and ruthless competition for jobs among all men that would generate economic growth for the South and individual freedom for blacks or retain a caste-bound society that permitted no growth and oppress the black population more fiercely to keep it subservient (Document 78). That the options Blair posed had been narrowed to an artificial Hobson's choice disconnected from real issues of freedom became evident from the perspectives of workers in the South in the 1880s and 1890s. Those views (as in Document 79) suggested that a variety of experiences for both black and white could lead to the same conclusion: The real goal of freedom could not be found in either the oppression of one race by another or the equal freedom of all to be exploited in a competitive market. Freedom could be found, these miners argued, only in the brotherhood of man and the liberation of all from the pressures generated by a compelled struggle for the right to survive.[24] Indeed, the market in this view, instead of liberating man from social repressions, became but another huge system of gain for a few at the expense of the many. And racial competition, as much as individual competition, served to perpetuate the power of the few by preventing a real brotherhood of man from becoming an effective political and social force. Not surprisingly, given the origins of the system of race relations in America, this issue had been apparent in the making of slavery in the South two centuries earlier. The efficacy of this system of racial subordination had been proven beyond a doubt.

By the end of the nineteenth century a maze of internal contradictions plagued the nation and especially the South. The market provided both opportunity and oppression. It carried hopes and fears with it into the South with obvious manifestations in the crop-lien system and farm tenancy and the gradual migration of blacks to the cities and the North in search of better lives. And an economy that had come to depend on the market found itself ravaged by depression in the 1890s. It was precisely at that moment of general social debilitation that new forms of oppression were launched against blacks. The ferocious wave of extralegal violence directed at blacks in intense and repeated surges was unprecedented in that it was sustained over a period of years. Jim Crow became a permanent fixture. The law countenanced the disfranchisement of black voters. In institutional forms and in behavioral aspects the contact between the races at the end of the nineteenth and beginning of the twentieth centuries resembled closely the forms of tribal warfare in a situation of colonial oppression. As Frantz Fanon suggested, the viciousness involved in such warfare usually centered around quests for dignity and self-respect; the external situation of the colonized peoples permitted very little pride.[25] The irony was that nearly three centuries earlier, in a much more literal colonial system, flexibility and the possibility of interracial cooperation had been evident.

What had happened in the intervening period was the transformation of power relationships. The development of a market society had indeed shifted the antagonism in society in a powerful fragmenting process from a struggle between the rulers and the ruled to disputes between the ruled themselves. The source of the antagonism evident in race relations lay partly in a regional power struggle and colonial system, but it was associated really with the larger struggle over the structure and purpose of organized power in the nation. The eruption of racial violence in the urban centers of the North suggests that the system that led to racial antagonism in the South was now part of a much larger, national, system. Instead of resolving the problems of racial subjugation and social harmony, the problems changed form and managed to emerge in an ever more resilient and durable package. The legacy of slavery, the legacy of indentures, the legacy of paternalism, the legacy of emancipation, and the legacy of a powerful and ubiquitous force of social transformation, by the dawn of the twentieth century would be the legacy of fear, the fear that greater freedom for some must mean a loss of freedom for others. Freedom itself, which had in the nineteenth century become placed in market terms of opportunities, by the end of the century had become a commodity to be gained in competition. That would be not just the legacy for the twentieth century; it would be the challenge.

NOTES

1. This approach to the analysis of social and cultural issues that are broadly political in their implication rests in part on the formulations found in Raymond Williams, *The Long Revolution* (New York, 1961), pp. 48-71; Raymond Williams, *Culture and Society 1780-1950* (New York, 1958); E. P. Thompson, "Anthropology and the Discipline of Historical Context," *Midland History*, 1 (Spring 1972): 41-55; Anthony F. C. Wallace, "Revitalization Movements," *American Anthropologist*, 58 (April 1956): 264-81; and Karl Polanyi, *The Great Transformation* (Boston, 1957).

2. Two analyses of this conceptualization of the market that have been especially provocative are C. B. Macpherson, *The Political Theory of Possessive Individualism: Hobbes to Locke* (New York, 1962); and James Willard Hurst, *Law and the Conditions of Freedom in the Nineteenth-Century United States* (Madison, Wis., 1956).

3. Christopher Hill, *Puritanism and Revolution: Studies in Interpretation of the English Revolution of the 17th Century* (New York, 1958); Christopher Hill, *Refor-*

mation to Industrial Revolution (Baltimore, 1967); R. H. Tawney, *Religion and the Rise of Capitalism* (New York, 1926).

4. The following discussion rests heavily on Winthrop D. Jordan, *White Over Black: American Attitudes Toward the Negro 1550-1812* (Chapel Hill, N.C., 1968), pp. 3-43.

5. Edmund S. Morgan, "The Labor Problem at Jamestown, 1607-18," *American Historical Review*, 76 (June 1971): 595-611; and Edmund S. Morgan, *American Slavery, American Freedom: The Ordeal of Colonial Virginia* (New York, 1975).

6. See especially Macpherson, *Political Theory of Possessive Individualism*, pp. 282-86; and Timothy H. Breen, "A Changing Labor Force and Race Relations in Virginia 1660-1710," *Journal of Social History*, 7 (Fall 1973): 3-25.

7. Hill, *Reformation to Industrial Revolution*, pp. 70-71.

8. The most sensitive and perceptive discussion of this problem, one that this treatment depends upon, is that of Timothy Breen in his "A Changing Labor Force and Race Relations," cited above.

9. Ibid., pp. 13-18.

10. Macpherson, *Political Theory of Possessive Individualism*, pp. 46-70. See also Eugene D. Genovese's discussion of George Fitzhugh's analysis of slavery, in which Genovese presents Fitzhugh as the defender of a traditional or status society and critic of Macpherson's notion of possessive market society, in Genovese, *The World the Slaveholders Made: Two Essays in Interpretation* (New York, 1969), pp. 124 ff.

11. For a vigorous discussion of the issues surrounding the nature of antebellum society in the South see especially: Charles S. Sydnor, *American Revolutionaries in the Making: Political Practices in Washington's Virginia* [originally *Gentleman Freeholders*] (Chapel Hill, 1952); William R. Taylor, *Cavalier and Yankee: The Old South and American National Character* (New York, 1961); Genovese, *The World the Slaveholders Made*; Clement Eaton, *The Freedom of Thought Struggle in the Old South* (New York, 1964); and, of course, W. J. Cash, *The Mind of the South* (New York, 1941).

12. Bernard Bailyn, *The Ideological Origins of the American Revolution* (Cambridge, Mass., 1967), pp. 232-45.

13. Hurst, *Law and the Conditions of Freedom*, pp. 3-32. Hurst's perspective on this major thrust of American law should not be applied without consulting two alternative views: Harry N. Scheiber, "At the Borderland of Law and Economic History: The Contributions of Willard Hurst," *American Historical Review*, 85 (February 1970), 744-56; and Morton J. Horwitz, *The Transformation of American Law* (Cambridge, Mass., 1977).

14. Hurst, *Law and the Conditions of Freedom*, p. 25.

15. Again, see Genovese's discussion of Fitzhugh in *The World the Slaveholders Made*, pp. 115-244.

16. On the issues surrounding slave culture and the notion of a "living space" see Eugene D. Genovese, *Roll, Jordan, Roll: The World the Slaves Made* (New York, 1974); Herbert G. Gutman, *The Black Family in Slavery and Freedom, 1750-1925* (New York, 1976); M. J. Cassity, "Slaves, Families, and 'Living Space': A Note on Evidence and Historical Context," *Southern Studies*, 17 (Summer 1978), 209-15; and Lawrence W. Levine, *Black Culture and Black Consciousness* (New York, 1977), pp. 3-135.

17. See E. P. Thompson, "Time, Work-Discipline, and Industrial Capitalism," *Past and Present*, 38 (December 1967), 56-97; Genovese, *Roll, Jordan, Roll*, pp. 295-324.

18. Jordan, *White Over Black*, pp. 136-78.

19. In addition to the formulations of the significance of the Civil War in the rise of market society in the South see Barrington Moore, Jr., *Social Origins of Dictatorship and Democracy: Lord and Peasant in the Making of the Modern World* (Boston, 1966), pp. 111-55.

20. Anthony F. C. Wallace's discussion of similar forms of social action provides a valuable conceptualization of the phenomena; Wallace, "Revitalization Movements."

21. Levine, *Black Culture and Black Consciousness*, pp. 136-55.

22. Joel Williamson, *After Slavery: The Negro in South Carolina During Reconstruction 1861-1877* (Chapel Hill, 1965), pp. 164-75, contains a cogent discussion of the initial steps in the change in agriculture.

23. Williamson, *After Slavery*, pp. 180-208.

24. Herbert G. Gutman, "The Negro and the United Mine Workers of America: The Career and Letters of Richard L. Davis and Something of their Meaning: 1890-1900," reprinted in Gutman, *Work, Culture, and Society in Industrializing America: Essays in American Working-Class and Social History* (New York, 1976).

25. Frantz Fanon, *The Wretched of the Earth* (New York, 1963), pp. 93-95; J. Glenn Gray, "Understanding Violence Philosophically," in *On Understanding Violence Philosophically and Other Essays* (New York, 1970). This problem is discussed further in the headnote to Document 85. While George M. Frederickson, *The Black Image in the White Mind: The Debate on Afro-American Character and Destiny, 1917-1941* (New York, 1971), and C. Vann Woodward, *American Counterpoint: Slavery and Racism in the North-South Dialogue* (Boston, 1971), pp. 243-46, approach this problem in their use of Pierre L. van der Berghe's notion of *"Herrenvolk* democracy," they emphasize the importance of competition between black and white instead of the emergence of a competitive, market society which dislocates both.

I

Seventeenth Century Beginnings

1 The Perception of Color

White and black, the ends of the spectrum, have long held positive and negative connotations. Whether stemming from an association with life and death, with day and night, or some other natural process, they long ago developed firm associations with good and evil. The ethnocentric elements of English culture confirmed the rule of white as good, even sublime, white being the color of the Englishman's skin. As contact with other, darker, peoples increased in the years after the fifteenth century particularly, that positive-negative imagery may even have been sharpened. At the very least color became a cultural quality, a badge of worth and character, and to some, even a sign of God's blessing or curse. The *Oxford English Dictionary* has noted a variety of meanings for these colors, meanings that would reinforce the ethnocentrism that produced them and that would shape the negative perception of peoples who were dark-skinned.

Source: Oxford English Dictionary (Oxford, 1933; 1961 edition), Vol. 1, B, pp. 889-90, Vol. 12, W, pp. 72-73.

Black.

5. Deeply stained with dirt; soiled, dirty, foul.

8. Having dark or deadly purposes, malignant; pertaining to or involving death, deadly; baneful, disastrous, sinister.

9. Foul, iniquitous, atrocious, horribly wicked.

10. Clouded with sorrow or melancholy; dismal, gloomy, sad.

10.b. Of the countenance, the "look" of things, prospects: Clouded with anger, frowning; threatening, boding ill; the opposite of *bright* and *hopeful*.

11.   Indicating disgrace, censure, liability to punishment, etc.

White.

4.b. Honourable; square-dealing.

7.   Morally or spiritually pure or stainless; spotless, unstained, innocent.

7.b. Free from malignity or evil intent; beneficent, innocent, harmless, esp. as opposed to something characterized as *black*.

8.   (Chiefly of times and seasons) Propitious, favourable; auspicious, fortunate, happy.

9.   Highly prized, precious; dear, beloved, favourite, "pet", "darling". Often as a vague term of endearment.

10. Fair-seeming, specious, plausible.

2 The Obedient Servant

Independent of the perception of color, another precondition that shaped the development of black-white relations in the seventeenth century, was that of the nature of servitude. The notion of the "servant" in England included far more than people who attended to the needs of others. It could include anyone from a slave to a journeyman. Those who were free, even by the standards of the Levellers at mid-century, were thus a small group. This breadth of the notion of servitude is clear in the following extract from a 1643 discourse on the meaning of the Apostle Paul's epistle to the Ephesians. There is, however, an additional two-fold meaning to the document. It obviously was designed to reinforce the bonds of servitude in society with a theological buttress and justification, but it also indicates that many of those "servants" in society were less than dutiful, obedient, and respectful and that such tension and the number of servants "altogether rebellious" actually generated the need for this admonition. It may also be noted that even this early the author identifies permanent servitude with blacks.

Source: Paul Bayne[s], *An Entire Commentary Upon the Whole Epistle of the Apostle Paul to the Ephesians* (London, 1643), pp. 694-96.

[Ephesians, Chap. 6.] Verse 5. *Servants be obedient unto them that be your masters according to the flesh, with fears and trembling, in singlenesse of your hearts, as unto Christ.*

... The first thing to be marked is, *That servants stand charged from God with dutiful obedience.*...

... Service is a state of subjection, grounded partly in the curse of God for sin; partly in Civill constitution: for though it bee not a sinfull condition, yet it is a miserable condition, which entreth through sinne. Now servants are either more slavish, or else more free and liberall: the first are such whose bodies are perpetually put under the power of the Master, as Blackmores with us, of which kinds servants are made sometime forcibly, as in captivity: sometime voluntarily, as when one doth willingly make himselfe over: sometime naturally, as the children of servants are borne the slaves of their Masters: and this was the most frequent kinde of service, wherein parties are upon certaine termes or conditions for a certaine time onely under the power of a man: such are our Apprentises, Journeymen, maideservants, &c. Now because there were mercenary servants as well as bond-men in these times we must conceive all sorts of servants here schooled by the Holy Ghost.... You must know generally that our obedience doth note a subjecting of our soules in all things, *Tit. 3.* whether they command in God's name the religious carriage of our outward man, or anything concerning domesticall affaires, nothing is excepted which is not sinfull: for if wee were the vassals bought with money, that must not be yeilded to. *Gen. 39. Iosephs* example refusing his Mistresse in her unchastness. *I Sam. 21. Sauls* servant, not yeilding to run upon the Priests.

But for more particular direction three things are to be conceived in which they must obey.

1. They must suffer themselves to be directed in their businesses and the things that they goe about by their Masters; his command is thy watchword. *Mat. 8.* I (saith the Centurion) am a man in authority, and I say to one, goe, he goeth, come, and he cometh, doe this, hee doth it. And when God doth lay this upon the Master and Mistresse, to give direction, as is gathered by proportion, *Prov. 31. 13.* he will then have the servants to be subject, which is to be marked of such selfe-conceited ones, as thinke nothing will doe well, but what they take up of their owne head.

2. They must obey them in corrections whether by word or blow, if rebuked, they must not mumble and answer againe, *2 Tim.* if corrected they must humble themselves under it, *Gen. 16.* yea though the governours would causelesly and beyond measure take on, yet they must be indured, *1 Pet. 2. 18.*

3. We must stand to their allowance in diet, apparell, for liberty; for the Master is to measure these things to us, we are not to be our owne carvers, *Prov. 3. 13.* If they be such as through unmercifull hardnesse trouble the house, (for as he said of the Massilians, it is better be their sheepe then children: so it may be said of some, it is better bee their horse then servant) if they be thus, we may relieve ourselves with meeke complaints to the Magistrate, who are both their Masters and owners.

This therefore thus opened doth shew how reproveable the course of many is, who if they bee bid doe a thing: will sometimes denie, sometime say, well, but doe nothing, who if they be called to religious duties, think they are not bound to anything, but to doe thier worke for which they are hired, who are so selfe-conceited, that they love to follow thier owne minds, like these forward lapwings that will runne on a head, when the shell is not off their head, and before they be their trades masters, love to goe with their owne direction; hence bidden doe a thing thus, they will tell you of this way, and that, of some other thing, forgetting that God did not file their tongues to talke, but boare their eares that they might heare and obey. And he that is a servant must not doe his owne will, but his masters whome he serveth. For reproofe, they will give work for word, for blowes they will take none, rule their Masters hands if they cannot his tongue, else they will shew a paire of heeles, as *Hagar* did runne away from her mistresse. For their allowance some so mancher mouthed, that if their bread be a little courser, they will grumble at it: and so in the rest, if their mindes be not all out pleased, in stead of being dutifull they are altogether rebellious: but we that are the servants of Christ, must lay up this sentence, *obey your Masters in all things*, we must count it our glory to be ruled in all things, and make their wills ours: yea to bite in the lip with patience, though they be too strait and deale crookedly with us.

3 The Servant in the New World

The problems faced by those who settled Virginia are legend. Many of the problems came from the objective conditions of the New World; some came from the habits and attitudes about work and authority carried across the Atlantic; some came from the apprehensions about such a project harbored by those in England. William Bullock in 1649 attempted to dispel "myths" and misapprehensions about the servant problem. Many believed that servants who went to Virginia were sold into slavery. Some believed that servants sent to Virginia were idle, were unlikely to do well in that environment, and were prone to become disappointed and disgruntled. These observations suggest the possible commonality of the plight of white English servants with blacks who wound up there. In this regard it should be noted that the "spirits" to whom Bullock referred were well known at the time for securing servants for the New World in a way that Bullock neglected to mention; they would indeed "spirit away," through coercion or trickery, unwilling servants, a feature that added a further common element in the experience of the black and white "servant." "Idleness" suggests the prevalence of pre-industrial work habits among the servants. Two further assumptions of Bullock could also bear examination. The notion of the servant as property to be transferred at the whim of the Master would later prove crucial and already indicated the transition from a paternalistic set of relations to market relations; and Bullock's formula for indentured servitude considered not just the necessity of a bound term of service, at least four years, but also closely calculated the costs to the master as amortized over that period—logic that could lead to slavery.

Source: William Bullock, *Virginia Impartially Examined, and left to publick view, to be considered by all Iudicious and honest men* (London, 1649), pp. 13-14, 52-53.

...It hath beene a constant report amongst the ordinaire sort of people, That all those servants who are sent to *Virginia*, are sold as slaves: whereas the truth is that the Merchants who send servants, and have no Plantations of their owne, doe only transferre their Time over to others, but the servants serve no longer then the time they themselves agreed for in *England*: and this is an ordinarie course in *England*, and no prejudice or hurt to the servant.

And lastly, the unfitnesse of the people transported for the Work, or being fit, not well ordered, hath hindred the Countries recoverie very much.

The usuall way of getting servants, hath been by a sort of men nicknamed *Spirits*, who take up all the idle, lazie, simple people they can intice, such as have professed idlenesse, and will rather beg then work; who are perswaded by these *Spirits*, they shall goe into a place where food shall drop into their mouthes: and being thus deluded they take courage, and are transported. But not finding what was promised, their courage abates, & their minds being dejected, their work is according: nor doth the Master studie any way how to encourage them, but with sowre looks for which they care not; and being tyred with chafing himselfe, growes carelesse, and so all comes to nothing. More might be said upon this subject, were it fit: 'tis most certaine, that one honest labouring husbandman shall doe more then five of these.

* * *

I should have fitted you with Servants, before your comming into the Countrey, but since it is onely our fancies have beene there to take a view against our persons come, wee'le not goe without Servants.

And of Servants the best are best cheape.

Therefore Ile not advice the Spiriting way, which sends Drones to the Hive, in stead of Bees, but that you take stout Labourers and good Worke-men, giving them honest wages from 3.li. to 10.li. a yeare according to the quality of the men, for if we in *England* can pay 2. or 300.li. *per annum* rent for a Farme, and give great wages, we may much better give wages where our ground is twice as good, and no rent paid.

Besides it keepes a Servant in heart, and makes him at alltimes willing to put forth his strength in that Masters service that gives him meanes to thrive, and taking this course you may pick and chuse your Servants.

Onely this I must advise, that you agree with your Servant for foure yeares at least, and considering that you pay his passage, and are at other charges with him, let the charge be proportioned upon the foure or more yeares wages that he is to serve you, and so deduct every yeare.

And for Servants encouragement, they shall finde themselves at the very first in the condition of Journymen for foure or five yeares, and before seven yeares end he shall have a faire estate.

4 Securing the Servant

That there actually were "Spirits" who set out to transport servants to the colonies not just by enticement and cheating but by outright kidnapping as well can be seen in the following document, an abstract taken from the English Public Record Office. The shortage of women made females especially attractive targets for the efforts of the kidnappers who would transport them to Virginia, in this case to be sold. This account and the others like it read much like the accounts of the slave traders who engaged in similar efforts along the African coast.

Source: *Virginia Magazine of History and Biography*, 6 (January 1899): 229-30.

1618, Oct. 19, Nethersham.

Sir Edward Hext, Justice of the Peace of Somerset to the Privy Council, Complaint having been made to him that one Owen Evans, had commanded the constable of the hundred of Whitleighe and others to press him divers maidens to be sent to the Bermudas and Virginia, he issued a warrant for his apprehension. Evans on being examined said he was a messenger of the Chamber and showed his badge of office. The constable affirmed that said Owen required him in His M. name to press him five maidens with all speed for the service aforesaid, and on demanding to see his commission reviled and threatened that he should answer it in another place—Another affirmed that Evans delivered 5^s to one and 12^d to another to press six maidens, and to a third he delivered his badge and required him to press some maidens, else would he procure him to be hanged—Sends an acquittance inclosed—Evans confessed all, and that he had no commission at all and so fell upon his knees and humbly confessed his fault. Has committed him to gaol. His undue proceedings breed such terror to the poor maidens as forty of them fled out of one parish into such obscure and remote places as their parents and masters can yet have no news what is become of them.

1618, Nov. 13.

Inclosure.

Examinations of Francis Prewe, of Ottery, Thomas Crocker, William Mitchell and John Watts, taken before Sir Edward Hext the 16th and 31st of October, 1618. In reference to the proceedings of Owen Evans in endeavoring to press Maidens to be sent to the Bermudas and Virginia—that same bred such terror as above forty young women fled out of the parish of Ottery and were not yet to be found: that he threatened Prewe should answer his conduct in another place, if he failed, that Thomas Crocker should be hanged in the morning if he failed to press him some maidens, that Mitchell compounded with Evans for ten shillings to be free: and that Evans gave John Watts four shillings to press him four maidens and bring them to him at Sherborne Co., Dorset, and twelve pence to one Jacob Cryste to press Evans his [Cryste's] daughter.

5 White Slavery at Mid-Century

The enticing or kidnapping of servants and children to be sold as servants or slaves in Virginia remained a common practice and perhaps grew in the century to accommodate the large demand for labor in the plantation. In 1657 when Lionel Gatford prepared and published a tract on the problems afflicting the Virginia colony he singled out this practice of stealing away labor as a central problem sufficient in itself to bring down a curse on the whole effort. Moreover, he argued, lodging for servants in Virginia proved so miserable it could only be compared to the kenneling of dogs and their food even worse than that of dogs. Again, the description of the source of labor and the conditions of servitude in the colony of Virginia for English servants bears a striking similarity to the experiences of Africans kidnapped, transported, and abused in servitude.

Source: Lionel Gatford, *Publick Good Without Private Interest, or A Compendious Remonstrance of the present sad State and Condition of the English Colonie in Virginea* (London, 1657), pp. 4-5, 10-11.

That very many Children and servants sent into that Plantation, that were violently taken away, or cheatingly duckoyed without the consent or knowledge of their Parents or Masters by some praestigious Plagiaties (commonly called Spirits) into some private places, or ships, and there sold to be transported; and then resold there to be slaves or servants to those that will give most for them. A practice proper for Spirits, namely the Spirits of Devils, but to be abhored and abominated of all men that know either what men are, or whose originally they are, (even his that made them) or what their relations are, either natural, civil, or Christian. A practice condemned by the very Heathen, and a Law called *Lex plagiaria*, made by them against it. And if it should be tollerated, or connived at by Christians, and known so to be of the Heathen, Let it never be expected that any of those Heathen should turn Christians. For they may well conclude, That they that will take by force or fraud those that are Christians either children from their Parents, or servants from their Masters or any of any relation from their friends and relations, and sell them for slaves or servants to others, will never make any conscience or scruple at all, either of taking away by force, or surreptitiously stealing, or otherwise unjustly possessing or selling those Heathen themselves, or their children, servants, goods, lands, or ought else they can lay their hands on. And if they should become Christians, they are foresaught by sufficient examples, that they being Christians would be no security or protection to them or theirs. And how this diabolical practice does, in this and many other respects, cry unto God for vengeance in the cries, and moanes, and complaints, and lamentations, made by those poor inslaved children and servants and by all their Parents, friends and relations, may be more easily gessed at than expressed; and may in probability, be enough of itself to pull a curse and vengeance upon the whole Plantation.

* * *

The Planters, many of them doe very much abuse and oppress their poor servants, by not allowing them that lodging and food which is meet, causing many of them either to ly all the time of their servitude in ash heaps, or otherwise to kennel up and down like dogs, where they can find room; scarce feeding them so well as our scornfull servants here in England feed our dogs; though men of honesty and conscience do discharge their consciences there in the good use of their servants, as the like do here.

6 A Tendency Toward Disobedience

By 1640 there were but few Africans in Virginia. The fate of those who had been transported remains obscure, but the following document sheds some light. It appears that the conditions of being captured or tricked into servitude in the colonies, of an unspeakable voyage across the Atlantic, and of servitude, subjugation, and work once arrived were sufficiently similar to those of white Englishmen that they could occasionally find common cause. The classic manifestation of that common cause was the effort to escape and run away. The chances for this were enhanced by virtue of the fact that, at least prior to 1680, the Africans were shipped initially to Barbados and then later to Virginia, a circumstance that provided them the opportunity to learn some English. Both groups tended to run away and in some instances they attempted to run away *together*. Punishment levelled against those runaways was not uniform. Even when the black man, John Punch, was sentenced to servitude for the rest of his life, as opposed to three years additional for the others, it is apparent that John Punch had been previously serving only a limited period of indenture and was not a slave. One should also note that among those who attempted to escape was a chirurgeon—a surgeon—thus again suggesting the breadth of the servant status.

Source: "Decisions of the General Court," *The Virginia Magazine of History and Biography*, 5 (January 1898), 236-37.

9th of July, 1640. Whereas Hugh Gwyn hath, by order from this board, Brought back from Maryland three servants formerly run away from the said Gwyn, the court doth therefore order that the said three servants shall receive the punishment of whipping and to have thirty stripes apiece; one called Victor, a Dutchman, the other a Scotchman called James Gregory, shall first serve out their times with their master according to their Indentures, and one whole year apiece after the time of their service is Expired By their said Indentures in recompence of his Loss sustained by their absence, and after that service to their said Master is Expired to serve the colony for three whole years apiece, and that the third being a negro named John Punch shall serve his said master or his assigns for the time of his natural life here or else where.

July 22d, 1640. Whereas complaint has been made to this Board by Capt. Wm. Pierce, Esqr., that six of his servants and a negro of Mr. Reginald's has plotted to run away unto the Dutch plantation from their said masters, and did assay to put the same in Execution upon Saturday night, being the 8th day July, 1640, as appeared to the Board by the Examinations of Andrew Noxe, Rich'd Hill, Rich'd Cookeson and John Williams, and likewise by the confession of Christopher Miller, Peter Milcocke and Emanuel, the foresaid Negro, who had, at the foresaid time, taken the skiff of the said Capt. Wm. Pierce, their master, and corn, powder and shot and guns to accomplish their said purposes, which said persons sailed down in the said skiff to Elizabeth river, where they were taken and brought back again, the court taking the same into consideration as a dangerous precedent for the future time (if left unpunished), did order that Christopher Miller, a Dutchman (a prime agent in the business), should receive the punishment of whipping, and to have thirty stripes and be so burnt in the cheek with the letter R and to work with a shackle on his legg for one whole year and longer if said master shall see cause, and after his full time of service is Expired with his said master to serve the colony for seven whole years, and the said Peter Milcocke to receive thirty stripes and to be Burnt in the Cheek with the letter R, and after his term of service is Expired with his said master to serve the colony for three years, and the said Rich'd Cockson, after his full time Expired with his master, to serve the colony for two years and a half, and the said Rich'd Hill to remain upon his good behavior untill the next offence, and the said Andrew Noxe to receive thirty stripes, and the said John Williams, a Dutchman and a chirurgeon after his full time of service is Expired with his master, to serve the colony for seven years, and Emanuel, the Negro, to receive thirty stripes and to be burnt in the cheek with the letter R and to work in shackles one year or more as his master shall see cause, and all those who are condemned to serve the colony after their time are Expired with their masters, then their said masters are required hereby to present to this board their said servants so condemned to the colony.

7 A Tearme Soe Scandalous

That slavery had emerged in some form by the mid-seventeenth century is apparent, yet the conditions and circumstances of the institution remained ill-defined. Its relationship with other forms of servitude and its identification with Africans exclusively had not been resolved. In October 1663 the Maryland Assembly considered the case of a father who feared for the fate of his daughter, that her apprenticeship would be turned into slavery. He also, and indeed more eloquently, feared that this would hurt the good name of the apprentices and cause those "free borne Christians" to decline to come to the colony as servants. While the court dismissed his complaint, the charge does indicate well that the forms of servitude had not crystallized nor had slavery become exclusively associated with black people.

Source: William Hand Browne, ed., *Archives of Maryland: Proceedings and Acts of the General Assembly of Maryland*, 1 (Baltimore, 1883) 464.

Now soe itt is that the Complt intending to returne out of this province into England with his wife there to Reside, and to leave the managem^t of his affayres in this Province with Richard Hotchkeyes and Mrs Anne Tilney one John Nicholls an Inhabitant of this Province who had been long and much indebted to the Complt, and from yeare to yeare forborne by him without ever takeing one penny of him for the damage of non payments being growne very poore and vnable by his labo^{rs} to pay his debts, and mayntayne himselfe wife and Children did some two or three moneths before the Complt^s departure for England in the yeare 1659 sell the Complt his plantacon And more to lessen his Charge did by the mediation of the s^d Richd Hotchkeys M^{rs}. Anne Tilney and others earnestly Importune the Complt & his wife to take his eldest daughter named Hester being ab^t 10 or 11 yeares ould, an Apprentice for five yeares which the Complt refused and yhett att last by the earnest sollicitacōn of the sd Nicholls himselfe and others in his behalfe. And in Commiseracōn of his poore Estate and the sd childs who was in a very poore Condicōn for want of Cloathes as well Linnen as woollen, did Condiscend to accept for her seaven years, And accordingly an Jndenture was drawne Signed & Sealed by the said Nicholls and his daughter in the p^{r}sence of the s^d Hotchkeys and John Abington without any other Condition than w^t was Conteyned in the s^d Jndent^r. And whereas in a pet^n to this hono^{ble} Court...Jtt is falsly alledged by the s^d Nicholls that the Complt did earnestly press him for his s^d daughter promising she should doe nothing else but wayte vpon his wife who itt is well knowne wanted noe Attendants of farr better fashon, And was shortly intended to goe for England with the same mayd she brought with her, with noe Resolucōn as was well knowne to the s^d Nicholls of returning againe into this Province. And to bee att the Charge of transporting or keeping such a Rude Rawe ill bred Childe for or in England where Servants of all sorts may be had on Easyer tearmes, is altogether Jmprobable yett how otherwise she should doe nothing else but wayte vpon his wife or that he the s^d Capt should take as much Care for her as his owne Child which is also Sworne by his Confederate Edward West, he humbly desires this hono^{ble} Court to take into their serious Consideracōn as alsoe the last Clause of the s^d Nicholls his pet^d wherein he Craves that his daughter may not be made a Slaue a tearme soe Scandalous that if admitted to be the Condicōn or tytle of the Apprentices in this Province will be soe distructive as noe free borne Christians will ever be induced to come over servants....

8 The Penalties of an Accomplice

Among the myriad problems facing legal authorities serving as mid-
wives in the birth of the institution of slavery was how to determine
and administer the proper punishment against the persistent tendency of slaves to join with other servants in making an escape. By
making servitude perpetual they had lost one of the harshest devices—the addition of time to the contract of indenture of servitude.
In 1663 the Maryland General Assembly proposed to deal with that
dilemma by assigning liability and responsibility to the English servants for damages to the owners or masters (an apparent distinction
in the terms of servitude) of the slave. Yet again, however, the
reference is to "Negroes or other Slaves," a category fraught with
baleful implications for those who were black but one that kept alive
the possibility that some slaves might not be black.

Source: William Hand Browne, ed., *Archives of Maryland: Proceedings and Acts of the General Assembly of Maryland* (Baltimore, 1883), 489.

An Act concerning English Serv^{ts}
th^t Runn away in Company of
Negroes or other Slaves. [1663]

Whereas div^{rs} English Serv^{ts} Runn away in Company wth Negroes & other
Slaves, who are incapeable of makeing Stisfaccōn by Addicōn of Tyme Bee itt
enacted...th^t any English Servt or Serv^{ts} th^t shall run away in the Company of
any Negroe or other Slaves shalbe able to pay either Singly or pporconably if
more then one all such Just Dammage to the owners or Mast^{rs} of the same as

shalbee made appeare before any Co^{rt} of Record in this pvince.

The vpp^r house have Assented
John Gittings Clke

The Low^r howse have Assented
Wm Bretton Clke.

9 A Still Troublesome People

In 1664 the Maryland General Assembly finally focused squarely on the issue of perpetual servitude in the hope, possibly, of resolving this thorny issue. At best, however, the issue became more complicated. Blacks and whites, servants and slaves, and women and men refused to fit the neat categories hoped for by established authorities. Not only did slaves and servants run away together, not only did blacks and whites sometimes associate in ways that authorities considered shameful and disgraceful, they even married one another—servant and slave, free and slave, black and white. In their effort to resolve the issue the government of Maryland moved the identification of slavery with black people a large step forward.

Source: William Hand Browne, ed., *Archives of Maryland: Proceedings and Acts of the General Assembly of Maryland*, 1 (Baltimore, 1883), 533-34.

An Act Concerning Negroes & other Slaues [1664]

Bee itt Enacted... That all Negroes or other slaues already within the Prouince And all Negroes and other slaues to bee hereafter imported into the Prouince shall serue Durante Vita And all Children born of any Negro or other slaue shall be Slaues as their ffathers were for the terme of their liues And forasmuch as divers freeborne English women forgettfull of their free Condicōn and to the disgrace of our Nation doe intermarry with Negro Slaues by which alsoe divers suites may arise touching the Issue of such woemen and a great damage doth befall the Masters of such Negros for preuention whereof for deterring such freeborne women from such shamefull Matches Bee itt further Enacted by the Authority advice and Consent aforesaid That whatsoever free borne woman shall inter marry with any slaue from and after the Last day of this present

Assembly shall Serue the master of such slaue dureing the life of her husband And that all the Issue of such freeborne woemen soe marryed shall be Slaues as their fathers were And Bee itt further Enacted that all the Issues of English or other freeborne women that haue already marryed Negroes shall serve the Masters of their Parents till they be Thirty yeares of age and noe longer.

10 White Over Black

While the Maryland Assembly seemed distraught mainly over the possibility of a free woman bearing the child of a slave, the white gentlemen of Virginia pondered the implications of black women bearing their children. Thus in 1662 Virginia law, which had already made interracial fornication a crime, doubled the penalty on the "Christians" so inclined and declared children to be slave or free depending upon the condition of the mother. Again race, abetted by the pejorative of the color connotation, was becoming more specifically identified with perpetual servitude.

Source: William W. Hening, ed., *Laws of Virginia* (Philadelphia, 1823), Vol. 2, 170.

Negro womens children to serve according to the condition of the mother. [1662]

WHEREAS some doubts have arrisen whether children got by any Englishman upon a negro should be slave or ffree, *Be it therefore enacted and declared by this present grand assembly*, that all children borne in this country shalbe held bond or free only according to the condition of the mother, And that if any christian shall committ ffornication with a negro man or woman, hee or shee soe offending shall pay double the ffines imposed by the former act.

11 Always a Slave?

The term slave in the seventeenth century may not always have suggested lifetime servitude. While both lamenting the severities of life in the colony and extolling the opportunities to be found there the Rev. Alexander Moray observed that some former slaves were now masters. Moray makes no comment on the race of those former slaves who have become masters, but he does suggest a certain openness in that plantation society that could generate turmoil within the white or free ranks once efforts were made to restrict or tighten the system of authority. Put another way, the expectations of freedom and certain opportunities could engender further "arrogance" and "rebelliousness" among those people to whom that freedom was denied. And that could be a decisive development itself.

Source: Alexander Moray to Sr. Robert Moray, June 12, 1665, in "Letters Written by Mr. Moray, A Minister to Sr. R. Moray, from Ware River in Mock-Jack Bay, Virginia," *William and Mary Quarterly*, 2nd Series, Vol. 2 (July 1922), 159-60.

I should think my self very happy in living in this Country: being so pleasant, so fertil & so plentiful a country: but that the emulations, and differences betwixt us and the English, not only givs discouragement but that when wee have occasion, we meet with many disappointments in justice, both for securing states [?] & persons & our peace: however we must take the bitt and the busket with it, and they tell us, we are like the jews, we thrive being crost: I hope our afflictions work for our good: for they make us spare, and ther prosperity make them spend so as generally the condi°n betwixt the English and us, is not farr different as to outward things, many of our Country men, living better then ever ther forfathers, and that from so mean a beginning as being sold slavs here, after hamiltons engagement and Worster fight are now herein great masters of many servants themselfs. . . . .

12 Toward a New Enclosure

The preponderance of white labor as servants in the colonies, labor that had been procured often by the privations generated by enclosure, by trickery, or even by kidnapping, tended to blur distinctions in servitude. It was possibly this feature which actively mitigated slave bondage. Another effect, though, was to drain labor from England proper. That vast mobile population set into motion by the enclosure movement was finding a new sanctuary, bleak though it might be, in the New World. Colonization could even serve, in the eyes of those eager to promote economic growth in England, to undermine the enclosure stimulus to cheap labor. Thus the pressure mounted on the government in England to restrict that flow of labor and to enforce more vigorously the laws prohibiting such "spiriting." The following letter indicates one Englishman's concern with this problem as he hoped that his majesty would "discourage this enterprise." In 1682 Charles II did so in a royal proclamation. The consequences of this action on race relations in the colonies would be felt for centuries.

Source: John Reresby to the Earl of Danby, July 17, 1677, in C. H. Firth, ed., "Emigration from Yorkshire to West Jersey, 1677," *American Historical Review*, 2 (April 1897), 472-73.

To Thom. Earle of Danby Ld. high Treasurer
   of England.
May it please y^r Lordship
   ...My Lord I thought it my duty to offer another matter to y^r Lordshipps Consideration vizt severall persons with their wiues and children (in all to near the nomber off 200) many of them Quaquers and other dissenters inhabitants about sheffield and the adjoining parts of Nottinghamshire and Darbysh^r haue lately gone and are euery day as yet going by the way of Hull to transport

themselves to an Island in America called west Jarsey, and are dayly followed by others upon the same design; Insomuch as soe many leaving the Country togather giues some discouragement to thes parts, that suffer already ffor want of people; Others going from us frequently for London Ireland and other plantations.

One of the Menagers of this Affair (whom I bound over to the last sessions for enticeing away servants from their masters) owned publiquely that they had noe leaue from this Ma^{ty} or the Council to depart the realme; that they had purchased the Island being 200 Miles in length and 60 Miles ouer for 1500 of his Highness the D. of York; that it was as yet uninhabited, but that He hoped it would be peopled in a short time soe as to giue a good Account of their Adventure.

My L^d if his Maiesty thinke fitt to discourage this enterprise I humbly conceive it will be necessary that a speedy stop be put to all ships bound for that island from Hull and if y^r Lordship please to order me to give y^u any further Account as to the names of the undertakers or any other perticulers, I shall doe the best I can to inform my selfe of them, and to observe y^r Lordsh^{ps} Commands therein that am y^r serv^t.

J. R.

13 The Watershed of Rebellion

In the seventeenth century black and white servants sharing similar fates in transportation and labor and life in Virginia found substantial common ground. Their efforts to run away together generated law after law punishing such behavior but produced no changes in the labor system itself. The discontent and dissatisfaction festered under the pressures of markets, Indian attacks, and an unresponsive social system. Indeed as land was being taken up the opportunities for those who left their bondage diminished. Out of a complex variety of circumstances the turmoil reached explosive proportions in Virginia in 1676 as Nathaniel Bacon led a rebellion against the established governor. The composition of the followers of Bacon, a group that included freemen, servants, and slaves, testifies to the common experiences and identities felt by these people. Confirming the diversity of the rebellious people, the author singles out one of the lieutenants in the rebellion named Larance for particular condemnation because of his uninhibited amorous association with a black slave, thus crossing racial and status lines.

The amnesty provided freedom for those who surrendered, a freedom from the terms of their bondage, but it was a short run solution to the rebellion. A more permanent arrangement would soon be forthcoming that would make such interracial cooperation more difficult and at any rate less likely. After this volatile event the troublesome white servants would be increasingly replaced with black slaves and those blacks would be more sharply restricted in their activities. Within a short period of time a caste system would be strongly evident and slavery would be the predominant system of labor. Bacon's rebellion, the coincident reduction of servants from England, and the increasing need for labor marked a clear watershed in the evolution of American race relations.

Source: The History of Bacon's and Ingram's Rebellion, 1676, in Charles M. Andrews, ed., Narratives of Insurrections 1675-1690 (New York, 1915), pp. 94-95, 96.

What number of Soulders was, at this time, in Garrisson at West Point, I am not Certane: It is saide about 250, sum'd up in freemen, searvants and slaves; these three ingredience being the Compossition of Bacons Army, ever since that the Governour left Towne. These was informed (to prepare the way) two or three days before that Grantham [a loyalist captain serving as intermediary between the governor and the rebels] came to them, that there was a treaty on foote betwene there Generall and the Governour; and that Grantham did manely promote the same, as he was a parson that favoured the cause, that they were contending for.

When that Grantham arived amongst these fine fellowes, he was receved with more then an ordnary respect; which he haveing repade with a suteable deportment, he aquaints them with his Commission, which was to tell them, that there was a peace Concluded betwene the Governour and there Generall; and since him self had (in som measures) used his indeviours, to bring the same to pass, hee beg'd of the Governour, that he might have the honour to com and aquaint them with the terms; which he saide was such, that they had all cause to rejoyce at, then any ways to thinke hardly of the same; there being a Compleate satisfaction to be given (by the Articles of agreement) according to every ones particular interss; which he sum'd up under these heads. And first, those that were now in Arms (and free Men) under the Generall, were still to be retained in Arms, if they so pleased, against the Indians. Secondly, And for those who had a desire for to return hom, to there owne abodes, care was taken for to have them satisfide, for the time they had bin out, according to the alowance made the last Assembly. And lastly, those that were sarvants in Arms, and behaved them selves well in there imployment, should emediately receve discharges from there Indentures, signed by the Governour, or Sequetary of State; and there Masters to receve from the publick a valluable Satisfaction, for every Sarvant so set free (Marke the words) proportionally to the time that they have to serve.

Upon these terms, the Soulders forsake West-Point, and goe with Grantham to kiss the Governours hands (still at Tindells point) and to receve the benifitt of the Articles mentioned by Grantham; where when they came (which was by water, them selves in one vessill, and there Arms in another; and so contrived by Grantham, as he tould me him selfe, upon good reason) the Sarvants and Slaves was sent hom to there Masters, there to stay till the Governour had leasure to signe there discharges, or to say better, till they were free, according to the Custom of the Countrey; the rest was made prisoners, or entertain'd by the Governour, as hee found them inclin'd.

*   *   *

Larance was late one of the Assembley, and Burgis for Towne, in which he was a liver. He was a Parson not meanely aquainted with such learning (besides his natureall parts) that inables a Man for the management of more then ordnary imployments, Which he subjected to an eclips, as well in the transactings of the present affaires, as in the darke imbraces of a Blackamoore, his slave: And that in so fond a Maner, as though Venus was cheifely to be worshiped in the Image of a Negro, or that Buty consisted all together in the Antiphety of Complections: to the noe meane Scandle and affrunt of all the Vottrisses in or about towne.

14 The Hardening of Caste Lines

The classic response to insurrection, amelioration in the short run to quell the rebellion and a division of the potential revolutionaries in the long run, found expression in Virginia in the years following Bacon's Rebellion. The law came to identify slave servitude increasingly with blacks and to associate with them particular cultural attributes that distinguished them from white society. The title and first sentence of the 1680 Virginia law restricting Negroes makes abundantly clear that it was they who were the objects of restraint rather than white servants in general. The fear that motivated the new law may have been either a fear of black insurrection or of a united black and white slave/servant insurrection. The careful inclusion of the term "any negroe or other slave" testifies to a reluctance to abandon completely the possibility of class tension in favor of racial division. The burden of the turmoil in society was being laid at the doorstep of the least powerful and hence the most convenient group instead of on the structure of authority itself. The main function of the law, then, was perhaps to assuage the fears and doubts of those in power by making the problem of social unrest a racially identifiable one and thereby concomitantly to promote racial solidarity with previously disaffected whites. It should be noted, incidentally, that the first sentence offers a slightly revealing comment on black culture in the colony. Blacks were indeed meeting frequently for feasts and burials which likely were remnants, or even blossomings, of tribal customs suggestive of an African dignity and strength troubling to the new masters.

As with earlier and later legislation, the 1680 measure went for naught. Two years passed and the same "insurrectionary" practices continued. Believing that the law was ineffective only because people did not know about it, in 1682 the parish churches were assigned the responsibility of making its provisions public and the Master the obligation of more carefully watching his slaves.

Source: William W. Hening, ed., *Laws of Virginia* (Philadelphia, 1823), Vol. 2, 481-82, 492-93.

An Act for preventing Negroes Insurrections. [1680]

WHEREAS the frequent meeting of considerable numbers of negroe slaves under pretence of feasts and burialls is judged of dangerous consequence; for prevention whereof for the future, *Bee it enacted*...that from and after the publication of this law, it shall not be lawfull for any negroe or other slave to carry or arme himselfe with any club, staffe, gunn, sword or any other weapon of defence or offence, nor to goe or depart from of his masters ground without a certificate from his master, mistris or overseer, and such permission not to be granted but upon perticuler and necessary occasions; and every negroe or slave soe offending not haveing a certificate as aforesaid shalbe sent to the next constable, who is hereby injoyned and required to give the said negroe twenty lashes on his bare back well layd on, and soe sent home to his said master, mistris or overseer. *And it is further enacted*...that if any negroe or other slave shall presume to lift up his hand in opposition against any christian, shall for every such offence, upon due proofe made thereof by the oath of the party before a magistrate, have and receive thirty lashes on his bare back well laid on. *And it hereby further enacted*...that if any negroe or other slave shall absent himself from his masters service and lye hid and lurking in obscure places, comitting injuries to the inhabitants, and shall resist any person or persons that shalby and lawfull authority be imployed to apprehend and take the said negroe, that then in case of such resistance, it shalbe lawfull for such person or persons to kill the said negroe or slave soe lying out and resisting, and that this law be once every six months published at the respective county courts and parish churches within this colony.

An additionall act for the better preventing insurrections by Negroes. [1682]

WHEREAS...an act preventing negroes insurrections hath not had its intended effect for want of due notice thereof being taken; *It is enacted* that for the better putting the said act in due execution, the church wardens of each parish in this country at the charge of the parish by the first day of January next provide true coppies of this present and the aforesaid act, and make or cause entry thereof to be made in the register book of the said parish, and that the minister or reader of each parish shall twice every yeare vizt. some one Sunday or Lords day in each of the months of September and March in each parish church or chappell of ease in each parish in the time of divine service, after the reading of the second lesson, read and publish both this present and the aforerecited act under paine such church-warden minister or reader makeing default, to forfeite each of them six hundred pounds of tobacco, one halfe to the informer and the other halfe to the use of the poore of the said parish. And for the further better preventing such insurrections by negroes or slaves, *Bee it likewise enacted*...that noe master or overseer knowingly permitt or suffer, without the leave or licence of his or their master or overseer, any negroe or slave not properly belonging to him or them, to remaine or be upon his or their plantation above the space of four houres at any one time, contrary to the intent of the aforerecited act upon paine to forfeite, being thereof lawfully convicted, before some one justice of peace within the county where the fact shall be comitted, by the oath of two witnesses at the least, the summe of two hundred pounds of tobacco in cask for each time soe offending to him or them that will sue for the same, for which the said justice is hereby impowered to award judgment and execution.

15 Lascivious & Lustful Desires

As in Virginia, so too in Maryland: the laws too often failed to have their desired effect. Whether encouraged by their masters and mistresses, or simply out of the need to satisfy their own lust, freeborn white women were being attracted (despite the previous law) to black men. The eternal answer, a new law to rectify the weaknesses of the old, emerged. In this measure of 1681 the central thrust is to promote a division of the labor force (white women servants being the objects of the prohibition) along racial lines, a division that was not naturally forthcoming. This may also be one of the last instances in which the impulse toward interracial sex is attributed to the "Lascivious & Lustful desires" of white women. In future years that libidinous quality would be considered a characteristic of black people.

Source: William Hand Browne, ed., *Archives of Maryland: Proceedings and Acts of the General Assembly of Maryland*, 7 (Baltimore, 1889), 203-5.

An Act concerning Negroes & Slaves [1681]

Bee itt enacted . . . that all Negroes & other Slaues already Imported or heereafter to bee Imported into this Province shall serve (durante vita) & all the Children already borne or heereafter to bee borne of any Negroes or other Slaues within this Province shall bee Slaues to all intents & purposes as theire fathers were for the Terme of theire naturall Lives.

And for as much a diuerse ffreeborne Englishe or White-woman sometimes by the Instigacon Procuremᵗ or Conievance of theire Masters Mistres or dames, & always to the Satisfaccon of theire Lascivious & Lustful desires, & to the disgrace not only of the English butt allso of many other Christian Nations, doe Intermarry with Negroes & Slaues by which meanes diuerse Inconveniencys Controuersys & suites may arise Touching the Issue or Children of such ffreeborne women aforesaid, for the pʳvencon whereof for the future, Bee itt further enacted...that if any Ma^r M^{irs} or dame haueing any ffreeborne Englishe or white woman Servt as aforesaid in theire possession or property, shall by any Instigacon procurem^t knowledge permission or Contriveance whatsoeuer, suffer any such ffreeborne Englishe or Whitewoman Servt in theire possession & wherein they haue property as aforesaid to Intermarry or Contract in Matrimony with any Slaue...That then the said M^r Mi^{rs} or dame of any such ffreeborne women as aforesaid, soe married as aforesaid, shall forfeite & Loose all theire Claime & Title to the service & servitude of any such ffreeborne woman & alsoe the said woman Servt soe married shall bee & is by this p^{r}sent Act absolutely discharged manymitted & made free Instantly upon her Intermarriage as aforesaid, from the Services Imploym^{ts} vse Claime or demands of any such M^r Mi^{rs} or dame soe offending as afforesaid, And all Children borne of such ffreeborne women, soe manymitted & ffree as aforesaid sahll bee free as the women soe married as aforesaid, as also the said Ma^r Mi^{rs} & dame shall forfeite the sume of Tenn Thousand pounds of Tobacco, one halfe thereof to the Lord Prop^{ry} & the other halfe to him or them that shall Informe & sue for the same to bee Recouered in any Court of Record within this Province by Bill plaint or Informacon, wherein noe Essoyne proteccōn or wager of Law to bee allowed, And any presit Minister Majestrate or other person whatsoeuer, within this Province that shall from & after the Publicacon heereof Joyne in Marriage any Negroe or other Slaue to any Englishe or other Slaue to any English or other Whitewoman Servt ffreeborne as aforesaid shall forfeite & pay the sume of Tenn Thousand pound of Tobacco, one halfe to the Lord Prop^{ry} & the other halfe to the Informer or the person greived.....

16 A Permanent Wedge by Law

By 1691 the authorities in Virginia had moved far in erecting a caste system of barriers for blacks. In that year a new law provided further restraints on slaves. Those runaways who refused to surrender could now be killed and their owners (no longer just masters) compensated, a feature which crudely underscored the lifetime proposition of the bondage. Those who intermarried with blacks could now be banished forever, white women could be fined for having a bastard with a black father, and servant women who married blacks would be sold upon the termination of their indenture (as recently as 1681 Maryland had granted freedom to those same servant women). Moreover free blacks would not be permitted to remain in Virginia. A more systematic code to associate servitude with negritude would be difficult to imagine at this point, in contrast to the former loose and broad terms of servant control.

Source: William W. Hening, ed., *Laws of Virginia* (Philadelphia, 1823), Vol. 3, 86-88.

An act for suppressing outlying Slaves. [1691]

WHEREAS many times negroes, mulattoes, and other slaves unlawfully absent themselves from their masters and mistresses service, and lie hid and lurk in obscure places killing hoggs and committing other injuries to the inhabitants of this dominion, . . . *Be it enacted . . . and it is hereby* that in all such cases upon intelligence of any such negroes, mulattoes, or other slaves lying out, two of their majesties justices of the peace of that county, whereof one to be of the quorum, where such negroes, mulattoes or other slave shall be, . . . are hereby impowered and commanded to issue out their warrants directed to the sherrife of the same county to apprehend such negroes, mulattoes, and other slaves, which said sherriffe is hereby likewise required upon all such occasions to raise such and soe many forces from time to time as he shall think convenient and necessary for the effectual apprehanding such negroes, mulattoes and other slaves, and in case any negroes, mulattoes or other slave or slaves lying out as aforesaid shall resist, runaway, or refuse to deliver and surrender him or themselves to any person or persons that shall be by lawfull authority employed to apprehend and take such negroes, mulattoes or other slaves that in such it shall and may be lawfull for such person and persons to kill and distroy such negroes, mulattoes, and other slave or slaves by gunn or any otherwaise whatsoever.

Provided that where any negroe or mulattoe slave or slaves shall be killed in pursuance of this act, the owner or owners of such negro or mulatto slave shall be paid for such negro or mulatto slave four thousand pounds of tobacco by the publique. And for prevention of that abominable mixture and spurious issue which hereafter may encrease in this dominion, as well by negroes, mulattoes, and Indians intermarrying with English, or other white women, as by their unlawfull accompanying with one another, Be it enacted . . . that for the time to come, whatsoever English or other white man or woman being free shall intermarry with a negroe, mulatto, or Indian man or woman bond or free shall within three months after such marriage be banished and removed from this dominion forever, and that the justices of each respective countie within this dominion make it their perticular care, that this act be put in effectuall execution. And be it further enacted . . ., That if any English woman being free shall have a bastard child by any negro or mulatto, she pay the sume of fifteen pounds sterling, within one moneth after such bastard child shall be born, to the Church wardens of the parish where she shall be delivered of such child, and in default of such payment she shall be taken into the possession of the said Church wardens and disposed of for five yeares, and the said fine of fifteen pounds, or whatever the woman shall be disposed of for, shall be paid, one third part to their majesties for and towards the support of the government and the contingent charges thereof, and one other third part to the use of the parish where the offence is committed, and the other third part to the informer, and that such bastard child be bound out as a servant by the said Church wardens untill he or she shall attaine the age of thirty yeares, and in case such English woman that shall have such bastard child be a servant, she shall be sold by the said church wardens, (after her time is expired that she ought by law to serve her master) for five yeares, and the money she shall be sold for divided as is before appointed, and the child to serve as aforesaid.

And forasmuch as great inconveniences may happen to this country by the setting of negroes and mulattoes free, by their either entertaining negro slaves from their masters service, or receiveing stolen goods, or being grown old bringing a charge upon the country; for prevention thereof, Be it enacted . . ., That no negro or mulatto be after the end of this present session of assembly set free by any person or persons whatsoever, unless such person or persons, their heires, executors or administrators pay for the transportation of such negro or negroes out of the countrey within six moneths after such setting them free, upon penalty of paying of tenn pounds sterling to the Church wardens of the parish where such person shall dwell with, which money, or so much thereof as shall be necessary, the said Church wardens are to cause the said negro or mulatto to be transported out of the countrey, and the remainder of the said money to imploy to the use of the poor of the parish.

17 Slavery: 1702

In 1701 and 1702 when Francis Louis Michel visited Virginia, he observed an institution that was unmistakably identifiable as Negro slavery. His visit coincided with the end of what Timothy Breen has calculated to be the greatest decade of growth in the slave population in American history. His remark that slaves constituted the premier form of wealth in the commonwealth thus should be considered as one only just then accurate. Moreover, he refers only to blacks as slaves, not to any other population group, and he observed slaves coming from Guinea, something relatively recent. Previously the slaves had most frequently undergone a "seasoning" in the West Indies; now some arrived straight from the midpassage across the Atlantic clad only in their native corals. The social significance of this feature could well be determinative. The similarities in black and white workers were rapidly declining in language, conditions of transportation, terms of servitude, and social organization. The two races were indeed growing more distant. His comment on the "animal-like people" he saw deserves comment. The association of this darker people with base, black qualities in the context of a form of servitude had solidified: while neither color nor the status of being a "servant" a half century or so before could positively shape race relations in a caste direction, now the logic of caste drew upon both for justification in the creation of a system of authority designed mainly to serve the needs of the market and to prevent any system of class unity.

Source: William J. Hinke, trans. and ed., "Report of the Journey of Francis Louis Michel from Berne, Switzerland, to Virginia, October 21, 1701-December 1, 1702," *Virginia Magazine of History*, 24 (April 1916), 116-17.

There are many people who have plantations for rent. Two to five pounds secures a good dwelling, and as much land as one can work. Most of the wealth consists in slaves or negroes, for if one has many workmen, much food-stuff and tobacco can be produced. These negroes are brought annually in large numbers from Guiné and Jamaica, (the latter of which belongs to England) on English ships. They can be selected according to pleasure, young and old, men and women. They are entirely naked when they arrive, having only corals of different colors around their neck and arms. They usually cost from 18-30 pounds. They are life-long slaves and good workmen after they have become acclimated. Many die on the journey or in the beginning of their stay here, because they receive meagre food and are kept very strictly. Both sexes are usually bought, which increase afterwards. The children like the parents must live in slavery. Even if they desire to become Christians, it is only rarely permitted, because the English law prescribes that after seven years' service they are [in that case] to be freed, in accordance with the Mosaic law. When a slave is bought from the captain of a ship, he is not paid at once, but the slave so bought usually plants tobacco, in order that the captain may be paid with it. Lately, before my departure, I was over night on a ship, which several days before had come from Guiné with 230 slaves. They get them there for a small sum, as also gold and ivory, but a hundred of them died on the journey to Virginia. It is said to be a very unhealthy country. Half of the sailors died also, including the brother of the captain, who had sailed along as clerk. The others were sickly and yellow in their faces. It often happens that the ships must be left in Guiné because everybody dies of sickness.... I was surprized at the animal-like people, The savages [Indians] are a far better breed. Among such people food tastes so badly, that one can hardly stand it. The negro fever is due to this, because it is their common sickness. It clings to people for a long time and emaciates them very much.

18 Fait Accompli: 1708

If there could be any doubt about the transformation in labor relations and race relations worked in the colonies since around 1680,
two letters by Edmund Jennings, President of the Council of Virginia
to the Lords of Trade, in 1708 should suggest how much change
there had been. The decline of white servants, the assumed association of Negroes and slavery, the direct trade with Africa, the rapid
increase in the number of blacks and the nature of the labor force—
all pointed to one conclusion: African slavery had been established
in North America.

Source: William L. Saunders, ed., *The Colonial Records of North Carolina* (Raleigh, 1886),
Vol. 1, 692-94.

VIRGINIA NOVEMBER Y^e 27th 1708

May it please yor Lordships
    ... I have computed the labouring Tithable persons to be about thirty thou-
sand, whereof about twelve thousand Negros, the rest being almost all Free
men; for the number of white servants is so inconsiderable, that they scarce
deserve notice.... So ... the number of Tithable persons (among which are
included all masters of familys and their male children above the age of sixteen)
have increased within these three years about three thousand, partly by the
Natives coming of age, but chiefly by the importation of Negros. It is possible
that ... yor Lordships may be induced to expect a far greater encrease to our
number, but to satisfy your Lordships therein I beg leave to acquaint yor Lordships, that besides the distempers usual among new Negros wch carry off not a
few of them, many of our poorer sort of Inhabitants daily remove into our

neighboring Colonies, especially to North Carolina which is the reason that the number of our Inhabitants doth not increase proportionally to what might be expected.

My Lords

Your Lord^{ps} most obedient Servt

E. JENINGS

VIRGINIA NOVEMBER ye 27th 1708

May it please yor Lordsps,

    ... [I] have herewith sent yor Lordships an account of all the Negros imported into this Colony from the 24th of June 1699 to the 12th of October last past distinguishing those imported by the Royal African Company (679), and those by seperate Traders (5928), wherein yor Lordships will perceive the latter have had much the greater Share. As to the particular Rates at which those Negros have been sold, they have been variable according to the different times of their coming in and the quality & ages of the Slaves, but the medium for men & women may be reckoned from 20 to 30 pounds a head for those sold by the Company & from 20 to 35£ a head for the like kinds sold by the seperate Traders, who in gen^{ll} have sold theirs at a higher rate than the Company.

    ... Before the year 1680 what negros were brought to Virginia were imported generally from Barbados for it was very rare to have a Negro ship come to this Country directly from Africa since that time, and before the year 1698, the Trade of Negros became more frequent, tho not in any proportion to what it hath been of late, during which the Affrican Company sent several Ships and others by their Licence (as I have been informed) having bought their Slaves of the Company brought them in hither for Sale, Among which I remember the late Alderman Jeffrys & Sr Jeffry Jeffrys were principally concerned, but all this time the price of the Negros was currant from 18 to 25 per head for men and women & never exceeded that Rate. Whether the opening the Trade to Africa having created an Emulation between the Company and the Seperate Traders which should outbid the other in the purchase of their Slaves there, or whether the dexterity of their Factors there in taking advantage of the prevailing humour of our Inhabitants for some years past of buying Negros even beyond their abilities, or the Concurrence of both, hath raised the Rates of Negros so extravagantly I shall not pretend to determine but this I may venture to say that it will be much harder to lower the price again now tis raised unless there be the same Freedom of Trade continued as formerly for tho the Inhabitants of this Country in gen^{ll} will not be so fond of purchasing Negros as of late being sensibly convinced of their Error which has in a manner ruined the Credit of the Country yet there will still be some that must, & others that will at any rate Venture to buy them, & if the Company alone have the Management of the Trade, they'l find pretences enough to keep up the price if not to impose what higher rate they please, which the buyer must submit to, knowing he cannot be supplyed by any other hand. As for Vessells trading directly from this place to the Coast of Africa I never knew of any nor is the same practicable this Country not being provided with Comoditys suitable for carrying on such a Trade.....

My Lords
Your Lordships
most obedient servant
E. JENINGS

II

Slavery and Social Relationships

19 Race, Slavery, and the Double-Bind

The institutionalization and codification of slavery should not be mistaken for the cementing of a rigid pattern of race relations where there previously had been flexibility. The complexities and the inherent contradictions of human bondage remained and had to be managed, by blacks and whites, on a day-to-day basis. Particularly relevant in understanding those contradictions is Gregory Bateson's anthropological formulation of the "double-bind," a notion that focuses on the ambiguous, even schizophrenic, response offered to persons in authority when they transmit to those under them conflicting messages of, say, love and understanding and rejection and distance. With exactly such conflicting demands of subservience tempered with humanity and independence in work, the master/slave, white/black relationship became clouded. On the one hand the situation required blacks to cope with an incredibly complex situation simply trying to figure out what was indeed required of them and what they might be limited to. On the other hand, the ambiguity of the circumstances reflected as much on the white owners and overseers who wrestled with the problem of what they could allow and what they could expect within this slave/race relationship. Their responses may well be all the more revealing given the paternalistic self-image owners often liked to promote. The following two extracts from letters sent by Henry St. George Tucker to his father four months apart reflect the conflicting feelings and expectations plaguing a master. On the one hand this master detected that his slave felt all too much his equal and exhibited too much confidence; on the other hand, having disposed of that slave, Tucker discovered that his new slave had human emotions and feelings similar to his own. One can only wonder how long it was before the new slave, thus assured of his master's understanding, took the fateful step of assuming it and also acting as an equal and thus evoking Tucker's reprisal once again. The other possibilities are that he delicately maneuvered around that double-bind by offering a deliberately ambiguous response; or that he began to offer the unthinking, automatically ambiguous response of the schizophrenic.

Source: Mrs. George Coleman, ed., *Virginia Silhouettes: Contemporary Letters Concerning Negro Slavery in the State of Virginia* (Richmond, 1934), pp. 8-10.

Winchester Oct. 10th 1803

—Charles, I presume, informed you that I have advertised Johnny for sale. Human forbearance could not have waited longer, and I have therefore been willing to comply with your directions. Indeed, my dear Sir, you cannot imagine the vexation I have met with. Today I have detected him wearing my clothes even. I cannot then hesitate about parting with him. Yet I fear it will be a difficult matter, he has become so well-known. Will you let me know what are the lowest terms on which you will part with him. I have been offered three hundred dollars, payable May next, with security as good as the bank. I suppose however this is less than his value. If I cannot dispose of him here, had I not better send him down to Williamsburg?

Winchester Feb. 17th 1804

—I enclose a short note from Bob to his mother. Poor little fellow! I was much affected at an incident last night. I was waked from a very sound sleep by a most piteous lamentation. I found it was Bob. I called several times before he waked. "What is the matter Bob?," "I was dreaming about my mammy Sir"!!! cried he in a melancholy & still distressed tone: "Gracious God!" thought I, "how ought not I to feel, who regarded this child as insensible when compared to those of our complexion." In truth our thoughts had been straying the same way. How finely woven, how delicately sensible must be those bonds of natural affection which equally adorn the civilized and savage. The American and African—nay the man and the brute! I declare I know not a situation in which I have been lately placed that touched me so nearly as that incident I have just related.

20 A Paternalistic Dilemma

The questions surrounding the proper relationship between white and black in slavery touched all social relations. Again, given the paternalistic model many planters posed, the family of the planter would be shaped somehow by the existence of other wards. In what way would children be different from slaves? By the logic of the planter mentality, the racial characteristics should determine some difference; yet the stereotype of the black slave as child-like meant there would be virtually none. In this observation by an English governess who tutored the children of Governor John Milton of Florida in 1861, some of the complexities of the situation can be seen. Curiously the teacher attributes to the children of the governor precisely the qualities often attributed to the blacks: a lack of discipline and a lack of appreciation of "the delights of any kind of labor." Who mirrored whom?

Source: Sarah L. Jones, "Governor Milton and His Family," *Florida Historical Quarterly*, 2 (July 1909), 47-49, 49-50.

As no sound of the word *study* was heard, I began to suggest some sort of commencement, but Mrs. Milton said, "The girls have had so little time to themselves, that they don't feel inclined to begin this week;" and that my predecessor had not long departed. Five girls, and a boy of about the age of Johnny Quence, also called Johnny, were to be my pupils. The rest were too young. We had our school house across the "yard," as that trodden portion of the woods was called; it was a large room with seven windows and two doors, not one of which had a fastening. Books, slates, torn fragments and old covers were littered all over this apartment, in which were some old shabby rickety desks, an antique piano, and benches.

For a time I labored hard to establish some system of order and tidiness, but in spite of blockade and scarcity, torn, worn, scribbled books, broken slates and lost pencils were of every-day occurrence. A great long row of books that I had arranged on the old piano, was one morning missing entirely; no one knew what had become of them, no one had touched them or seen them, but they were gone!

... I tried hard to get locks or some kind of fastenings put upon the doors, which should "certainly be done;" but every time any one went into town the locks were forgotten, and as each week produced a great scarcity and a higher price for articles they were "quite forgot" until not procurable at all.

Necessarily immense patience and some very grave faces required to be summoned over all these baneful habits. The pleasantest smiles and readiest promises responded to my expostulations, and there the responsibilities of the young ladies ceased. Their mother thanked me frequently for endeavoring to make her children orderly and systematic, which she said none of their governesses had ever troubled themselves to do, excepting one English lady, who she was so very sorry had gone away. She had tried very much herself, she said, to enforce these things upon her children, but she could not induce them to pay attention. No; Southern parents who have been reared on the same principles do not understand the discipline necessary to *enforce* any system. They are too indulgent, too much accustomed to control an inferior class, and to allow their children to control that class, to reconcile to themselves the idea of compelling obedience in their own children when once past infancy, which would perhaps be placing them too much on a par with the negroes.

* * *

Johnny and I managed to lay out a few garden beds, but William, the head and chief, as well as the chief head of the domestic establishment, was required by His Excellency at Tallahassee; and as for "Jim" and any of the other mischievous negro children, one could never secure them when wanted. The elder negroes were too busy planting, or ploughing, or chopping wood, or doing something else to render any assistance. When the weather permitted, I worked harder on those garden beds, than the united labour of any three slaves on the place, while Johnny and the girls stood and watched me in astonishment, entreating me not to take so much trouble. I endeavoured in vain to persuade them to come and help, and that it was a delightful amusement. None of them could comprehend the delights of any kind of labour. Even Johnny called to a negro boy to hold his spade or to carry a root, and at last for want of physical strength myself, and finding it impossible to create a taste for exertion in any one else, the garden was almost abandoned.

21 The Limits of Paternalism

While the paternalistic pose was designed to emphasize the responsibilities the master assumed for his dependents and the rewarding qualities such responsibility naturally produced, the familial model was less than universal. The parental tyrant could be the model as well. In this episode from a 1784 news account, such paternal tyranny is clear.

Source: "The Unbridled Fury of a North Carolina Planter," *The North Carolina Historical Review*, 3 (April 1926), 371.

Charleston, Nov. 1, 1784.

—The following is, perhaps, as singular an instance of unrelenting tyranny, as is to be met with in the histories of base actions, which individuals have left to be recorded for the mortification of mankind. A Planter in North Carolina, being seized with a dangerous disease, conceived himself neglected by the Negro girl that attended him, ordered his son to put her immediately to death; the young gentlemen being unwilling to punish with such severity, a fault which was unvoluntary, remonstrated against the dictatorial mandate with so much feeling and humanity, as to put the old brute out of all patience. He commanded the son to quit the room, and sent for a lawyer to whom he gave orders for such an alteration in his will, as left his son a beggar; he then called the girl to his bedside, and, whilst the attendants held her, animated with fury and revenge, he raised himself up in the bed and cut off all her toes, after which nature being exhausted by the violence of the exertion, he expired.

22 A Lazy Libertine?

The work habits of black slaves never ceased to be a favorite subject of speculation and philosophizing by those whites who occupied themselves in the leisurely custom of watching blacks work. The normal judgment was unequivocal: blacks were lazy, whether because of heredity or the bond situation, though more and more laziness came to be considered hereditary and slavery all the more necessary. Yet the habits the masters usually describe focus not so much on their slaves' perpetual idleness as on the seasonal nature of that idleness. Here the observation may have had a germ of truth stemming as it does from the intrinsic nature of agricultural labor, which by its very essence demands alternating periods of intensive work and rest. It is based more on the natural rhythms of the sun and seasons than on the mechanical discipline of the clock which would later become the measure of work and productivity. Moreover, the same habits of laziness and uninspired work would repeatedly be attributed to other groups who, like blacks, either operated in pre-industrial, pre-market circumstances or who were freshly emerged from such circumstances into a more mechanically oriented activity. Notice how the following description of Louisiana slaves around 1800 begins with the truism that the Negro is lazy and winds up a few sentences later arguing that "their toils are nevertheless excessive."

Source: Berquin-Duvallon, ed., *Travels in Louisiana and the Floridas in the Year 1802*, trans. by J. Davis (New York, 1806), pp. 84-85.

From this digression let us return to the examination of the negro slave of Louisiana. He has the faults of a slave. He is lazy, libertine, and given to lying, but not incorrigibly wicked. His labour is not severe, unless it be at the rolling of sugars, an interval of from two to three months, when the number of labourers is not proportionate to the labour; then he works both by day and night. It must be allowed that forty negroes rolling a hundred and twenty thousand weight of sugar, and as many hogsheads of syrup, in the short space of two cold, foggy, rainy months (November and December) under all the difficulties and embarrassments resulting from the season, the shortness of the days, and the length of the nights, cannot but labour severely; abridged of their sleep, they scarce retire to rest during the whole period. It is true they are then fed more plentifully, but their toils are nevertheless excessive.

23 The Duty of Race

The transfer of the cultural qualities of pre-industrial workers in servitude to a particular race involved generation upon generation, but the process was as certain as it was powerful. The result was that a seasonal and task orientation to labor came to be viewed as inherent black laziness; a belief in the immanence of the supernatural in any other than a narrowly conceived Christianity became superstition inherent in blacks; and the necessity of mutual societal obligations in a pre-market, pre-contractual sense came to be the obligations of the black race to the white. The following selections from the Rev. Charles Colcock Jones, *The Religious Instruction of Negroes in the United States,* illuminate some of the exact contours of a condescending paternalism. Jones was a planter slave-owner in Georgia. In the first passage he considers the superstitiousness of the blacks; in the second he calls attention to "the degraded moral character" of blacks; and in the third he expresses the necessary obedience due masters, not just by servants, but by Negroes. It should be noted that Jones was attempting to construct a model of a pre-market society in which competition determined nothing and in which the obligations of heredity and inherent capabilities and limits shaped the destinies of peoples, destinies that could be altered only through religious inculcation. The superstitions he bemoans were common in Europe two centuries earlier. The commandment toward obedience was similar in many ways to Paul Baynes' injunctions of 1643. The social and psychic origins of the rampant immorality associated with blacks by the mid-nineteenth century remain obscure, but Jones hints slightly at them with his reference to it as a licensed culture, as a quality of people who live almost in a state of child-like innocence who do not yet conceive sin and the fall of Adam.

Source: Charles Colcock Jones, *The Religious Instruction of the Negroes in the United States* (Savannah, 1842), pp. 127-28, 103-4, 198-201.

They believe in second-sight, in apparitions, charms, witchcraft, and in a kind of irresistible Satanic influence. The superstitions brought from Africa have not been wholly laid aside. Ignorance and superstition render them easy dupes to their teachers, doctors, prophets, conjurers; to artful and designing men. When fairly committed to such leaders, they may be brought to the commission of almost any crime. Facts in their history prove this. On certain occasions they have been made to believe that while they carried about their persons some charm with which they had been furnished, they were invulnerable. They have, on certain other occasions, been made to believe that they were under a protection that rendered them invincible. That they might go any where and do any thing they pleased, and it would be impossible for them to be discovered or known; in fine, to will was to do—safely, successfully. They have been known to be so perfectly and fearfully under the influence of some leader or conjurer or minister, that they have not dared to disobey him in the least particular; not to disclose their own intended or perpetrated crimes, in view of inevitable death itself; notwithstanding all other influences brought to bear upon them. Their superstition is made gain of by the conjurers and others like them. They are not only imposed and practiced upon to their hurt, by these more prominent characters, but by each other more privately, by "tricking" as it is called, for the gratification of revenge, or of lust, or of covetousness. A plain and faithful presentation of the Gospel, usually weakens if not destroys these superstitions.

* * *

From childhood we have been accustomed to their slovenly, and too frequently, their scanty dress; to their broken English, ignorance, vulgarity, and vice. What in them would disgust or grieve a stranger, or truly afflict us if seen in white persons, we pass by with little or no impression, as a matter of course;—they are Negroes. Their character is held in low estimation, throughout the United States; and, considering what it is, not without reason; for that character cannot be esteemed which in itself is not estimable. Whatever is idle, dissolute, criminal, and worthless, attaches to them. Unconsciously, or rather, instinctively, we determine what the fruits must be from their known character, condition, and circumstances; and when they do appear, we are not surprised, We say, "what better can be expected?"

Such a general corruption of morals as would blast the reputation of any white community, is known to exist among them; and yet how unaffected are we by it? Indeed, the habit of our mind is to consider them in a state of moral degradation; to expect little that is truly excellent and praiseworthy; and to feel lightly, and to pass over as well as we can, what is revolting in them. We are disposed not to try them as we would others by that standard which is holy, just, and good; but by a low and worldly standard, accommodated to their character and circumstances. Vice seems to lose its hideousness in proportion as it shades itself in black; as in painting, with black we obliterate the warm light and soft shades, and native hues, which gave depth and life and beauty to the picture, and the eye rests upon the dark, dead surface without emotion.

The Gospel recognizes the condition in which the Negroes are, and inculcates the duties appropriate to it. Ministers are commanded by the Apostle Paul to "exhort servants to be obedient to their own masters and to please them well in all things; not answering again, not purloining; but showing all good fidelity, that they may adorn the doctrine of God our Saviour in all things; for the grace of God, that bringeth salvation, hath appeared to all men; teaching us that denying ungodliness and worldly lusts, we should live soberly righteously and godly in this present world."—Titus 2: 9-12....

Such are the commands of the Gospel to servants, as comprehensive of their duties as any master could desire; and all excuses for unfaithfulness and insubordination carefully guarded against. Yea, we hear the Apostle Paul exclaim, "let every man abide in the same calling wherein he was called. Art thou called being a servant? Care not for it; but if thou mayest be free choose it rather. For he that is called in the Lord being a servant, is the Lord's freeman; likewise also, he that is called being free is Christ's servant. Ye are bought with a price, be not ye the servants of men. Brethren let every man wherein he is called, therein abide with God."—1 Cor. 7: 20-24....

We now ask, will the duties of servants to their masters be neglected, and their authority despised, by instructions of this sort, and by a careful adherence to the example of the Apostle Paul on the part of the ministers of the Gospel? No never. Is not the discharge of duty made more sure and faithful, and respect for authority strengthened by considerations drawn from the omniscience of God and the retribution of eternity? The fact is not to be questioned. Joseph exclaimed "how can I do this great wickedness and sin against God?" And what was the reply of the Christian Negro when the ground of his obedience and fidelity to his master was inquired into? "Sir, I fear God, whose eyes are in every place beholding the evil and the good: therefore do I obey and am faithful as well behind my master's back as before his face."

What parent considers the religious instruction of his children, as having a tendency to make them more wicked and rebellious? Should neglect of duty and insubordination ensue upon the religious instruction of servants, the fault will be discovered in imperfect instruction, or in the mismanagement of the master.

24 A Licensed Culture

What Charles Colcock Jones saw as the innately degraded moral character of blacks came to be viewed by others as an unrestrained libido. That quality had been noticed or expressed since Europeans had first made contact with blacks, but within slavery it became a hardened cultural attribute in the eyes of whites. Yet in a system of social control as thorough as slavery pretended to be and as thorough as its antagonists claimed, the wanton lust that so many white people, like Dr. Francis Le Jau in his 1708 letter below, perceived must be explained. Much of that explanation rests upon the whites themselves. As Le Jau observed, black promiscuity was "tollerated or at least Connived at by us under a pretence of Impossibility" to cure.

Source: Frank J. Klingberg, ed., *The Carolina Chronicle of Dr. Francis Le Jau, 1706-1717* (University of California Publications in History), Vol. 53 (Berkeley, 1956), pp. 41-42.

Another scruple which I must not conceal from the Honble Society is, whether or no we are not to answer for grievous sins dayly Committed by all our Slaves here and elsewhere, and tollerated or at least Connived at by us under a pretence of Impossibility to remedy them; tho' I'm sure we cou'd prevent all those evils if we wou'd take pains about it, but Masters are content if their slaves labour much and cost them little trouble and Charges; The evil I complain of is the constant and promiscuous cohabiting of Slaves from different Sexes and Nations together; When a Man or Woman's fancy dos alter about his Party they throw up one another and take others which they also change when they please this is a General Sin, for the exceptions are so few they are hardly worth mentioning.

25 The Stimulus to Licentiousness

That whites were doing more than tolerating the depravity they attributed to blacks, free or slave, is apparent in the following account of blacks and mulattoes in New Orleans at the beginning of the nineteenth century. Whites appear to have been attributing to blacks the qualities that they most envied and the passions they most enjoyed. Indeed, the implication of Berquin-Duvallon's observation is that the mulatto women of New Orleans may have valued their commitments to their husbands and race more than did the white men who enjoyed their embraces.

Source: Berquin-Duvallon, *Travels in Louisiana and The Floridas in the Year 1802*, trans. by J. Davis (New York, 1806), p. 80.

The mulatto women have not all the faults of the men. But they are full of vanity, and very libertine; money will always buy their caresses. They are not without personal charms; good shapes, polished and elastic skins. They live in open concubinage with the whites; but to this they are incited more by money than any attachment. After all we love those best, and are most happy in the intercourse of those, with whom we can be the most familiar and unconstrained. These girls, therefore, only affect a fondness for the whites; their hearts are with men of their own color.

26 A Fitting Punishment

The following excerpt from the laws of North Carolina, and the records of the execution of that law following it, focuses upon castration as a punishment for crimes perpetrated by blacks. A correct understanding of the significance of this treatment would begin with the consideration that rape and murder were excluded from this punishment. It applied to lesser crimes, and notably, not sex-related crimes. With that in mind, the law and its execution suggest not that the black man was dominated by his testes, but that the white man may have been possessed of a threat to his own by this libidinous people. What more fitting punishment then for a black man who had dared challenge the system of authority?

Source: Walter Clark, ed., *The State Records of North Carolina*, Vol. 23, *Laws 1715-1716* (Goldsboro, N.C., 1904), pp. 488-89; Vol. 22, *Miscellaneous* (Goldsboro, N.C., 1907), pp. 818-19, 824-25.

An additional Act to an Act, intituled, An Act concerning Servants and Slaves. [1758]

I. Whereas many great Charges have arisen to the Province of Punishment of Slaves who having Liberty from their Owners to hire themselves out, and having committed Robberies; by the Importation of Slaves from Foreign Parts for Crimes by them committed; by the condemnation of Slaves to Death for capital Crimes, for want of a punishment adequate to the Crimes they have been guilty of; and by the High Valuation of Slaves condemned to Death, or killed by Virtue of an Outlawry;

II. Be it Enacted, by the Governor, Council, and Assembly, and by the Authority of the same, That no Person who shall Permit any Slave to hire himself or herself out, shall be intitled to receive any Pay from the Public, should they be punished for any Crimes by them committed during the Time of such Permission; any Usage or Custom, to the contrary, notwithstanding.

III. And be it further Enacted, by the Authority aforesaid, That no Person hereafter purchasing any Slave, transported for Crimes from foreign Parts into this Province, shall be intitled to receive any Payment from the Public, should such Slave afterwards be convicted and punished for any Crimes committed within this Province; unless he first make Oath, in the Court appointed for trying such Slave, that he did not at the Time of his purchasing, know that such Slave had been transported here for any Crimes committed in Foreign Parts.

IV. And be it further Enacted, by the Authority aforesaid, That no male Slave shall for the First Offence, by condemned to Death, unless for Murder or Rape; but for every other Capital Crime, shall for the First Offence, suffer castration, which punishment every Court trying such Slave, shall be impowered, and are hereby directed to cause to, be inflicted; and the Sheriff shall cause such Judgment to be duly Executed; for which he shall have and receive, from the Public, Twenty Shillings, Proclamation Money, and no more; any Usage or Custom to the contrary, notwithstanding.

V. Provided always, That such Slave be valued by the Court Trying him, in the Usual Manner, that in case Death should ensue the Owner might be paid by the Public; and that the Sum of Three Pounds, Proclamation Money, shall be allowed and paid by the Public, to defray the expense of the Cure, of each slave Castrated.

VI. And be it further Enacted, by the Authority aforesaid, That there shall not be allowed by the Public to the owner of any Slave which shall hereafter happen to be convicted of any Capital Offence, killed on outlawry, or in being apprehended when run away, more than the Sum of Sixty Pounds, Proclamation Money; any Law or Custom to the contrary, notwithstanding.

27 The Greater Abomination

From 1733 to 1765 Johann Martin Bolzius served as a religious leader in the young colony of Georgia. Drawing upon his experiences there he attempted to answer a series of questions about Georgia and Carolina to inform Europeans of the state of matters there. Much of his attention focused upon slavery. In his discussion of intermarriage and the clothing of slaves Bolzius indicates again the hand of the white man in shaping the licentious culture, or at least one that they so perceived. As whites fathered children of black mothers and kept their slaves near naked, the origins of this "licentiousness" become clear.

Source: Klaus G. Loewald, Beverly Starika, and Paul S. Taylor, trans. and eds., "Johann Martin Bolzius Answers a Questionnaire on Carolina and Georgia," *William and Mary Quarterly*, Third Series, 14 (April 1957), 235, 236. Reprinted with the kind permission of Paul S. Taylor, Klaus G. Loewald, and Beverly Starika Tangri.

15th Question. Whether white servants may marry Negresses, & vice versa, white servant girls may marry Negroes, and how the freedom of the children of such marriages is determined.

Answer. Such mixings or marriages are not allowed by the laws; but just as all manner of terrible abominations are rampant in Carolina, I have learned of 2 white women, one French and one German, who have secretly disgraced themselves with Negroes and have borne black children. However, an abomination more common and all too common in Carolina is that white men live in sin with Negresses and father half-black children who walk around in large numbers to the shame of the Christian name. They are perpetual slaves just like their mothers.

* * *

In winter the Negroes must be kept warm, but in summer they go naked, except that the men cover their shame with a cloth rag which hangs from a strap tied around the body. The women have petticoats; the upper body is bare. The children of both sexes go about in summer just as they left the mother's womb. In winter Negro men and women have shoes, none in summer. One does not give the children any work beyond guarding the rice in the field from the rice birds, and possibly serving at table. They are spared from work so that they may grow big and strong. In winter Negro clothing consists of a woolen blue or white camisole, a pair of long pants of cloth down to the shoes, no shirt, and a woolen cap. At night they lie around the fire, and have woolen blankets. The clothing for each Negro comes to about 10s. or 4 1/2 fl. (except for the carpets or woolen blankets). When the masters drive or ride to town with Negroes, they give them better clothes. The skilled Negroes in Charlestown, who are used in the offices and shops or who are mistresses are very well dressed. Food for a Negro does not come to much over 8d. or 16 kr. a week. They have to take as their wives or husbands whomever their master gives them without ceremonies. Most of them live in whoredom.

28 Not So Singular a Sight

Increasingly it becomes clear that a widespread nudity or near nudity when weather permitted was associated with the slaves. Nor was it just the hands in the field. The relationship between the races seems to have had a highly sexed charge whether in the big house, the field, or at the auction block. When George Grieve translated the *Travels* of the Marquis de Chastellux he added his own note to the original text commenting on his own observations of sexual propriety in the South during the Revolutionary War. For further documentation of this point concerning immodesty in the big house see the Alfred J. Morrison trans. and ed., edition of Johann David Schoepf, *Travels in the Confederation [1783-1784]* (Philadelphia, 1911), 1, 357; 2, 147; and Winthrop D. Jordan's quotation of a Pennsylvania military officer in 1781 observing the waiters at tables in Virginia: "I am surprized this does not hurt the feelings of this fair Sex to see these young boys of about Fourteen and Fifteen years Old to Attend them, these whole nakedness Expos'd and I can Assure you It would Surprize a person to see these d—d black boys how well they are hung." Jordan, *White Over Black: American Attitudes Toward the Negro, 1550-1812* (Chapel Hill, 1968), 159.

Source: Howard C. Rice, Jr., trans. and ed., *Travels in North America in the Years 1780, 1781, and 1782 by the Marquis de Chastellux* (Chapel Hill, 1963), p. 585.

It was a singular sight for an European to behold the situation of the negroes in the southern provinces during the war, when clothing was extremely scarce. I have frequently seen in Virginia, on visits to gentlemen's houses, young negroes and negresses running about or basking in the courtyard naked as they came into the world, with well characterized marks of perfect puberty; and young negroes from sixteen to twenty years old, with not an article of clothing, but a loose shirt, descending half way down their thighs, waiting at table where were ladies, without any apparent embarrassment on one side, or the slightest attempt at concealment on the other.

29 "This Is Not Right"

The testimony of a former slave on this matter adds weight to the suspicion of the origin of the "degraded moral character" evident under slavery. John Brown was born a slave and lived his first decade in the area of Virginia where shortly afterwards Nat Turner would lead possibly the most famous slave insurrection in the history of the South.

Source: L. A. Chamerozow, ed., *Slave in Georgia: A Narrative of the Life, Sufferings, and Escape of John Brown, A Fugitive Slave, Now in England* (London, 1855), as reprinted in F. N. Boney, "The Blue Lizard: Another View of Nat Turner's Country on the Eve of Rebellion," *Phylon*, 31 (Winter 1970), 354.

The children of both sexes usually run about quite naked, until they are from ten to twelve years of age. I have seen them as old as twelve, going about in this state, or with only an old shirt, which they would put on when they had to go anywhere very particular for their mistress, or up to the great house.

The clothing of the men consists of a pair of thin cotton pantaloons, and a shirt of the same material, two of each being allowed them every year. The women wear a shirt similar to the men's, and a cotton pitticoat, which is kept on by means of braces passing over their shoulders. But when they are in the field, the shirt is thrown aside. They also have two suits allowed them every year. These, however, are not enough. They are made of the lowest quality of material, and get torn in the bush, so that the garments soon become useless, even for the purposes of the barest decency. We slaves feel that this is not right, and we grew up with very little sense of shame; but immorality amongst ourselves is not common, for all that.

30 Eros and Civilization

It would not, of course, be sufficient simply to suggest that the view of blacks as highly sexed beings stemmed from the projection of white desires onto a group of people already in subjection. The need for explanation remains. And it is here that evidence and theory become most contentious as relations fade off into a blur of social, sexual, racial, and, indeed, historical cloudiness. Yet some suggestions and clues can be found. One hint emerges from an observation by Timothy Ford in his diary when he was in Charleston, South Carolina. What he noticed was an excessive formality in their social functions, excessive in that he observed it when people were at their most relaxed. This distance of formality may indeed be the same phenomenon to which Berquin-Duvallon obliquely referred (Document 25) when he suggested that the greater passionate release comes with those with "whom we can be the most familiar and unconstrained." It could be that in the effort to create a paternalistic set of social relations the family relations, whether parents and children or husband and wife, were becoming stylized, even being sacrificed, to a pontifical set of images that could justify subjection and supremacy along racial lines. What on one scale included the formalization of relations between family members (and members of society at large?) and the abandonment of frankness and straightforward habits of discipline (Document 20), on the other scale meant the establishment of libidinous images and relations or projections of desires in the only socially permissible way: the invention of an erotic people and environment for the psychic or even physical release of tensions produced by a de-sexed, sterile forum devoted to a form of racial superiority and cultural "civilization." Only then, with such an artificial division, could the illusion of higher morality, and the justification it provided for slavery, be sustained and the psychic equilibrium of eros and performance be secured. It may well be, as a consequence, that the claims of slaveholders to a paternalistic system merit legitimacy; if so, this circumstance may testify to the complete artificiality of such a system in the American South in the eighteenth and nineteenth centuries. Finally, that such sacrifice, illusion, and self-conscious striving for paternalism should emerge with such enormous cost reinforces the emphasis on the psychic benefits of paternalism as a system of social relations preferable to the competitive individualistic, even atomistic, relations of the marketplace. At its worst this system represented a fraud perpetrated on one race by another for illusory gains. At its best it represented a desperate and possibly even well meaning effort to create social relations different from and superior to those of the market.

Source: Joseph W. Barnwell, ed., "Diary of Timothy Ford, 1785-1786," *The South Carolina Historical and Genealogical Magazine*, 13 (October 1912), 190-91.

The citizens as would naturally be expected relax in some degree that rigid formality for which they are remarked—but still they retain more than enough. It is hard that hospitality should thus want its most essential part (sociability) and that a person cannot be made an object of politeness without being also made an object of formality. The ladies carry formality & scrupulosity to a considerable extreme; a stranger makes his female acquaintance by slow gradations interspersed with niceties & punctilios w^h. often disconcert the forward & intimidate the bashful. The maxims of the country have taught them & custom has forced them to almost consider a sociability on their part with gentlemen as an unbecoming forwardness—& they are by this means circumscribed within such narrow bounds as exclude the frankness & care which are necessary to put people on the most agreeable footing and constitutes the principal charms of Society.

31 A Red-Hot Experience

In the passage that follows Frederick Law Olmsted described a whipping that he figured to be "by no means unusual in its severity." The precise form in this instance, however common or uncommon, was accepted in a matter of fact way by both the overseer and the boy, and indeed seems not to have come as too much of a surprise to the woman whipped. And that form raises a variety of questions. After all, the punishment begins in almost a ritualistic way with the eighteen-year-old woman kneeling, not for supplication but possibly in a symbolic fellatio, and then proceeds to a particularly sexually oriented flagellation as he whips the naked woman's front across the loins and thighs while taking in all of her "writhing, grovelling, and screaming." It concludes with her abandonment to her own "choking, sobbing, spasmodic groans." The overseer could then laugh and observe that the blacks had trouble initially adjusting to his ways but then they got used to him "and like him better than any of the rest." The psychic electricity involved in this brief episode boggles the mind with its complexity. What mental gratification was involved here? Who was fooling whom? As Olmsted admitted, it was a red-hot experience for him partly because of the restraint he used in suppressing his outward feelings about it all. The overseer and the boy appear to have exercised more restraint. Might it not have been something more than red-hot for them? For us, at any rate, it can provide a searing insight into the volatile world of race relations under slavery.

Source: Frederick Law Olmsted, *The Cotton Kingdom: A Traveller's Observations on Cotton and Slavery in the American Slave States* (New York, 1861), Vol. 2, pp. 204-8.

I happened to see the severest corporeal punishment of a negro that I wit-
nessed at the South while visiting this estate. I suppose, however, that punishment equally severe is common; in fact, it must be necessary to the maintenance
of adequate discipline on every large plantation. It is much more necessary than
on shipboard, because the opportunities of hiding away and shirking labour,
and of wasting and injuring the owner's property without danger to themselves,
are far greater in the case of the slaves than in that of the sailors, but, above
all, because there is no real moral obligation on the part of the negro to do what
is demanded of him. The sailor performs his duty in obedience to a voluntary
contract; the slave is in an involuntary servitude. The manner of the overseer
who inflicted the punishment, and his subsequent conversation with me about
it, indicated that it was by no means unusual in severity. I had accidentally
encountered him, and he was showing me his plantation. In going from one
side of it to the other, we had twice crossed a deep gully, at the bottom of which
was a thick covert of brushwood. We were crossing it a third time, and had
nearly passed through the brush, when the overseer suddenly stopped his horse
exclaiming, "What's that? Hallo! who are you, there?"

It was a girl lying at full length on the ground at the bottom of the gully,
evidently intending to hide herself from us in the bushes.

"Who are you, there?"

"Sam's Sall, sir."

What are you skulking there for?"

The girl half rose, but gave no answer.

"Have you been here all day?"

"No, Sir."

"How did you get here?"

The girl made no reply.

"Where have you been all day?"

The answer was unintelligible.
After some further questioning, she said her father accidentally locked her in,
when he went out in the morning.

"How did you manage to get out?"

"Pushed a plank off, sir, and crawled out."

The overseer was silent for a moment, looking at the girl, and then said, "That
won't do; come out here." The girl arose at once, and walked towards him. She

was about eighteen years of age. A bunch of keys hung at her waist, which the overseer espied, and he said, "Your father locked you in; but you have got the keys." After a little hesitation, she replied that these were the keys of some other locks; her father had the door-key.

Whether her story were true or false, could have been ascertained in two minutes by riding on to the gang with which her father was at work, but the overseer had made up his mind.

"That won't do;" said he, "get down." The girl knelt on the ground; he got off his horse, and holding him with his left hand, struck her thirty or forty blows across the shoulders with his tough, flexible, "raw-hide" whip (a terrible instrument for the purpose). They were well laid on, at arm's length, but with no appearance of angry excitement on the part of the overseer. At every stroke the girl winced and exclaimed, "Yes, sir!" or "Ah, sir!" or "Please, sir!" not groaning or screaming. At length he stopped and said, "Now tell me the truth." The girl repeated the same story. "You have not got enough yet," said he; "pull up your clothes—lie down." The girl without any hesitation, without a word or look of remonstrance or entreaty, drew closely all her garments under her shoulders, and lay down upon the ground with her face toward the overseer, who continued to flog her with the raw hide, across her naked loins and thighs, with as much strength as before. She now shrunk away from him, not rising, but writhing, grovelling, and screaming, "Oh, don't sir! oh, please stop, master! please, sir! please, sir! oh, that's enough, master! oh, Lord! oh, master, master! oh, God master, do stop! oh, God, master! oh, God, master!"

A young gentleman of fifteen was with us; he had ridden in front, and now, turning on his horse, looked back with an expression only of impatience at the delay. It was the first time I had ever seen a woman flogged. I had seen a man cudgelled and beaten, in the heat of passion, before, but never flogged with a hundredth part of the severity used in this case. I glanced again at the perfectly passionless but rather grim business-like face of the overseer, and again at the young gentleman, who had turned away; if not indifferent he had evidently not the faintest sympathy with my emotion. Only my horse chafed. I gave him rein and spur and we plunged into the bushes and scrambled fiercely up the steep acclivity. The screaming yells and the whip strokes had ceased when I reached the top of the bank. Choking, sobbing, spasmodic groans only were heard. I rode on to where the road, coming diagonally up the ravine, ran out upon the cottonfield. My young companion met me there, and immediately afterward the overseer. He laughed as he joined us, and said:

"She meant to cheat me out of a day's work, and she has done it, too."

"Did you succeed in getting another story from her?" I asked, as soon as I could trust myself to speak.

"No; she stuck to it."

"Was it not perhaps true?"

"Oh no, sir; she slipped out of the gang when they were going to work, and she's been dodging about all day, going from one place to another as she saw me coming. She saw us crossing there a little while ago, and thought we had gone to the quarters, but we turned back so quick, we came into the gully before she knew it, and she could do nothing but lie down in the bushes."

"I suppose they often slip off so."

"No, sir; I never had one do so before—not like this; they often run away to the woods, and are gone some time, but I never had a dodge-off like this before."

"Was it necessary to punish her so severely?"

"Oh yes, sir," (laughing again.) "If I hadn't, she would have done the same thing again to-morrow, and half the people on the plantation would have followed her example. Oh, you've no idea how lazy these niggers are; you Northern people don't know anything about it. They'd never do any work at all if they were not afraid of being whipped."

We soon afterward met an old man, who, on being closely questioned, said that he had seen the girl leave the gang as they went to work after dinner. It appeared that she had been at work during the forenoon, but at dinner-time the gang was moved, and as it passed through the gully she slipped out. The driver had not missed her. The overseer said that when he first took charge of this plantation, the negroes ran away a great deal—they disliked him so much. They used to say, 'twas hell to be on his place; but after a few months they got used to his ways, and liked him better than any of the rest. He had not had any run away now for some time. When they ran away they would generally return within a fortnight. If many of them went off, or if they stayed out long, he would make the rest of the force work Sundays, or deprive them of some of their usual privileges until the runaways returned. The negroes on the plantation could always bring them in if they chose to do so. They depended on them for their food, and they had only to stop the supplies to oblige them to surrender.

Accepting the position of the overseer, I knew that this method was right, but it was a red-hot experience to me, and has ever since been a fearful thing in my memory. Strangely so, I sometimes think, but I suppose the fact that the delicate and ingenuous lad who was with me, betrayed not even the slightest flush of shame, and that I constrained myself from the least expression of feeling of any kind, made the impression in my brain the more intense and lasting.

32 The "Living Space" of Slavery

A central theme of the paternalist argument defending slavery was its salutary and civilizing influence on Africans. Such a posture could be maintained only by interpreting the responses of black people to demands made upon them in a superficial, unanalytic way. Instead of considering the circumstances of the double-bind or even, at its most simple level, the need to get along with minimum conflict and restraint in an oppressive institution, the responses and behavior patterns of blacks would be considered only in the most self-serving and unambiguous light. Thus the stereotypes: stupid, immoral, lazy, heathen, docile, sexual, and rhythmic creatures. Some whites, however, were sufficiently perceptive and frank to move beyond the veil of oppression. In the following selection John Dixon Long demonstrated that, to those who had the sensitivity at least, some approach could be made in comprehending the meaning of slavery for those whose lives were at birth possessed by it. In so doing he immediately questioned by implication the paternalist logic, accepting the possibility of a legitimate culture among black people. His was a sensitivity to what Eugene D. Genovese has referred to as a "living space" in which slaves possess a certain latitude for the exercise of autonomy and initiative within the restraints of the institution of slavery.

Source: John Dixon Long, *Pictures of Slavery in Church and State* (Philadelphia, 1857), pp. 196-98.

The inevitable tendency of servitude is to make a slave a hypocrite toward the white man. If you approach him from the standpoint of authority, you will never get an insight into his real character. He is exceedingly shrewd.... Let a slave once know or suspect that you are seeking to "pump" him, and if you don't meet with your match for once, then I am mistaken; even though you be an Eastern Shore or Delaware Yankee, the keenest of all Yankees, the genuine Boston specimens not excepted. You must catch him at work. Listen to his songs while seated on his ox-cart hauling woods, or splitting rails. You must overhear his criticisms in the quarters—his holiday songs and his self-made hymns. His songs do not always indicate a happy state of mind. He resorts to them in order to divert his thoughts from dwelling on his condition. The loud, merry laughter of the prostitute does not prove that she is happy. The songs of a slave are word-pictures of every thing he sees, or hears, or feels. The tunes once fixed in his memory, words descriptive of any and every thing are applied to them, as occasion requires. Here is a specimen, combining the sarcastic and pathetic. Imagine a colored man seated on the front part of an ox-cart, in an old field, unobserved by any white man, and in a clear loud voice, ringing out these words, which wake up sad thoughts in the minds of his fellow-slaves:

"William Rino sold Henry Silvers;
        Hilo! Hilo!
Sold him to de Gorgy trader;
        Hilo! Hilo!
His wife she cried, and children bawled,
        Hilo! Hilo!
Sold him to de Gorgy trader;
        Hilo! Hilo!

Here is a specimen in the religious vein.

"Working all day,
And part of the night
And up before the morning light.
Chorus.—When will Jehovah hear our cry,
And free the sons of Africa?"

33 The African Aura

The persistence of an African legacy in slave culture is obvious. Even those who denied the existence of an African civilization could observe the old ways, languages, beliefs, and customs interfering with what would no doubt otherwise be a more compliant work force. Among the blacks themselves this heritage took many forms, and not the least of them was a certain family pride in tracing their lineage back to Africa. Usually relayed by word of mouth from one generation to another, the stories could be very specific (witness Alex Haley's *Roots*) or only vague recollections. Possibly most were like the account that follows.

Source: A.M.H. Christensen, *Afro-American Folklore: Told Round Cabin Fires on the Sea Islands of South Carolina* (Boston, 1898), pp. 4-5.

But I was gwine to tell you 'bout my ol' gran'daddy. I ofting yeardy him tell how 'e was bring ober from Arfrica in a ship when 'e was a boy. De white man lef' de ship behin' and gone asho' in a small boat; an' when dey meet up wid my gran'daddy an' a whole parcel more, young boys like, all from de same village, dey hir dem wid piece ob red flannel an' ting for go 'long wid dem. But when dey git dem on bo'd de ship dey bring dem ober to dis country an' sell dem for slave. Dey bring my gran'daddy to Charleston an' ol' Marse Heywood buy um. When I was a small leetle boy 'e ben bery ol', too ol' for work, an' I use for hab it for my tarsk for min'um. So 'e tell me heap o' dese story, ef I only could 'member um, dat 'e used to yeardy way ober in Arfrica.

34 Race Pride and the High Yaller

In addition to pride in their African origin and legacy, a certain racial pride could be found among blacks. The fruit of the master's passion with one of his slave women did not command the natural respect and preferential treatment whites often expected to result from this "improvement" of the race. Indeed, in the passage below from one of the WPA interviews in the 1930s with ex-slaves, Dora Franks recalls her bitter experience as a mulatto in Mississippi.

Source: George P. Rawick, ed., *The American Slave: A Composite Autobiography*, Vol. 7, *Mississippi Narratives* (Westport, Conn., 1972), p. 49.

"My mammy come from Virginny. Her name was Harriet Brewer. My daddy was my young Marster. His name was Marster George Brewer an' my mammy always tol' me dat I was his'n. I know dat dere was some dif'ence 'tween me an' de res' o' her chillun, 'cause dy was all coal black, an' I was even lighter dan I is now. Lawd, it's been to my sorrow many a time, 'cause de chillun used to chase me 'round an' holler at me, 'Old yellow Nigger,' Dey didn't treat me good, neither.

35 A Forbidden Title

Evidence abounds that blacks in slavery had enormous difficulties maintaining a stable family life. Yet more and more historians have perceived that although threatened by the auction block, unprotected, discouraged, or prohibited by law, and ignored or discouraged by whites, black marriages and families not only existed but became an important part of the slaves' "living space." There private thoughts, values, and habits constituted the basic elements of a black culture that was to some degree independent of the culture imposed upon them by the white masters. One clue to this phenomenon is the number of slaves who maintained a surname independent of their masters and frequently unknown to them. The family name inherited by Jacob Stroyer is a clear example of this pattern.

Source: Jacob Stroyer, *My Life in the South* (Salem, 1885), pp. 15-16.

I said that my father was brought from Africa when but a boy, and was sold to old Col. Dick Singleton....

.... Father said that his father's name in Africa was Moncoso, and his mother's Mongomo, but I never learned what name he went by before he was brought to this country. I only know that he stated that Col. Dick Singleton gave him the name of William, by which he was known up to the day of his death. Father had a surname, Stroyer, which he could not use in public, as the surname Stroyer would be against the law; he was known only by the name of William Singleton, because this was his master's name. So the title Stroyer was forbidden him, and could be used only by his children after the emancipation of the slaves.

There were two reasons given by the slave holders why they did not allow a slave to use his own name, but rather that of the master. The first was that if he run away, he would not be so easily detected by using his own name, as if he used that of his master instead. The second was, that to allow him to use his own name would be sharing an honor which was due only to his master, and that would be too much for a negro, said they, who was nothing more than a servant. So it was held as a crime for the slave to be caught using his own name, which would expose him to severe punishment. But thanks be to God that those days have passed, and we now live under the sun of liberty.

36 A Question of Priority: Marriage vs. Freedom

It is also apparent that the family life formed by slaves was often more than the matter of convenience it appeared to the master. The premium that slaves placed on marriage and family can be seen vividly in this 1815 petition of Lucinda, a manumitted slave in Virginia who was willing to sacrifice her freedom in order to remain with her husband.

Source: U. B. Phillips, ed., *Plantation and Frontier Documents: 1649-1863* (Cleveland, 1909), Vol. 2, pp. 161-62.

To this Legislature of the Commonwealth of Virginia, the petition of Lucinda, lately a slave belonging to Mary Matthews of King George county, respectfully sheweth that the said Mary Matthews, by her last will and testament, among other things, emancipated all her slaves, and directed that they should be removed by her executor to some place where they could enjoy their freedom by the laws there in force: That all the slaves so emancipated (except your petitioner) were removed this year to the State of Tennessee; but your petitioner declined going with them, as she had a husband belonging to Capt. William H. Hoe in the King George county, from whom the benefits and privileges to be derived from freedom, dear and flattering as they are, could not induce her to be separated: that, in consequence of this determination on her part, a year has elapsed since the death of her late mistress Mary Matthews, and your petitioner is informed that the forfeiture of her freedom has taken place under the law prohibiting emancipated slaves from remaining in this State; and that the Overseers of the poor might now proceed to sell her for the benefit of the poor of the county: Your petitioner, still anxious to remain with her husband, for whom she has relinquished all the advantages of freedom, is apprehensive that, in case of a sale of her by the Overseers of the poor, she may be purchased by some person, who will remove her to a place remote from the residence of her husband:

to guard against such a heart rending circumstances, she would prefer, and hereby declares her consent, to become a slave to the owner of her husband, if your honorable body will permit it, and for that purpose she prays that you will pass a law vesting the title to her in the said William H. Hoe and directing that all proceedings on the part of the Overseers of the Poor for King George county to effect the sale of her may be perpetually staid, And your petitioner will pray &c.

Nov 27th 1815.   LUCINDA.

37 Against Her Will

No one would probably argue that all the marriages on the plantation were freely made and enjoyed any more than all marriages contracted in freedom could be so characterized. Yet neither should it be assumed that those coerced marriages were quickly assented to or taken lightly. In this WPA interview Rose Williams described first her childhood and her family which was fortunately purchased together, and then how her new master, who was in other respects kindly, forced a husband on her. The continued and determined resistance that she mounted to the imposed "marriage" suggests the value placed upon a certain kind of marriage and family, not just one imposed, and also something about morality within the slave quarters.

Source: George P. Rawick, ed., *The American Slave: A Composite Autobiography*, Vol. 5, *Texas Narratives* (Westport, Conn., 1972), pp. 174-78.

"I has de correct mem'randun of when de war start. Massa Black sold we'uns right den. Mammy and pappy powerful glad to git sold, and dey and I is put on de block with 'bout ten other niggers. When we'uns gits to de tradin' block, dere lots of white folks dere what come to look us over. One man shows de intres' in pappy. Him named Hawkins. He talk to pappy and pappy talk to him and say, "Dem my woman and chiles. Please buy all of us and have mercy on we'uns. Massa Hawkins say, 'Dat gal am a likely lookin' nigger, she am portly and strong, but three am more dan I wants, I guesses.'

"De sale start and 'fore long pappy am put on de block. Massa Hawkins wins de bid for pappy and when mammy am put on de block, he wins de bid for her. Den dere am three or four other niggers sold befo' my time comes. Den massa Black calls me to de block and de auction man say, 'What am I offer for dis portly young wench. She's never been 'bused and will made de good breeder.'

"I wants to hear Massa Hawkins bid, but him say nothin.' Two other men am biddin' 'gainst each other I sho' has de worryment. Dere am tears comin' down my cheeks 'cause I's bein' sold to some man dat would make sep'ration from my mammy. One man bids $500 and de auction man ask, 'Do I hear more? She am gwine at $500.00.' Den someone say, $525.00 and de auction many say, 'She am sold for $525.00 to Massa Hawkins. Am I glad and 'cited! Why, I's quiverin' all over.

"Massa Hawkins am good to he niggers and not force 'em work too hard. Dere am as much diff'ence 'tween him and old Massa Black in de way of treatment as 'twixt de Lawd and de devil. Massa Hawkins 'lows he niggers have reason'ble parties and go fishin', but we'uns am never tooken to church and no books for larnen'. Dere am no education for de niggers.

"Dere am one thing Massa Hawkins does to me what I can't shunt from my mind. I knows he don't do it for meanness, but I allus holds it 'gainst him. What he done am force me to live with dat nigger, Rufus, 'gainst my wants.

"After I been at he place 'bout a year, de massa come to me and say, "You gwine live with Rufus in dat cabin over yonder. Go fix it for livin'.' I's 'bout sixteen year old and has no larnin', and I's jus' igno'mus chile. I's thought dat him mean for me to tend de cabin for Rufus and some other niggers. Well, dat am start de pestigation for me.

"I's took charge of de cabin after work am done and fixes supper. Now, I don't like dat Rufus, 'cause he a bully. He am big and 'cause he so, he think everybody do what him say. We'uns has supper, den I goes here and dere talkin', till I's ready for sleep and den I gits in de bunk. After I's in, dat nigger come and crawl in de bunk with me 'fore I knows it. I say, 'What you mean, you fool nigger?' He say for me to hush de mouth. 'Dis am my bunk, too,' he say.

"You's teched in de head. Git out,' I's told him, and I puts de feet 'gainst him and give him a shove and out he go on de floor 'fore he knew what I's doin'. Dat nigger jump up and he mad. He look like de wild bear. He starts for de bunk and I jumps quick for de poker. It am 'bout three feet long and when he comes at me I lets him have it over de head. Did dat nigger stop in he tracks? I's say he did. He looks at me steady for a minutes and you's could tell he thinkin' hard. Den he go and set on de bench and say, 'Jus wait.' You thinks it am smart, but you's am foolish in de head. Dey's gwine larn you somethin'.

"Hush yous big mouth and stay 'way from dis nigger, dat all I wants," I say, and jus' sets and hold dat poker in de hand. He jus' sets, lookin' like de bull. Dere we'uns sets and sets for 'bout an hour and den he go out and I bars de door.

"De nex' day I goes to de missy and tell her what Rufus wants and missy say dat am de massa's wishes. She say, 'Yous am de portly gal and Rufus am de portly man. De massa wants you'uns for to bring forth portly chillen.'

"I's thinkin' 'bout what de missy say, but say to myse'f, 'I's not gwine live with dat Rufus.' Dat night when him come in de cabin, I grabs de poker and sits on de bench and says, 'Git 'way from me, nigger, 'fore I busts your brains out and stomp on dem.' He say nothin' and git out. De nex' day de massa call me and tell me, 'Woman, I's pay big money for you and I's done dat for de cause I wants yous to raise me chillens. I's put yous to live with Rufus for dat purpose. Now, if you doesn't want whippin' at de stake, yous do what I wants.

"I thinks 'bout massa buyin' me offen de block and savin' me from bein' sep'rated from my folks and 'bout bein' whipped at de stake. Dere it am. What am I's to do? So I 'cides to do as de massa wish and so I yields.

"I never marries, 'cause one 'sperience am 'nough for dis nigger. After what I does for de massa, I's never wants to truck with any man. De Lawd forgive dis cullud woman, but he have to 'scuse me and look for some others for to 'plenish de earth."

38 The Courtship of Lucy Dunn

In striking contrast to the rapid, forced pairing off that Rose Williams suffered in Texas, Lucy Dunn experienced a courtship that would make many another marriage, black or white, appear to be of dubious propriety. While it is unclear from her comments in the interview if this took place during slavery or after emancipation, the values and standards evident were obviously those that had been nurtured by her family, and her culture, during the years of bondage.

Source: George P. Rawick, ed., *The American Slave: A Composite Autobiography*, Vol. 14, *North Carolina Narratives* (Westport, Conn., 1971), Part 1, pp. 281-83.

"Hit wus in de little Baptist church at Neuse whar I fust seed big black Jim Dunn an' I fell in love wid him den, I reckons. He said dat he loved me den too, but hit wus three Sundays 'fore he axed ter see me home.

"We walked dat mile home in front of my mammy an' I wus so happy dat I aint thought hit a half a mile home. We et cornbread an' turnips fer dinner an' hit wus night 'fore he went home. Mammy wouldn't let me walk wid him ter de gate. I knowed, so I jist sot dar on de porch an' sez good night.

"He come ever' Sunday for a year an' finally he proposed. I had told mammy dat I thought dat I ort ter be allowed ter walk ter de gate wid Jim an' she said all right iffen she wus settin' dar on de porch lookin'.

"Dat Sunday night I did walk wid Jim ter de gate an' stood under de honeysuckles dat wus a-smellin' so sweet. I heard de big ole bullfrogs a-croakin' by de riber an' de whipper-wills a-hollerin' in de woods. Dar wus a big yaller moon, an' I reckon Jim did love me. Anyhow he said so an' axed me ter marry him an' he squeezed my han'.

"I tol' him I'd think hit ober an' I did an' de nex' Sunday I tol' him dat I'd have him.

"He aint kissed me yet but de nex' Sunday he axes my mammy fer me. She sez dat she'll have ter have a talk wid me an' let him know.

"Well all dat week she talks ter me, tellin' me how serious gittin' married is an' dat hit lasts a powerful long time.

"I tells her dat I knows hit but dat I am ready ter try hit an' dat I intends ter make a go of hit, anyhow.

"On Sunday night mammy tells Jim dat he can have me an' yo' orter seed dat black boy grin. He comes ter me widout a word an' he picks me up outen dat cheer an' dar in de moonlight he kisses me right 'fore my mammy who am a-cryin'.

"De nex' Sunday we wus married in de Baptist church at Neuse. I had a new white dress, do times wus hard.

"We lived tergether fifty-five years an' we always loved each other. He aint never whup ner cuss me an' do we had our fusses an' our troubles we trusted in de Lawd an' we got through. I loved him durin' life an' I love him now, do he's been daid now fer twelve years."

The old lady with her long white hair bowed her head and sobbed for a moment then she began again unsteadily.

"We had eight chilluns, but only four of dem are livin' now. De livin' are James, Sidney, Helen an' Florence who wus named fer Florence Nightingale.

"I can't be here so much longer now case I'se gittin' too old an' feeble an' I wants ter go ter Jim anyhow." The old woman wiped her eyes, "I thinks of him all de time, but seems lak we're young agin when I smell honeysuckles er see a yaller moon."

39 The Ambiguity of the Family

When T. T. Bradley wrote the following letter to the father of a slave he had recently purchased, he demonstrated that the family was an institution that was of crucial significance to the slaves and to the masters. The two vastly different perspectives represented in these letters concur on one broad point. The family ties between the slave David and his parents were sufficiently strong to warrant a special letter sanctioned and penned by the son's new owner to preserve those ties, or at least, to respect them. The motivation and concern of David is obvious and understandable. On one level he simply sought to retain contact or to respond to the worries his parents had expressed in writing him to learn of his trip and circumstances with a new master. On another level, though, it is quite possible that David's concern may have had a more protective source—the fear that his parents and kin might take dangerous risks because of their anxiety over their son and the hope that a reassuring letter, no matter what the real circumstances of his new home, could alleviate those concerns and prevent such risks. This possibility is made all the more likely by the fact that Bradley had relatives living near enough to David's parents to be acquainted with him. In any case, before David had been sold, whatever his age at that time, he had learned well the importance of family obligations and his parents were not going to let him forget.

The action of the young slave's new owner is even more complex and opaque. Either paternalism or fear—or a combination of both—could lead Bradley to write such a letter to the parents of his new slave. If the circumstances of a comfortable well-being that David related to his parents were authentic and accurate, there is every reason to believe that the master permitted and helped with the letter in the same spirit that inspired him to care for the material needs of his new ward. On the other hand, the ambiguity of the slave relationship, despite the real paternalist possibilities, suggests other motivations, different from, but not necessarily inconsistent with that paternalism. After all, the desirability of a stable system of control, subtle or otherwise, could mean that an owner who wanted to protect his investment (or however he conceived of his slave) might attempt to reassure both elements of the family he divided. A complete cynic would even raise the further possibility that the young slave never knew of the letter from his parents or the response to them in his name. Such is the ambiguity of this piece of evidence. All that can be finally concluded from it is that in this instance, at least, family bonds required serious attention from all concerned.

Source: T. T. Bradley Letters, 1859. State Historical Society of Missouri, Columbia, Mo. Reprinted by permission of the director.

July the 11. AD 1859

McKinney
Collen County
Texas

[To A. Higgans, Spring Fork, Pettis County, Missouri]
Dear Sir this is a letter to your Negro man Gabe from his Sun Dave
Dear father and mother: I received your letter and was very glad to hear from you. you was anxious to no whether I had got home safe or not. I have bin at home 3 weeks and I am very well pleased with my home dont be uneasy a bout me for I would not Swap my home for no other. I would like to se you and mother and my Sisters and Brothers but we are two fur a part to think a bout that   I have a good master and mistress. I war good Cloths and I have plenty to eat   I eat Just Such as my master and mistress eats   we eat Cakes and Coffe bacon and Beans milk and Butter molasses and hunney pickle Beets and Cucumbers we will soon have lots of Sweet potatoes and we have Rosten nears for 2 or 3 weeks. this is all   So well now father you and mother Content your Selves a bout me the best you Can.
So no more at present but Still remain your Sun David until deth.

Mr. A Higgens. a few lines to Gabe your Nigro man in relation to his Sun dave well Gabe I Suppose I own your Sun Dave   I did not no it when I bought him tho I am well pleased with him   I never have had to Speak a Short word to him yet and I am in hopes I never will I Bought him to keep and if Dave holds out to be a good boy I will keep him as long as we Both live and I will treat him well   I could Sel dave for twelve hundred dollars but money Caint by him.
T T Bradley

40 The Boldness of the Exhorters

Forced or willingly contracted as a means to control slaves or as a haven for independence, the slave family represented an ambiguous and a politically neutral ground. The actual content of the "living space" depended upon what the blacks themselves put into it. On the other hand, various expressions of religion formed a much more politically charged area and one whose explosive potential was seldom lost upon either slaves or masters. The egalitarian notion of something approaching the priesthood of all believers was evident during the Great Awakening when a new religious enthusiasm seemed to take hold in the colonies. Charles Chauncey, the staid Congregational minister who opposed the revivalistic fervor, lamented many of its qualities but especially the "vanity" it encouraged by providing opportunities for all kinds of people not only to participate but to lead and preach, even "yea, *Negroes*," being moved to preach.

Source: Charles Chauncey, *Seasonable Thoughts on the State of Religion in New England* (Boston, 1743), p. 226.

Another Thing that very much tends, as I apprehend, to do Hurt to the Interest of Religion, is the Rise of so many *Exhorters*. A Stranger to this Land, and the present Appearance in it, may be at a Loss to know, who are meant by *these Exhorters*: And I'm really asham'd to say, that the Persons pointed out by them, are *Men* of all *Occupations*, who are vain enough to think themselves fit to be *Teachers* of others; Men who, though they have *no Learning*, and but *small* Capacities, yet imagine they are able, and without Study too, to speak to the *Spiritual Profit* of such as are willing to hear them: Nay, there are among these Exhorters, *Babes* in *Age*, as well as Understanding. They are *chiefly* indeed *young Persons*, Sometimes *Lads*, or rather *Boys*: Nay, *Women* and *Girls*; yea, *Negroes*, have taken upon them to do the Business of *Preachers*. Nor has this been *accidental* only, or in a *single Place*, or at a *private House*; but there is scarce a Town in *all the Provinces*, where this Appearance has been, but there have been also *these Exhorters*, in smaller or greater Numbers: Neither have they contented themselves to speak in the *more private Meetings* of Christians, but have held forth in the *publick Congregations*.

41 The Promise of Deliverance

Insofar as masters would permit religious instruction and preaching to their blacks the usual text would come from the Apostle Paul or another part of Scripture emphasizing the need for humility and obedience in this world. Yet the discussion of salvation and conversion raised interesting possibilities, and the discussion of the bondage of the Israelites and their deliverance from slavery was too close an analogy to be missed by anyone. The following letter from the Hon. James Habersham of Savannah, Georgia, written in 1775, illustrates both the readiness of blacks to use these analogies and the sensitivity of whites to their implications. Again, this may well serve as an example of the double-bind, the conflicting expectations presented to blacks. On the one hand Habersham in a previous letter commented that "the souls of my poor benighted Blacks have long lain heavy on my Heart." When the preacher David presented some of the obvious lessons of the Scripture, however, he was accused of showing "some impudent Airs," and meaning "to raise rebellion amongst the negroes."

Source: "The Letters of Hon. James Habersham, 1756-1775," *Collections of the Georgia Historical Society*, 6 (1904), 238, 241-42, 243-44.

To Mr Robert Kean.   In London.
                    Savannah in Georgia the 11th of May 1775
Dear Sir

This day I received a Letter from Mr Piercy in Charlestown, dated the 8th Instant, and another two or three days agoe, dated the 3d. In the latter, he desired I wou'd enquire into some misconduct of black David's in her Ladyship's Family, and if after smart reproof, He remained incorrigable, and did not amend, immediately to dismiss him, her Ladyship's Service, without putting her to one farthing more Expense. David had shown some impudent Airs, since Mr Piercy left Bethesda, of which he had been informed, but before I had an opportunity of making such Enquiry. I received the above mentioned Letter of the 8th wherein is the following.

> In my last, I advised you to have nothing to do with paying, David's Passage to England; but I now find it absolutely necessary in order to save his Life. The Gentlemen of this Town are so possessed with an opinion that his Designs are bad, that they are determined to puruse, and hang him, if they can lay hold of him. I have only therefore to beg of you to send him off privately, in the first vessel, that sails for home. I wou'd indeed be very sorry that the poor fellow should lose his life.

You may not perhaps have been acquainted with the ground of the Disgust he gave the People of Charlestown, I will inform you of what I have heard. The Person who received and lodged Mr Cossen in Charlestown entertained David likewise, and desired him to preach to several white People and Negroes, who had collected together to hear him. David in the Course of his exhortation, dropped some unguarded Expressions, such as, that he did not doubt; but "God would send Deliverance to the Negroes, from the power of their Masters, as He freed the Children of Israel from Egyptian Bondage."

Some thing similar to this was construed, as tho' he meant to raise rebellion amongst the negroes. It was undoubtedly wrong, and he thereby shewed his Ignorance and Folly. In consequence of this and other things, Information was given to the Grand Jury who presented the Person who kindly entertained him, for suffering him to preach Doctrine in his house contrary to the Peace of Society, and accordingly he is prosecuted and must stand his Tryal and abide by the consequence. Our Laws are very severe and pointed in this respect. Upon the whole, I am rather glad David is going, as I think he wou'd have done more harm than good to her Ladyships Negroes, having by no means the spirit of a true missionery amongst the Heathen. His Business was to preach a Spiritual Deliverance to these People, not a temporal one, but he is, if I am not mistaken, very proud, and very superficial, and conceited, and I must say it's a pity, that any of these People should ever put their Feet in England, where they get totally spoiled and ruined, both in Body and Soul, through a mistaken kind of compassion because they are black, while many of our own colour and Fellow Subjects, are starving through want and Neglect. We know these People better than you do. I am told nothing could please him at Bethesda, although he was provided for as well as any Person there. I have agreed with Capt Inglis of the Ship Georgia Planter, to take him as a Steerage Passenger, for which he asks eight Guineas, which I think a great deal of money, however I think it is best to get him away at any rate, which you will please pay him.

You may depend that David is a fugitive Slave, and his Story about being stole from the Coast of africa is not Truth, but I have done with him, I have done all I can for him, and am Dear Sir

Your Affectionate Friend and Servant——

42 Inspiration for Rebellion

Further evidence that the religion believed and used by the slaves was not always the same that their masters had in mind can be discerned in the following confession given by Ben Woolfolk concerning the abortive rebellion of more than a thousand slaves near Richmond under the leadership of Gabriel Prosser in 1800. From the source of legitimacy to the strategic formulations undertaken, religious notions pervaded the preparations for war.

Source: H. W. Flournoy, ed., *Calendar of Virginia State Papers and Other Manuscripts*, Vol. 9, Jan. 1, 1799 to Dec. 31, 1807 (Richmond, 1890), 150-52.

On the day of the sermon, George called on Sam Bird to inform how many men he had; he said he had not his list with him, but he supposed about 500. George wished the business to be deferred some time longer. Mr. Prosser's Gabriel wished to bring on the business as soon as possible. Gilbert said the summer was almost over, and he wished them to enter upon the business before the weather got too cold. Gabriel proposed that the subject should be referred to his brother Martin to decide upon. Martin said there was this expression in the Bible, delays breed danger; at this time, he said, the country was at peace, the soldiers were discharged, and the arms all put away; there was no patrolling in the country, and that before he would any longer bear what he had borne, he would turn out and fight with his stick. Gilbert said he was ready with his pistol, but it was in need of repair; he gave it to Gabriel, who was put it in order for him. I then spoke to the company and informed them I wished to have something to say. I told them that I had heard in the days of old when the Israelites were in service to King Pharoah, they were taken from him by the power of God, and were carried away by Moses. God had blessed him with an angel to go with him, but that I could see nothing of that kind in these days. Martin said in reply: I read in my Bible where God says if we will worship Him we should have peace in all our land; five of you shall conquer an hundred, and a hundred a thousand of our enemies. After this they went on consultation upon the time they should execute the plan. Martin spoke and appointed for them to meet in three weeks, which was to be of a Saturday night. Gabriel said he had 500 bullets made. Smith's George said he was done the corn and would then go on to make as many cross-bows as he could. Bowler's Jack said he had got 500 spiers or bayonets fixed at the end of sticks. The plan was to be as follows: We were all to meet at the briery spot on the Brook; 100 men were to stand at the Brook bridge; Gabriel was to take 100 more and go to Gregory's tavern and take the arms which were there; 50 more were to be sent to Rocketts to set that on fire, in order to alarm the upper part of the town and induce the people to go down there; while they were imployed in extinguishing the fire Gabriel and the other officers and soldiers were to take the Capitol and all the arms they could find and be ready to slaughter the people on their return from Rocketts. Sam Bird was to have a pass as a free man and was to go to the nation of Indians called Catawbas to persuade them to join the negroes to fight the white people. As far as I understood all the whites were to be massacred, except the Quakers, the Methodists, and the Frenchmen, and they were to be spared on account as they conceived of their being friendly to liberty, and also they had understood that the French were at war with this country for the money that was due them, and that an army was landed at South Key, which they hoped would assist them. They intended also to spare all the poor white women who had no slaves.

43 The Spiritual Strain on Social Bonds

The following letter from William Eaton concerning his observations as he toured Virginia indicates two especially noteworthy tendencies. One is the tendency toward aristocracy, a closed society, that seemed deeply concerned with preserving that system of authority (certainly more than with productive industry and farming). The second is that even within that system the religious habits of the countryside, especially the prevalence of the camp meetings, were tending to undermine that system of authority.

Source: Louis B. Wright, ed., "William Eaton Takes a Dismal View of Virginia," *William and Mary Quarterly*, Third Series, 5 (January 1948), 106-7. This letter of William Eaton to Col. Alexander Sessions, June 24, 1804, is in the Eaton Collection in the Huntington Library, San Marino, California, and is reproduced by permission of the Huntington Library.

Since I left the city of Washington I have made the tour of Virginia. Have passed through its capital, and all its chief commercial towns—as well as the interior of the state. Though we hear so much about *democracy* from this quarter the state approaches nearer a pure aristocracy than any other state in the Union. The great landholders are Lords; and their tenants, as decidedly as their negroes, are slaves. They are amused, indeed, with *incantations* of *republicanism, liberty,* and *equality;* whereas in truth, their *public affairs* are in an absolute monopoly by the rich. The poor have, unquestionably, the liberty to quarrel about the support of a patron at an election; but as to *equality* it no more exists here than it does in the French, English, or Turkish Dominions. The representatives from this state clamor a great deal about taxation, and display a great deal of talent, in projects to promote the agricultural interest. They ought verily to be concerned to promote it by law; for they probably never will do it by industry nor good management. They are certainly the worst farmers in the United States. As to police, they seem to exhibit no proofs of it but what they show in their statutes. They have no free schools.

A traveller may ride hundreds of miles through the most populous parts of the state without meeting a district schoolhouse. And as for religion, *it is left to shift for itself!* They have, however, a great number of methodist preachers rambling about the country, preaching to such as will hear them—sometimes in old court houses, sometimes in rough built half finished meeting houses—but more frequently in the open fields. To these *camp meetings* they are followed by vast numbers of blacks both bond and free—and by hordes of whites, of all sexes and ages, a degree below the blacks both in point of manners and understanding. These itinerant declaimers I consider most dangerous to the political existence of this state: for, while they affect to inculcate into the minds of the slaves principles of subordination and passive obedience, they inspire them with sentiments calculated to prompt their ideas to hopes of freedom, and of leveling their tyrants to a standard which nature intended for the sphere of man. These sentiments, together with the loud declamations about liberty and equality which the political motives of the prevailing majority have raised among all classes of people here, aided by the awful example of St. Domingo, will ere long bring the slaves of this state into insurrections; and, I predict, the consequence will be a total revolution. Impressed with these alarming apprehensions I appreciate more justly than ever our New England institutions; especially those of religion and education; and I feel more and more convinced of the duty incumbent on every citizen, who wishes well to life and posterity, to support those institutions.

44 A Passionate Spirit

Religion in the slave community not only held a different emphasis and supplied a different logic but also found expression in strikingly different forms. The difference in religious expression was carefully noted by Frederika Bremer in her 1850 visit to the Charleston area when she attended a camp meeting where both whites and blacks worshipped. She touches on many points, from the separation of the races at the meeting to the dull emphasis on moralizing by whites as compared to the fiery and exciting black appeals for salvation and conversion. But one central leitmotif prevails: the black preachers and believers, with the exception of a Wesleyan minister, were free and exuberant as compared to those white preachers who "did not believe, or rather did not livingly *feel*, that which" they preached. Restraint, order, and decorum were the watchwords of the whites. Belief, passion, sincerity, and the fullest expression of commitment guided the blacks. This may yet again be related to the licensed nature of black culture; part of the enthusiasm may stem from African religious and cultural heritages. While attributing a passionate spirit, as even Bremer seems to agree, "to the impulsive negro temperament," the contrast may more properly be made with the inhibited and restrained culture that the whites (or at least those not associated with the Wesleyans) have identified with civilization. The anal retentive qualities of proper Calvinism may have become a defining element of white civilization. So long as blacks exhibited the lack of inhibition and the impulse toward emotional gratification it implied, so long would black people be viewed as more primitive beings. Yet, the hope remained that religion could provide the path for them to become "good Christians and orderly members of society." Which goal was really desired remains subject to serious question as the tensions of the double-bind surely intensified.

Source: Frederika Bremer, *Homes of the New World: Impressions of America* (London, 1853), Vol. 1, pp. 313-24.

Away we go, through forest and field, eighteen miles from Charleston. It is late in the afternoon and very warm. We stop; it is in the middle of a thick wood. There is wood on all sides, and not a house to be seen. We alight from the carriages and enter a fir-wood. After we have walked for an hour along unformed paths, the wood begins to be very animated. It swarms with people, in particular with blacks, as far as we can see among the lofty tree-stems. In the middle of the wood is an open space, in the centre of which rises a great long roof, supported by pillars, and under which stand benches in rows, affording sufficient accommodation for four or five thousand people. In the middle of this tabernacle is a lofty, square elevation, and in the middle of this a sort of chair or pulpit. All round the tabernacle, for so I call the roofed-in space supported on pillars, hundreds of tents and booths of all imaginable forms and colours, are pitched and erected in a vast circle, and are seen, shining out white in the wood to a great distance, and everywhere, on all sides, near and afar off, may be seen groups of people, mostly black, busied at small fires, roasting and boiling. Children are running about, or sitting by the fires; horses stand and feed beside the carriages they have drawn thither. It is a perfect camp, with all the varied particoloured life of a camp, but without soldiers and arms. Here everything looks peaceful and festive, although not exactly joyful.

By degrees the people begin to assemble within the tabernacle, the white people on one side, the black on the other; the black being considerably more numerous than the white. The weather is sultry; thunderclouds cover the heavens, and it begins to rain.... A tent is opened for us, and we are received into it by a comfortable bookseller's family. The family are red-hot Methodists, and not to be objected to. Here we have coffee and supper.

After this meal I went out to look around me, and was astonished by a spectacle which I never shall forget. The night was dark with the thunder-cloud, as well as with the natural darkness of night; but the rain had ceased, excepting for a few heavy drops, which fell here and there, and the whole wood stood in flames. Upon eight fire-altars, or fire-hills, as they are called, a sort of lofty table, raised on posts, standing around the tabernacle, burned, with a flickering brilliance of flame, large billets of fire-wood, which contains a great deal of resin, whilst on every side in the wood, far away in its most remote recesses, burned larger or smaller fires, before tents or in other places, and lit up the lofty fir-tree stems, which seemed like columns of an immense natural temple consecrated to fire. The vast dome above was dark, and the air was so still that the flames rose straight upwards, and cast a wild light, as of a strange dawn upon the fir-tree tops and the black clouds.

Beneath the tabernacle an immense crowd was assembled, certainly from three to four thousand persons. They sang hymns; a magnificent quire! Most likely the sound proceeded from the black portion of the assembly, as their number was three times that of the whites, and their voices are naturally beautiful and pure. In the tower-like pulpit, which stood in the middle of the tabernacle, were four preachers, who, during the intervals between the hymns, addressed the people with loud voices, calling sinners to conversion and amendment of life.

During all this, the thunder pealed, and fierce lightning flashed through the wood like angry glances of some mighty invisible eye. We entered the tabernacle, and took our seats among the assembly on the side of the whites.

Round the elevation, in the middle of which rose the pulpit, ran a sort of low counter, forming a wide square. Within this, seated on benches below the pulpit, and on the side of the whites, sat the Methodist preachers, for the most part handsome tall figures, with broad grave foreheads; and on the side of the blacks their spiritual leaders and exhorters, many among whom were Mulattoes, men of a lofty, noticeable and energetic exterior.

The later it grew in the night, the more earnest grew the appeals; the hymns short, but fervent, as the flames of the light wood ascended, like them, with a passionate ardour. Again and again they arose on high, like melodious, burning sighs from thousands of harmonious voices. The preachers increase in the fervour of their zeal; two stand with their faces turned towards the camp of the blacks, two towards that of the whites, extending their hands, and calling on the sinners to come, come, all of them, now at this time, at this moment, which is perhaps the last, the only one which remains to them in which to come to the Saviour, to escape eternal damnation! Midnight approaches, the fires burn dimmer, but the exaltation increases and becomes universal. The singing of hymns mingles with the invitations of the preachers, and the exhortations of the class-leaders with the groans and cries of the assembly. And now, from among the white people, rise up young girls and men, and go and throw themselves, as if overcome, upon the low counter. These are met on the other side by the ministers who bend down to them, receive their confessions, encourage and console them. In the camp of the blacks is heard a great tumult and a loud cry. Men roar and bawl out; women screech like pigs about to be killed; many having fallen into convulsions leap and strike about them, so that they are obliged to be held down. It looks here and there like a regular fight; some of the calmer participants laugh. Many a cry of anguish may be heard, but you distinguish no words excepting, "Oh, I am a sinner!" and "Jesus! Jesus!"

During all this tumult the singing continues loud and beautiful, and the thunder joins in with its pealing kettle-drum.

Whilst this spectacle is going forward in the black camp we observe a quieter scene among the whites. Some of the forms which had thrown themselves on their knees at the counter have removed themselves, but others are still lying there, and the ministers seem in vain to talk or to sing to them. One of these, a young girl, is lifted up by her friends and found to be "in a trance." She now lies with her head in the lap of a woman dressed in black, with her pretty, young face turned upwards, rigid, and as it appears, totally unconscious. The woman dressed in black and another also in the same coloured attire, both with beautiful though sorrowful countenances, softly fan the young girl with their fans and watch her with serious looks, whilst ten or twelve women—most of them young—stand around her, singing softly and sweetly a hymn of the resurrection; all watching the young girl, in whom they believe that something great is now taking place. It is really a beautiful scene in that thunderous night, and by the light of the fire-altars.

* * *

It was now past midnight; the weather had cleared and the air was so delicious, and the spectacle so beautiful, that I was compelled to return to the tent to tell Mrs. Howland, who at once resolved to come out with me. The altar-fires now burned low and the smoke hung within the wood. The transparently bright and blue heaven stretched above the camp. The moon rose above the wood, and the planet Jupiter stood brilliantly shining just over the tabernacle. The singing of hymns still ascended, though much lower; still the class-leaders exhorted; still the young girl slept her mysterious sleep; still the women watched and waited and fanned her, in their attire of mourning. Some oppressed souls still lay bowed upon the counter and still were the preachers giving consolation either by word or song. By degrees, the people assembled in the tabernacle dispersed, scattered themselves through the woods, or withdrew to their tents. Even the young sleeping girl awoke and was led by her friends away from the assembly. Mr. R. had now joined us, and accompanied by him we went the round of the camp, especially on the black side. And here all the tents were still full of religious exaltation, each separate tent presenting some new phasis. We saw in one, a zealous covert, male or female, as it might be, who with violent gesticulations gave vent to his or her newly-awakened feelings, surrounded by devout auditors; in another, we saw a whole crowd of black people on their knees, all dressed in white, striking themselves on the breast and crying out and talking with the greatest pathos; in a third, women were dancing "the holy dance" for one of the newly-converted. This dancing, however, having been forbidden by the preachers, ceased immediately on our entering the tent. I saw merely a rocking movement of women who held each other by the hand in a circle, singing the while. In a fourth, a song of the spiritual Canaan was being sung excellently. In one tent we saw a fat negro-member walking about by himself and breathing hard; he was hoarse, and sighing he exclaimed himself, "Oh! I wish I could hollo!" In some tents people were sitting around the fires, and here visits were received, greetings were made, and friendly, cheerful talk went on, whilst everywhere prevailed a quiet, earnest state of feeling, which we also experienced whenever we stopped to talk with the people. These black people have a something warm and kind about them which I like very much. One can see that they are children of the warm sun. The state of feeling was considerably calmer in the camp of the whites. One saw families sitting at their covered tables eating and drinking.

At length we returned to our tent, where I lay upon the family bed with our good hostess and her thirteen-year old daughter, and slept indifferently; yet, thanks to some small white globules of my Downing-medicine, I rested nevertheless, and became calm in the hot feverish night.

At sunrise I heard something which resembled the humming of an enormous wasp caught in a spider's web. It was a larum which gave the sign for the general rising. At half-past five I was dressed and out. The hymns of the negroes, which had continued through the night, were still to be heard on all sides. The sun shone powerfully—the air was oppressive. People were cooking and having breakfast by the fires, and a crowd already began to assemble on the benches under the tabernacle. At seven o'clock the morning sermon and worship commenced. I had observed that the preachers avoided exciting the people's feelings too much, and that they themselves appeared without emotion. This morning their discourses appeared to me feeble, and especially to be wanting in popular eloquence. They preached morality. But a mere moral sermon should not be preached when it is the heart that you wish to win; you should then tell, in the language of the heart, the miracle of spiritual life. It was, therefore, a real refreshment to me when the unimpassioned and well-fed preachers, who had spoken this morning, gave place to an elderly man with a lively and somewhat humourous expression of countenance, who from out the throng of hearers ascended the pulpit and began to speak to the people in quite another tone. It was familiar, fresh, cordial, and humourous; somewhat in the manner of Father Taylor. I should like to have heard him address these people, but then, I am afraid the negroes would have been quite beside themselves!

* * *

"Amen! Amen! Glory and glory!" cried the assembly, and never did I see such an espression of joy and rapture as I then saw beaming from the countenances of these children of Africa: the class-leaders in particular were regularly beside themselves; they clapped their hands, laughed, and floods of light streamed from their eyes. Some of these countenances are impressed upon my memory as some of the most expressive and the most full of feeling that I ever saw. Why do not the painters of the New World avail themselves of such scenes and such countenances? The delight occasioned by the speaker's narrative would here and there have produced convulsions, had not Mr. Martin, the principal preacher of the assembly, indicated, by the movements of his hand from his pulpit, its discontinuance, and immediately the increasingly excited utterance ceased. Already during the night had he warned the people against these convulsive outbreaks, as being wrong, and disturbing both to themselves and others. The Wesleyan preacher left the pulpit amid continued expressions of delight from the people.

The principal sermon of the day was preached about eleven o'clock by a lawyer from one of the neighbouring States, a tall, thin gentleman, with strongly marked keen features, and deep-set brilliant eyes. He preached about the Last Judgment, and described in a most lively manner, "the fork-like, cloven flames, the thunder, the general destruction of all things," and described it as possibly near at hand. "As yet, indeed," exclaimed he, "I have not felt the earth tremble under my feet; it yet seems to stand firm," and he stamped vehemently on the pulpit floor; "and as yet I hear not the rolling of the thunder of doom; but it may nevertheless be at hand," and so on; and he admonished the people therefore immediately to repent and be converted.

Spite of the strength of the subject, and spite of the power in the delineation, there was a something dry and soulless in the manner in which it was presented, which caused it to fail of its effect with the congregation. People seemed to feel that the preacher did not believe, or rather did not livingly feel, that which he described and preached. A few cries and groans were heard it is true, and some sinners came forth; but the assembly upon the whole continued calm, and was not agitated by the thunders of the Last Judgment. The hymns were, as on the former occasion, fervent and beautiful on the side of the negroes' camp. This people seem to have a keen perception of the most beautiful doctrines of religion, and understand particularly well how to apply them. Their musical talents are remarkable. Most of the blacks have beautiful, pure voices, and sing as easily as we whites talk.

After this service came the hour of dinner, when I visited various tents in the black camp, and saw tables covered with dishes of all kind of meat, with puddings and tarts; there seemed to be a regular superfluity of meat and drink. Several of the tents were even furnished like rooms, with capital beds, looking-glasses, and such like.

The people seemed gay, happy, and gentle. These religious camp-meetings—my little heart, thou hast now been at a camp meeting!—are the saturnalia of the negro-slaves. In these they luxuriate both soul and body, as is their natural inclination to do; but on this occasion every thing was carried on with decency and befitting reverence. These meetings have of late years greatly improved in moral character, and masters allow their servants and slaves to be present at them, partly for pleasure, and partly because they are often productive of good results. I did not observe the slightest circumstance which was repugnant to my feelings or unbecoming, except, if people will, the convulsive excitement. I had some conversation on this subject with the leader of the meeting, the amiable and agreeable Mr. Martin, the Methodist preacher, and he disapproved of it, as I had already heard. These excited utterances however, said he, appear to belong to the impulsive negro temperament, and these sudden conversions, the result of a moment of excitement, have this good result, that such converts commonly unite themselves to churches and ministers, become members of a so-called class, and thus obtain regular instruction in the doctrines of religion, learn hymns and prayers, and become generally from that time good Christians and orderly members of society.

45 A Consuming Grace

The exact experiences of conversion that led many observers to comment on the tendency of blacks to convulsions and emotionalism took many forms. It is quite possible that those conversions assumed an intensity and depth that could be realized by many people, white or black, only in an orgasmic context, and possibly not even then. Especially would this be true among those whose restraint and rigorous discipline have shaped all parts of their lives to a model of the systems of productivity and management, to a time-oriented work discipline, and an efficiency measure of the meaning of life. This religious experience among slaves could well have been the most intense and visible manifestation of a culture that had not been reduced to the constrictive maze-ways of a society dominated by materialism. This is an extract from a WPA interview with an unidentified former slave woman (Kelly————), entitled "Proud of that 'Ole Time' Religion."

Source: George P. Rawick, ed., *The American Slave: A Composite Autobiography*, Vol. 18, *The Unwritten History of Slavery* (Fisk University), (Westport, Conn., 1972), pp. 164-65. Reprinted with Permission of Fisk University Library.

Well, I went on like that for a long time, didn't know nothing 'bout nothin', bless yo' heart, but I jest felt something, didn't know what. I went on my way by myself, and one day I went behind the house and sat down to cry. Well, I got back there and went to sit down, and I tell you the gospel's truth, I kin go and put my hand on the spot right now, where I jest fell face foremost— something just struck me. "Ooh Lord!" I cried, "have mercy on me, a poor hell-deserving sinner." You heard me, I said I didn't know how to pray, but them words jest come to me from nowheres; chile, I fell to crying, jest like I was crazy; I felt right crazy, too, praise God, but I wasn't; it was jest the grace of God I had done been looking for, lo them many weeks. Oooh, merciful Jesus, honey, you ain't never been through all that has you? Why, I went three days and nights without eating and drinking; didn't want nothin', jest was uplifted and free from sin. Somehow or other that morning, I was jest as light as a feather. I got up and I had to go to the foot of the bed to git my clothes, and I stooped down to get 'em, and seem like something jest stopped me, just struck me still, ooh, Jesus, chile, I got right stiff; finally I got my clothes off the floor and wrapped my arms around them right tight, and then, great God, I got upon my knees and prayed the Lord with a prayer that tumbled from my lips, that the Lord had give me to pray hisself—ooh chile, I tell you it's a wonderful feeling when you feel the spirit of the Lord God Almighty in the tips of your fingers, and the bottom of yo' heart. I didn't know then what was the matter with me. I knows now when I feel that spirit arising in my body, yessiree.

Well, I tell you chile, when I got up from prayer, I felt like I was brand new—I had done been washed in Jesus' blood, ooh my great and holy Father! Sometimes I gits to thinking 'bout it and I git happy. Yessirree, chile, if you wants ole sister Kelly to tell you 'bout her 'ligious 'sperience, I sho' kin tell you that, 'cause I sho' been through a great fight with the devil, I tell you, ooh praise God. I didn't know no more 'bout nothin' than this rock, but honey you asks me now, I kin tell you with the very words what God put in my mouth.

46 The Other Side of Paradise

Besides providing a sense of hope and dignity and a set of values, religion could also provide faith in a sense of eternal justice. Rewards and punishments would be meted out differently in the next world. Here again is an unidentified interview with a former slave who spoke strongly of her tyrant of a mistress; she referred on two separate occasions in the interview to the duplicity in the slaves' expressions of remorse upon the deaths of the whites.

Source: George P. Rawick, ed., *The American Slave: A Composite Autobiography*, Vol. 18, *The Unwritten History of Slavery* (Fisk University), (Westport, Conn., 1972), pp. 134, 136. Reprinted with permission of Fisk University Library.

Yes, I was here in slavery. I will be 86 years old the 15th of August. My master had 47 slaves. We all lived right in the yard below the white people's house. There was about eight or nine cabins. My mother had eight children; all of us stayed at home. None of us was sold from her. Sometimes they was good and again they was mean. If you didn't do to suit them they would whip you. I have got a many beating over my head with a stick, cowhide, or anything that they could lay their hands on. I was so sassy. I would sass them to the very last. They would knock and beat me again, but I would sass them again. They would whip me 'cause I didn't mind. We would pick wool and have us all sitting around in the house, and I would go to sleep. After a while I would get a lick on my head for going to sleep. Old mistress got sick and I would fan her with a brush, to keep the flies off her. I would hit her all in the face; sometimes I would make out I was sleep and beat her in the face. She was so sick she couldn't sleep much, and couldn't talk, and when old master come in the house she would try to tell him on me, but he thought she meant I would just go to sleep. Then he would tell me to go out in the yard and wake up. She couldn't tell him that I had been hitting her all in the face. I done that woman bad. She was so mean to me.

Well, she died and all the slaves come in the house just hollering and crying and holding their hands over their eyes, just hollering for all they could. Soon as they got outside of the house they would say, "Old God damn son-of-a-bitch, she gone on down to hell."

*   *   *

When the white folks would die the slaves would all stand around and 'tend like they was crying but after they would get outside they would say, "They going on to hell like a damn barrell full of nails."

47 The Promise of Freedom New Orleans Style

New Orleans has probably always been unique in America because of the French influence and because of its status as virtually the sole commercial metropolis of the South of a size comparable to Northern cities. One quality repeatedly struck Northern visitors to the city: the prevalence of creoles, mulattos, blacks, and whites living together there with at least an outward equanimity. It is noteworthy that in the account below, Thomas Low Nichols compared New Orleans and the South at large favorably to the North in the treatment afforded blacks.

Source: Thomas Low Nichols, *Forty Years of American Life, 1821-1861* (n. p., 1864) 127-28.

There was nothing of the pomp and magnificence which one might have expected in a Catholic city—a city as rich as New Orleans—among a people as proud as the creoles. But, if there was little grandeur in the services of the church, there was something very interesting in the appearance of the worshippers. Never had I seen such a mixture of conditions and colours. A radiant creole beauty, with coal-black eyes, long silken lashes, a complexion of the lily, scarcely tinged with the rose, and a form of matchless elegance, dressed in black, with a gold-clasped missal and bouquet of roses, knelt on the pavement, and close at her side was a venerable descendant of Africa, with devotion marked on every feature. White children and black, with every shade between, knelt side by side. In the house of prayer they made no distinction of rank or colour. The most ardent abolitionist could not have desired more perfect equality; and, in New Orleans, as in all the South, the negro was certainly treated more like "a man and a brother" than I had ever seen him in the North.

Three-fourths of the congregation were females; a large proportion were of African blood; and the negroes seemed the most demonstrative in their piety.

The negro women with their clean, stiffly starched Sunday gowns, and handkerchiefs of red and yellow, not only appeared to attend to the services with great devotion, but their children, little boys and girls, nine or ten years old, showed a docility which, I fear, not many of our Northern children exhibit in religious services.

48 Integration and Social Control

The docility of the children in the church in New Orleans is enigmatic, but the suggestion is instructive. More positive evidence on the point comes from the comments of a former slave who as a girl lived in the big house and indeed at first slept in the same bed with her mistress and then on a pallet on the floor in the same room. It appears from this account that no pretense of equality was involved; slave status and black inequality were assumed and made the arrangement possible. Nor did the slave herself view this as an act of largesse. In fact, she was much more under her owner's control than were the other slaves who lived in separate quarters, and she was therefore suspect by her own fellow slaves who would not speak before her.

Source: George P. Rawick, ed., *The American Slave: A Composite Autobiography*, Vol. 18, *The Unwritten History of Slavery* (Fisk University), (Westport, Conn., 1972), pp. 182, 183, 184-85, 187. Reprinted with permission of Fisk University Library.

I have been in the white folks hands ever since I was so high. They took me in the white folks house and kept me there and till after the War, and if I went to any colored folks house I had to come back 'fore night. I cleaned up and toted water and scrubbed and washed dishes. I have washed dishes a long time, and done anything they asked me to. But when my mother died I was just throwed away 'cause she took care of me. I had a half-sister and a half-brother, but they is dead.

No'm, he was his own overseer. He wouldn't have an overseer; they beat the darkies too much, and he wanted to beat his own. He used to beat them right smart. I used to remember about him whipping them. I don't know much about colored folks before the War. I wasn't 'lowed to go to see them. I better not be seen talking to colored people; they would whip me. I couldn't talk to the

Negroes in the kitchen. I slept with ole mistiss till I was too big and used to kick her; and then they made me a pallet on the floor, and I never stayed in her bed any more. She told Mary, her daughter, to make me a tick and let me sleep on the floor. The girl said "Why?" and she said, "She kicked me, I didn't sleep a bit last night." And she got some straw and I slept right by her bed. When she died they wrote me a letter, and I didn't go. That was after the War. They had treated me so bad I wouldn't go back.

* * *

When I was a girl there was an ole white man, after the War, his name was John Hesley, and used to have the colored preacher to come to an ole shack to preach, and he would tell them to obey their masters and mistisses. I never will forget it. It was just a little ole shack. He just preached to the Negroes. I will never forget it. Yes, my ole mistiss used to take me behind her and carry me to the Rutledge Church, on her horse, and I had a cotton bonnet and a cotton dress on. This was after the War when John Hesley preached to us. People soon stopped going to hear him. My ole mistiss would carry me on her hoss to her church on Sunday. No, honey, I don't know if they would; if they had them I don't know, 'cause I wouldn't get out amongst the colored people, and I didn't know. There was a man came up from Wilson's farm and came here and got more colored people and brought them up on that farm, and you know they wouldn't 'low me to say anything to them, and I would get a whipping if I did.

* * *

No, they (the colored people) wouldn't say anything before me, 'cause I stayed in the house, and et in there, and slept in there. Yes, they were 'fraid to say anything 'fore me.

49 Freedom and Segregation

Again the irony: the practice of segregation of the races was more evident in the areas of freedom than in slavery. In 1817 and 1818 Henry B. Fearon toured America and related his travels in a book published in London. The following incident and then Fearon's reflections on the commonality of racial discrimination in the free state suggest how the troublesome questions of race relations were being resolved in the absence of slavery as an institutional framework. Caste notions of servility and servitude based on race, however informal, provided more social distance than did slavery.

Source: Henry Bradshaw Fearon, *Sketches of America* (London, 1818), pp. 58-61.

Soon after landing I called at a hair-dresser's in Broadway, nearly opposite the city-hall: the man in the shop was a negro. He had nearly finished with me, when a black man, very respectably dressed, came into the shop and sat down. The barber enquired if he wanted the proprietor or his boss, as he termed him, who was also a black: the answer was in the negative; but that he wished to have his hair cut. My man turned upon his heel, and with the greatest contempt, muttered in a tone of proud importance, "We do not cut coloured men here, Sir." The poor fellow walked out without replying, exhibiting in his countenance confusion, humiliation, and mortification. I immediately requested, that if the refusal was on account of my being present, he might be called back. The hair-dresser was astonished: "You cannot be in earnest, Sir," he said. I assured him that I was so, and that I was much concerned in witnessing the refusal from no other cause than that his skin was of a darker tinge than my own. He stopped the motion of his scissars; and after a pause of some seconds, in which his eyes were fixed upon my face, he said, "Why, I guess as how, Sir, what you say is mighty elegant, and you're an elegant man; but I guess you are not of these parts."

"I am from England," said I, "where we have neither so cheap nor so enlightened a government as yours, but we have no slaves."

"Ay, I guessed you were not raised here; you salt-water people are mighty grand to coloured people; you are not so proud, and I guess you have more to be proud of; now I reckon you do not know that my boss would not have a single ugly or clever gentleman come to his store, if he cut coloured men; now my boss, I guess, ordered me to turn out every coloured man from the store right away, and if I did not, he would send me off slick; for the slimmest gentleman in York would not come to his store if coloured men were let in; but you know all that Sir, I guess, without my telling you; you are an elegant gentleman too, Sir."

I assured him that I was ignorant of the fact which he stated; but which, from the earnestness of his manner, I concluded must be true.

"And you come all the way right away from England. Well! I would not have supposed, I guess, that you come from there from your tongue; you have no hardness like, I guess, in your speaking; you talk almost as well as we do, and that is what I never see, I guess, in a gentleman so lately from England. I guess your talk is within a grade as good as ours. You are a mighty elegant gentleman, and if you will tell me where you keep, I will bring some of my coloured friends to visit you. Well, you must be a smart man to come from England, and talk English as well as we do that were raised in this country."

At the dinner-table I commenced a relation of this occurrence to three American gentlemen, one of whom was a doctor, the others were in the law: they were men of education and of liberal opinions. When I arrived at the point of the black being turned out, they exclaimed, "Ay right, perfectly right, I would never go to a barber's where a coloured man was cut!" Observe, these gentlemen were not from the south; they are residents of New York, and I believe were born there. I was upon the point of expressing my opinion, but withheld it, thinking it wise to look at every thing as it stood, and form a deliberate judgment when every feature was finally before me. They were amused with the barber's conceit about the English language, which I understand is by no means a singular view of the subject.

The exclusion of blacks from the places of public worship where whites attend, I stated at the commencement. In perfect conformity with this spirit is the fact, that the most degraded white will not walk or eat with a negro; so that, although New York is a free state, it is such only on parchment: the black Americans are in it *practically* and politically slaves; the laws of the mind being, after all, infinitely more strong and more effective than those of the statute book; and it is these *mental* legislative enactments, operating in too many cases besides this of the poor negroes, which excite but little respect for the American character.

50 Segregation and Self-Help

Another traveller to the United States, Edward Abdy, was interested in the pattern of race relations, especially in the free states. Several features bear commentary in this account. First, the emphasis is less on the denial to blacks of equal accommodations and services than on the creation of entire categories of service left exclusively to blacks because of the servility they imply. The second feature is the observation of a broadly sustained spirit of self-help in the black community. If race pride and mutual assistance and cultural autonomy could be located in the "living space" of the slave community, so too might it have been thriving in the segregated life of blacks in the Northern communities.

Source: Edward S. Abdy, *Journal of a Residence and Tour in the United States . . .* (London, 1835), pp. 185-87.

In many of the cities in the Union, the free blacks are hackney coachmen; and some of them drive their own carriages, which are usually the best and the neatest on the stand. I asked one of them, whether the whites did not prefer them. He replied that they did, and added, that there were three reasons for the preference;—because they had no fear that they would assume any thing like equality,—because they could order them about in the tone of masters,—and still more, because it might be thought they were riding in their own carriages—like our cockneys, who put a livery-servant at the back of a glass-coach, and then pass it off as their own. Hence it is that these men are more attentive to the appearance both of themselves and their vehicles, and elevate their condition by the means employed to degrade it.

It is highly gratifying to see the pride of man defeating its own purposes, and enriching the very persons it would impoverish and depress. It is the same with the barbers, who are almost entirely colored men. The whites are too proud or too lazy to shave themselves; and one of the few employments they have left open to the despised race, has given it both wealth and influence. The barber's shop is a lounging place, and a reading-room; where the customers amuse themselves with caricatures and newspapers; while the conversation that passes makes the operator acquainted with the occurrences of the day. The information these men possess is astonishing. Most of them take in the abolition papers, which thus find a powerful support, and the best channel to convey their sentiments to the public. Were they to act in concert, their numbers would enable them to exercise a salutary check upon a large portion of the periodical press, by limiting their subscriptions to those publications that are friendly or less violent in their hostility to them. There are many who express themselves freely upon those topics, in which they are personally interested, who, in handling a colonizationist, are as ready with their logic as their razors, and can take off his arguments and his beard with equal dexterity.

The respectability of this class was proved a few years back, by a memorial they sent to the legislature of the State. According to statistical tables, the accuracy of which could not be disputed, they contributed 2500 dollars annually to the poor fund, and seldom received more than 2000 from it,—while but four per cent upon the whole amount of paupers, whether in or out of the almshouse, belonged to them;—eight and a quarter per cent being, in 1830, their proportion of the population in Philadelphia. They were paying annually for rents 100,000 dollars, and had six methodist meeting-houses, two Baptist, two Presbyterian, one Episcopalian, and one public hall, all supported by themselves, and valued at upwards of 100,000 dollars. They owned two Sunday schools, two tract societies, two Bible societies, two temperance societies, and one female literary institution. "We have among ourselves," say these ill-treated men, "more than fifty beneficent societies, some of which are incorporated, for mutual aid in times of sickness and distress." The members were liable to be expelled or suspended for misconduct. Upwards of 7000 dollars, raised among themselves, were expended annually in the relief of sickness or distress. "It is worthy of remark," they add, "that we cannot find a single instance of one of the members of these societies being convicted in any of our courts. One instance only has occurred of a member brought up and accused before a court, but this individual was acquitted."

51 The Restraints of Freedom

That abolitionists should repeatedly urge restraint upon freed blacks says something about their own paternalism regarding blacks, but it says even more about the conception of freedom prevalent in Northern society. Apparently the freedom they had in mind required *self*-restraint rather than externally imposed control. The internalization of discipline they had in mind was what had essentially been in conquest of spontaneity and liberty in white society, for it was, in the last analysis, an internalized discipline designed to promote productivity. Oddly enough they were calling upon the black man to forsake the very freedom and "living space" that had been his own in bondage.

Source: American Convention for Promoting the Abolition of Slavery . . ., *Minutes of the Proceedings of the Third Convention of Delegates from the Abolition Societies* . . . (Philadelphia, 1796), pp. 12-15.

The committee to whom was referred the address to the free Blacks, made report, which was read and adopted, as follows, *viz.*

TO THE
Free Africans and other free People of color
IN THE
UNITED STATES.

The Convention of Deputies from the Abolition Societies in the United States, assembled at Philadelphia, have undertaken to address you upon subjects highly interesting to your prosperity.

They wish to see you act worthily of the rank you have acquired as freemen, and thereby to do credit to yourselves, and to justify the friends and advocates of your color in the eyes of the world.

As the result of our united reflections, we have concluded to call your attention to the following articles of Advice. We trust, they, are dictated by the purest regard for your welfare, for we view you as Friends and Brethren.

In the first place, We earnestly recommend to you, a regular attention to the important duty of public worship; by which means you will evince gratitude to your CREATOR, and, at the same time, promote knowledge, union, friendship, and proper conduct amongst yourselves.

Secondly, We advise such of you, as have not been taught reading, writing, and the first principles of arithmetic, to acquire them as early as possible. Carefully attend to the instruction of your children in the same simple and useful branches of education. Cause them, likewise, early and frequently to read the holy Scriptures. They contain, among other great discoveries, the precious record of the original equality of mankind, and of the obligations of universal justice and benevolence, which are derived from the relation of the human race to each other in a COMMON FATHER.

Thirdly, Teach your children useful trades, or to labor with their hands in cultivating the earth. These employments are favorable to health and virtue. In the choice of masters, who are to instruct them in the above branches of business, prefer those who will work with them; by this means they will acquire habits of industry, and be better preserved from vice, than if they worked alone, or under the eye of persons less interested in their welfare. In forming contracts, for yourselves or children, with masters, it may be useful to consult such persons as are capable of giving you the best advice, who are known to be your friends, in order to prevent advantages being taken of your ignorance of the laws and customs of our country.

Fourthly, Be diligent in your respective callings, and faithful in all the relations you bear in society, whether as husbands, wives, fathers, children or hired servants. Be just in all your dealings. Be simple in your dress and furniture, and frugal in your family expenses. Thus you will act like Christians as well as freemen, and, by these means, you will provide for the distresses and wants of sickness and old age.

Fifthly, Refrain from the use of spirituous liquors. The experience of many thousands of citizens of the United States has proved, that these liquors are not necessary to lessen the fatigue of labor, nor to obviate the extremes of heat or cold; much less are they necessary to add to the innocent pleasures of society.

Sixthly, Avoid frolicking, and amusements which lead to expense and idleness; they beget habits of dissipation and vice, and thus expose you to deserved reproach among your white neighbours.

Seventhly, We wish to impress upon your minds the morals and religious necessity of having your marriages legally performed; also to have exact registers preserved of all the births and deaths which occur in your respective families.

Eighthly, Endeavour to lay up as much as possible of your earnings for the benefit of your children, in case you should die before they are able to maintain themselves—your money will be safest and most beneficial when laid out in lots, houses or small farms.

Ninthly, We recommend to you, at all times and upon all occasions, to behave yourselves to all persons in a civil and respectful manner, by which you may prevent contention and remove every just occasion of complaint. We beseech you to reflect, it is by your good conduct alone, that you can refute the objections which have been made against you as rational and moral creatures, and remove many of the difficulties, which have occurred in the general emancipation of such of your brethren as are yet in bondage.

With hearts anxious for your welfare, we commend you the guidance and protection of that BEING who is able to keep you from all evil, and who is the common Father and Friend of the whole family of mankind.

Resolved, That the above address be signed by the President and attested by the Secretary, and that three thousand copies thereof be printed in hand-bills, and transmitted to the several Abolition Societies in the United States; to be by them distributed in such manner as shall appear best calculated to promote its design.

III

The Market and the Conditions of Freedom

52 To Secure the Objects of Capital and Labor

The freedmen of Louisiana soon discovered the meaning of the Emancipation Proclamation. While the proclamation held an enormous potential in severing the chains of slavery, the race relations that would replace those fostered under slavery could only be guessed at. Before freedom could have any real meaning the U.S. government would have to act to specify the rights and responsibilities of the freedmen. The following order issued by the U.S. military command in Louisiana makes abundantly clear the market conception of the freedom presumed to replace slavery. It addresses itself first and foremost to the labor system in the area and specifies with great detail the obligations of the freedmen to labor and a wage-labor relationship with a lien on the crops to be produced.

Source: The War of the Rebellion: A Compilation of the Official Records (Washington, 1886), Series 1, Vol. 15, 666-67.

GENERAL ORDERS,   HDQRS. DEPARTMENT OF THE GULF,
   No. 12.   New Orleans, January 29, 1863

. . . The public interest peremptorily demands that all person without other means of support be required to maintain themselves by labor. Negroes are not exempt from this law. Those who leave their employers will be compelled to support themselves and families by labor upon the public works. Under no circumstances whatever can they be maintained in idleness, or allowed to wander through the parishes and cities of the State without employment. Vagrancy and crime will be suppressed by enforced and constant occupation and employment.

Upon every consideration labor is entitled to some equitable proportion of the crops it produces. To secure the objects both of capital and labor the sequestration commission is hereby authorized and directed, upon conference with planters and other parties, to propose and establish a yearly system of negro labor, which shall provide for the food, clothing, proper treatment, and just compensation for the negroes, at fixed rates or an equitable proportion of the yearly crop, as may be deemed advisable. It should be just, but not exorbitant or onerous. When accepted by the planter or other parties all the conditions of continuous and faithful service, respectful deportment, correct discipline, and perfect subordination shall be enforced on the part of the negroes by the officers of the Government. To secure their payment the wages of labor will constitute a lien upon its products.

This may not be the best, but it is now the only practicable system. Wise men will do what they can when they cannot do what they would. It is the law of success. In three years from the restoration of peace, under this voluntary system of labor, the State of Louisiana will produce threefold the product of its most prosperous year in the past.

53 Labor: A Public Duty

A fuller meaning of the new social order became apparent shortly as military authorities proceeded to lay down the ground rules of proper relations. Revealingly, this general order focused again mainly on economic relations as the basis of civil society. While proposing to be a neutral force between capital and labor (a narrower conception of the freedman-former slaveowner relationship than the relationship considered obligatory or oppressive under slavery), this general order also noted the gratitude due the planter for his special role in the nation's prosperity by hiring labor and granted him a "favor" in deliberately improving rather than impairing his position. Somehow the contribution of those who actually did the work in producing such prosperity seemed less valuable and certainly less deserving of favors. The freedman thus had the freedom of contracting with an employer but then the obligation of fulfilling the terms of that contract for the year "under the protection of the Government." Those who were slack would be turned over to the provost marshal and the punishment would be to work without pay. Clearly, the freedom of the contract, while liberating in a sense, came to this group of people not as a great uplifting moment, but with an iron hand.

Source: *The War of the Rebellion: A Compilation of the Official Records* (Washington, 1891) Series 1, Vol. 34, Pt. 2, 227-31.

GENERAL ORDERS,   HDQRS, DEPARTMENT OF THE GULF,

No. 23   New Orleans, February 3, 1864.

The following general regulations are published for the information and government of all interested in the subject of compensated plantation labor, public or private, during the present year, and in continuation of the system established January 30, 1863:

I. The enlistment of soldiers from plantations under cultivation in this department, having been suspended by order of the Government, will not be resumed except upon direction of the same high authority.

II. The provost-marshal-general is instructed to provide for the division of parishes into police and school districts, and to organize from invalid soldiers a competent police for the preservation of order.

III. Provision will be made for the establishment of a sufficient number of schools, one at least for each of the police and school districts, for the instruction of colored children under twelve years of age, which, when established, will be placed under the direction of the superintendent of public education.

IV. Soldiers will not be allowed to visit plantations without the written consent of the commanding officer of the regiment or post to which they are attached, and never with arms except when on duty, accompanied by an officer.

V. Plantation hands will not be allowed to pass from one place to another except under such regulations as may be established by the provost-marshal of the parish.

VI. Flogging and other cruel or unusual punishments are interdicted.

VII. Planters will be required, as early as practicable after the publication of these regulations, to make a roll of persons employed upon their estates, and to transmit the same to the provost-marshal of the parish. In the employment of hands, the unity of families will be secured as far as possible.

VIII. All questions between the employer and the employee, until other tribunals are established, will be decided by the provost-marshal of the parish.

* * *

XII. Laborers shall render to their employer, between daylight and dark, ten hours in summer and nine hours in winter, of respectful, honest, faithful labor, and receive therefore, in addition to just treatment, healthy rations, comfortable clothing, quarters, fuel, medical attendance, and instruction for children. Wages per month as follows, payment of one-half of which at least shall be reserved until the end of the year: For first-class hands, $8; second-class, $6; third-class, $5; fourth-class, $3. Engineers and foremen, when faithful in the discharge of their duties, will be paid $2 per month extra. This schedule of wages may be commuted, by consent of both parties, at the rate of one-fourteenth part of the net proceeds of the crop, to be determined and paid at the end of the year. Wages will be deducted in case of sickness, and rations, also, when sickness is feigned. Indolence, insolence, disobedience of orders, and crime will be suppressed by forfeiture of pay, and such punishments as are provided for similar offenses by Army Regulations. Sunday work will be avoided when practicable, but when necessary will be considered as extra labor, and paid at the rates specified herein.

XIII. Laborers will be permitted to choose their employers, but when the agreement is made, they will be held to their engagement for the year, under the protection of the Government. In cases of attempted imposition, by feigning sickness, or stubborn refusal of duty, they will be turned over to the provost-marshal of the parish, for labor upon the public works, without pay.

XIV. Laborers will be permitted to cultivate land on private account, as herein specified, as follows: First and second class hands, with families, 1 acre each; first and second class hands, without families, one-half acre each; second and third class hands, with families, one-half acre each; second and third class hands, without families, one-quarter acre each, to be increased for good conduct at the discretion of the employer. The encouragement of independent industry will strengthen all the advantages which capital derives from labor, and enable the laborer to take care of himself and prepare for the time when he can render so much labor for so much money, which is the great end to be attained. No exemption will be made in this apportionment, except upon imperative reasons, and it is desirable that for good conduct the quantity be increased until faithful hands can be allowed to cultivate extensive tracts, returning to the owner an equivalent of product for rent of soil.

XV. To protect the laborer from possible imposition, no commutation of his supplies will be allowed, except in clothing, which may be commuted at the rate of $3 per month for first-class hands, and in similar proportion for other classes. The crops will stand pledged, wherever found, for the wages of labor.

XVI. It is advised, as far as practicable, that employers provide for the current wants of their hands, by perquisites for extra labor, or by appropriation of land for share cultivation; to discourage monthly payments so far as it can be done without discontent, and to reserve till the full harvest the yearly wages.

* * *

XIX. The last year's experience shows that the planter and the negro comprehend the revolution. The overseer, having little interest in capital and less sympathy with labor, dislikes the trouble of thinking, and discredits the notion that anything new has occurred. He is a relic of the past, and adheres to its customs. His stubborn refusal to comprehend the condition of things occasioned most of the embarrassments of the past year. Where such incomprehension is chronic, reduced wages, diminished rations, and the mild punishments imposed by the Army and Navy will do good.

XX. These regulations are based upon the assumption that labor is a public duty, and idleness and vagrancy a crime. No civil or military officer of the Government is exempt from the operation of this universal rule. Every enlightened community has enforced it upon all classes of people by the severest penalties. It is especially necessary in agricultural pursuits. That portion of the people identified with the cultivation of the soil, however changed in condition by the revolution through which we are passing, is not relieved from the necessity of toil, which is the condition of existence with all the children of God. The revolution has altered its tenure, but not its law. This universal law of labor will be enforced upon just terms by the Government, under whose protection the laborer rests secure in his rights. Indolence, disorder, and crime will be suppressed. Having exercised the highest right in the choice and place of employment, he must be held to the fulfillment of his engagements until released therefrom by the Government. The several provost-marshals are hereby invested with plenary powers upon all matters connected with labor, subject to the approval of the provost-marshal-general and the commanding officer of the department. The most faithful and discreet officers will be selected for this duty, and the largest force consistent with the public service detailed for their assistance.

XXI. Employers, and especially overseers, are notified, that undue influence used to move the marshal from his just balance between the parties representing labor and capital will result in immediate change of officers, and thus defeat that regular and stable system upon which the interests of all parties depend.

XXII. Successful industry is especially necessary at the present time, when large public debts and onerous taxes are imposed to maintain and protect the liberties of the people and the integrity of the Union. All officers, civil or military, and all classes of citizens who assist in extending the profits of labor and increasing the product of the soil, upon which, in the end, all national prosperity and power depends, will render to the Government a service as great as that derived from the terrible sacrifices of battle. It is upon such consideration only that the planter is entitled to favor. The Government has accorded to him, in a period of anarchy, a release from the disorders resulting mainly from insensate and mad resistance to sensible reforms, which can never be rejected without revolution and the criminal surrender of his interests and power to crazy politicians, who thought by metaphysical abstractions to circumvent the laws of God. It has restored to him in improved, rather than impaired condition, his due privileges at a moment when, by his own acts, the very soil was washed from beneath his feet.

54 Submission Through Freedom

The "revolution," as the general orders referred to the change in relations, was evident to all. And its precise contours were noted by many. In the following interrogation of General Rufus Saxton by a Congressional committee in 1866, Saxton put his finger directly on the crucial system of incentives and compulsions that replaced the personalized control of the slaveowner. That Saxton noted the dependence of the freedmen on the wage system, and on their being a landless group of people, marks him as a perceptive observer. Yet that he should proceed into a discussion of the necessity of granting political rights to the freedmen, having already noted their economic dependency, suggests not a personal shortcoming but a narrow perception of the social nature of freedom. Such a narrow interpretation could well result from the fact that political freedoms, once divorced from economic reality, are much easier to grant, are much more visible and elaborate in their forms, and provide an appearance of precision in the description of social relations. Curiously, the slave and his master probably both knew better when they measured slavery not as an economic system but as a system of authority—social, economic, racial, political, and cultural. The hopes for real freedom dimmed substantially when the "protectors and friends" of the black population began to define both freedom and oppression in the narrowly categorized terms of economics and politics, presumably separate and unrelated realms of behavior.

Source: *Report of the Joint Committee on Reconstruction*, 39th Cong., 1st Session (Washington, 1866), Part 3, 101-2.

Question. Considering the negroes as a class by themselves what is your opinion of their disposition to labor if they are properly paid and properly treated?

Answer.   I think that the freedmen share with the rest of the human race a natural disinclination to labor, but to no greater extent than it is shared by the white race. I think that with proper stimulus to industry they would be as industrious as any other people. I know this to be the case, because I have tried the experiment myself. The only stimulus they formerly had to labor was that of the lash. That is removed; but the stimulus of wages, and their finding out that by the products of their own labor they can obtain those necessaries of life which they desire, will be sufficient to make them a thrifty and industrious people.

Question. What is their disposition in regard to purchasing land, and what is the disposition of the landholders in reference to selling land to the negroes?

Answer.   The object which the freedman has most at heart is the purchase of land. They all desire to get small homesteads and to locate themselves upon them, and there is scarcely any sacrifice too great for them to make to accomplish this object. I believe it is the policy of the majority of the farm owners to prevent negroes from becoming landholders. They desire to keep the negroes landless, and as nearly in a condition of slavery as it is possible for them to do. I think that the former slaveholders know really less about the freedmen than any other class of people. The system of slavery has been one of concealment on the part of the negro of all his feelings and his impulses; and that feeling of concealment is so ingrained with the very constitution of the negro that he deceives his former master on almost every point. The freedman has no faith in his former master, nor has his former owner any faith in the capacity of the freedman. A mutual distrust exists between them. But the freedman is ready and willing to contract to work for any northern man. One man from the north, a man of capital, who employed large numbers of freedmen, and paid them regularly, told me, as others have, that he desired no better laborers; that he considered them fully as easy to manage as Irish laborers. That was my own experience in employing several thousands of them in cultivating the soil. I have also had considerable experience in employing white labor, having, as quartermaster, frequently had large numbers of laborers under my control.

Question. If the negro is put in possession of all his rights as a man, do you apprehend any danger of insurrection among them?

Answer.   I do not; and I think that is the only thing which will prevent difficulty. I think if the negro is put in possession of all his rights as a citizen and as a man, he will be as peaceful, orderly, and self-sustaining as any other man or class of men, and that he will rapidly advance in the scale of civilization.

Question. It has been suggested that, if the negro is allowed to vote, he will be likely to vote on the side of his former master, and be inveighed in the support of a policy hostile to the government of the United States; do you share in that apprehension?

Answer.   I have positive information from negroes, from the most intelligent freedmen in those States, those who are leaders among them, that they are thoroughly loyal, and know their friends, and they will never be found voting on the side of oppression. I think all their instincts, that is, of all the intelligent ones, are on the side of the Union; and there are intelligent ones among them who will instruct the others how they should vote. I think it vital to the safety and prosperity of the two races in the south that the negro should immediately be put in possession of all his rights as a man; and the word "color" should be left out of all laws, constitutions, and regulations for the people; I think it vital to the safety of the Union that this should be done.

55 The Fear and Hope of Violence

Despite the persistent bonds of contracts rather than chains restraining the blacks, the potential fluidity of the contract generated apprehensions among the whites. After all, in the classic terms of contractual freedom rewards are determined by merit through the operation of the market rather than by hereditary status. In the transition from the traditional, status, or even paternalistic society that slavery represented, to a competitive, possessive market society characterized by large numbers of landless blacks and whites competing for both economic rewards and the social and psychic symbols of dignity and sources of self-respect, a broad fear often consumed whites. Often, those fears had been there a long time even though the system of mirrors and projections and self-serving illusions available in slavery could always set aside doubts and fears. Given the continuing stern reality, the blacks had no opportunity to realize their potential in a way sufficient finally to *prove* or *disprove* the elaborate assumptions. Without real proof the doubts multiplied into fears and the fears into a hysteria that could even produce genocide. In the following letter written from Memphis in December, 1865, some of that fear is evident. So too is another quality: even now the Negro cannot be burdened, given his nature, with the responsibility and autonomy of independent action. Should a revolt of the blacks emerge, it would be because the blacks were incited by the Yankees.

Source: D. L. Corbitt, ed., "A Letter by James E. Beasley to D. L. Swain Inquiring About North Carolina and North Carolinians," *North Carolina Historical Review*, 3 (April 1926), 376. Reprinted with permission of North Carolina Department of Cultural Resources, Division of Archives and History.

How are the *freedmen* getting along in N.C. We are anticipating some trouble here. Yesterday and day before two white men were murdered by them without provocation. One killed in his house and the other taken from his house and carried beyond the city limits. This I believe only to be a foretaste of what we may expect unless Congress will do away with Freedmen's bureau. We have in the city about 3 or 4 thousand negroes with arms. The white population are comparatively destitute of arms and if disposed the negroes could give us some serious trouble. I do not think they would be half as bad were it not for the Yankees that are here urging them on. In the city itself there will be no danger, but I fear those in the suburbs will suffer. Those of us that were in the army, may soon have occasion to listen again to the music of bullets. I do not care to see it but I believe firmly if some different course from the present is not persued, one race or the other will have to be exterminated and probably the sooner the better. I would like to have the pleasure of killing the scoundrels that are inciting the negro. "Sufficient unto the day is the evil thereof."

56 The Crowning Acts

When violence occurred in Memphis in 1866, it did so in a horrid, brutal fashion. Hardly a Negro uprising, the riot ensued when black soldiers took custody of a black prisoner from the Memphis police to protect him from the police and when the white police arrested two black soldiers. The official tabulation of the results, which was no doubt understated, figured forty-six blacks killed in the frenzy; more than twice that number of black homes and churches were burned. As August Meier and Elliott Rudwick have noted, this episode, like several others in the period, was not so much a riot as it was a pogrom, an actual effort at extermination. Perhaps more revealing than the statistics are the actual personal sufferings. That so many victims should have been weak and helpless suggests a deeper motivation than vengeance or retribution, at least on an individual scale. It was an act of psychological and social subjugation of vast ferocity and unlimited intensity. Again, only speculation can be offered; it does appear, however, that with the change in legal status of labor and race, with the attainment of freedom if only in a formalistic, legal, and market sense, the subjugation of blacks could no longer be an assumed certainty; it had to be proved, at least to the satisfaction of the perpetrators and presumably as an object lesson to the blacks. If the change generated by emancipation was indeed a revolution, there is no doubt that this was a large step in the counter-revolution.

Source: *Memphis Riots and Massacres*: Report of the Select Committee, House of Representatives, 39 Congress, 1st Session, Document No. 101 (Washington, 1866), 13-17.

The crowning acts of atrocity and diabolism committed during these terrible nights were the ravishing of five different colored women by fiends in human shape, independent of other attempts at rape. The details of these outrages are of too shocking and disgusting a character to be given at length in this report, and reference must be had to the testimony of the parties. It is a singular fact, that while this mob was breathing vengeance against the negroes and shooting them down like dogs, yet when they found unprotected colored women they at once "conquered their prejudices," and proceeded to violate them under circumstances of the most licentious brutality.

FRANCES THOMPSON
The rape of Frances Thompson, who had been a slave and was a cripple, using crutches, having a cancer on her foot, is one to which reference is here made. On Tuesday night seven men, two of whom were policemen, came to her house. She knew the two to be policemen by their stars. They were all Irishmen. They first demanded that she should get supper for them, which she did. After supper the wretches threw all the provisions that were in the house which had not been consumed out into the bayou. They then laid hold of Frances, hitting her on the side of the face and kicking her. A girl by the name of

LUCY SMITH
about sixteen years old, living with her, attempted to go out at the window. One of the brutes knocked her down and choked her. They then drew their pistols, and said they would shoot them and fire the house if they did not let them have their way. The woman, Frances Thompson, was then violated by four of the men, and so beaten and bruised that she lay in bed for three days. They then took all the clothes out of the trunk, one hundred dollars in greenbacks belonging to herself, and two hundred dollars belonging to another colored woman, which had been left to take care of her child, besides silk dresses, bed-clothing, &c. They were in the house nearly four hours, and when they left they said they intended "to burn up the last God-damned nigger, and drive all the Yankees out of town, and then there would be only some rebel niggers and butternuts left." The colored girl, Lucy Smith who was before the committee, said to be sixteen or seventeen years old, but who seemed, from her appearance, to be two or three years younger, was a girl of modest demeanor and highly respectable in appearance. She corroborated the testimony of Frances Thompson as to the number of men who broke into the house and as to the policemen who were with them. They seized her (Lucy) by the neck and choked her to such an extent that she could not talk for two weeks to any one. She was then violated by one of the men, and the reason given by another for not repeating the act of nameless atrocity was, that she was so *near dead he would not have anything to do with her.* He thereupon struck her a severe blow upon the side of the head. The violence of these wretches seemed to be aggravated by the fact that the women had in their room some bed-covering or quilting with red, white, and blue, and also some pictures of Union officers. They said, "You niggers have a mighty liking for the damned Yankees, but we will kill you, and you will have no liking for any one then." This young girl was so badly injured that she was unable to leave her bed for two weeks.

* * *

OTHER BURNINGS AND SHOOTINGS.

Witnesses testified as to the circumstances of other burnings and shootings. A house containing women and little children was set on fire, and was then surrounded by armed men. Scorched by the extending flames the terrified inmates rushed out, but only to be fired upon when fleeing from their burning dwelling. It was reported that the arm of a little child was shot off. A woman and her little son were in a house which was fired. She begged to be permitted to come out, but the murderer (Pendergrast) shot at her. She got down on her knees and prayed him to let her out. She had her little son with her. McGinn was in this crowd, and the scene moved even his adamantine heart to mercy. He said, "This is a very good woman; it is a pity to burn her up. Let her come out." She came out with her boy; but it happened he had on *blue clothes*. That seemed to madden them still more. They pushed him back and said, "Go back, you d——n son of a b——h." Then the poor heartbroken mother fell on her knees and prayed them to let the child out; *it was the only child she had*; and the boy was finally permitted to escape from the flames. Pendergrast went into a grocery and gave ammunition to a policeman to load his pistol. They then started up a negro man who ran up the bayou, and told him to come to them. He was coming up to them, when they put a pistol to his mouth, shot his tongue off, killing him instantly. This man's name was Lewis Robertson.

57 Don't Be Too Free

The physical and symbolic restraints placed upon the freedman were both real and visible. Other restraints, however, equally real but more subtle, also beset the freedman. The following document illustrates the nature of this restraint as in this instance it came from a black man, not a white, who espoused a cultural repression that sharply restricted the potential of freedom. Freedom was defined here within the limits of capitalism, promising the full potential of a market conception, defining satisfaction in terms of economics and the work ethic as the path to Heaven (certainly a far cry from prevalent religious conceptions in the black community), and even arguing that freedom must be earned.

Source: William Wells Brown, *The Negro in the American Rebellion: His Heroism and his Fidelity* (Boston, 1867), p. 114.

After several others had spoken, George Payne, another contraband, made a few sensible remarks, somewhat in these words: "Friends, don't you see de han' of God in dis? Haven't we a right to rejoice? You all know you couldn't have such a meetin' as dis down in Dixie! Dat you all knows. I have a right to rejoice; an' so have you; for we shall be free in jus' about five minutes. Dat's a fact. I shall rejoice that God has placed Mr. Lincum in de president's chair, and dat he wouldn't let de rebels make peace until after dis new year. De Lord has heard de groans of de people, and has come down to deliver! You all knows dat in Dixie you worked de day long, an' never got no satisfacshun. But here, what you make is yourn. I've worked six months; and what I've made is mine! Let me tell you, though, don't be too free! De lazy man can't go to heaven. You must be honest, an' work, an' show dat you is fit to be free; an' de Lord will bless you an' Abrum Lincum. Amen!"

58 Free to Starve

The vast uncertainty about the terms of freedom perceived by whites and blacks is clear in this following account by a white man in Alabama in 1866. The main message transmitted by the document is no doubt the increasingly bitter "estrangement between the races." Yet other elements of significance can also be detected. The equation of civilization with discipline and the persistence of an undisciplined black culture identified repeatedly as infantile and childlike is of course more than an unthinking racism; it is testimony to the intensity and distance of the separation. The fact that so many blacks armed themselves and were unwilling to make contracts suggests an apprehension about the breadth of their newfound freedom. And their hopes for land indicate perhaps a widespread aspiration for the full measure of freedom, starting with economic independence rather than with the freedom of the market. The limitations restricting whites should be noted also. Whites were unable to exercise the patriarchal protection needed; most were unable to pay wages, as the new system demanded; they offered as high a price for labor as they could afford; and they found themselves in the midst of a social revolution in which old certainties were being uprooted. It could well be that William F. Samford, in his reference to being "free to starve," was not speaking just of the fate of the freedman, but of the growing conquest of society by the market to the detriment of both white and black.

Source: George Petrie, "William F. Samford, Statesman and Man of Letters," *Transactions of the Alabama Historical Society*, 4 (June 1902), 479-81.

Emancipation is a fact. I have sworn to support it, and I shall keep my oath. Sambo is a freeman by force of presidential proclamation. But it is not unlawful to see certain evils of emancipation which call for the active interposition of the philanthropists. Sambo will flog his child unmercifully and Sally will neglect it in sickness, and so between paternal action and maternal non-action little Cuff has a "hard road to travel" for twenty-one years of his infancy—a terrible preparatory training for the bliss of being "free to starve."

The stupendous wrong and folly consists of taking a poor, ignorant childlike race from under the fostering care of a patriarchal government and withdrawing from it the protection of interest.

* * *

The Christmas holidays here are cold, rainy, cheerless. The heart of the South is beginning to sink in despair. The streets are full of negroes, who refuse to make contracts to labor the next year. The short crop of 1866 causes much dissatisfaction. They will not engage to work for anything but wages, and few are able to pay wages. They are penniless, but resolute in their demands. They expect to see the land all divided out equally between them and their old masters, in time to make the next crop. One of the most intelligent black men I know told me this day that in a neighboring village where several hundred negroes were congregated, he does not think that as many as three made contracts, although the planters are urgent in their solicitations, and offering the highest prices for labor they can possibly afford to pay. The same man informed me that the impression widely prevails that Congress is about to divide out the lands, and that this impression is given out by Federal soldiers at the nearest military station. It cannot be disguised that in spite of the most earnest efforts of their old masters to conciliate and satisfy them, the estrangement between the races increases in its extent and bitterness. Nearly all the negro men are armed with repeaters and many of them carry them openly, day and night. The status is most unsatisfactory, and really full of just apprehensions of the direst results. The negro children are growing up in ignorance and vice. The older ones, men and women, abandon themselves to dissipation of the lowest sort. Their schools, 'so-called,' are simply a farce.

* * *

Here, in a mile of me, is a negro woman dying, who says an old African hag put a snake in her four years ago, and the Obi doctor has gone to deliver her. Civilization is marching two steps backwards' like the truant boy went to school, to one forward in our "Africa" down here. The negroes here spend their time in going to "funerals," religious howlings, promiscuous sexual intercourse, thieving and "conjuring." At their "funerals" they bellow like cattle when one of their number is slaughtered.

59 The Burden of Teaching Freedom's Ways

Similar cultural confrontations emerged at other points with the coming of freedom, and the issues seemed remarkably similar regardless of where or when the confrontations occurred, or even who the principals were. The following extract from the diary of Laura M. Towne, one of a number of anti-slavery advocates who went into the Union-occupied Sea Islands of South Carolina to work with the blacks, describes the problems of teaching proper habits of agriculture and economics. There were, no doubt, great difficulties involved in teaching the freedmen that they should no longer allow *any masters* to claim them while they begged those in authority over them for the privilege of growing corn, something practical and edible, instead of cotton, something marketable. The logic of the system of production for the market rather than for subsistence and of being paid on account and then of paying high prices for the goods made from cotton no doubt struck many of the former slaves as strange if not thoroughly tainted. Yet this was definitely more than an economic endeavor for the economics were yet again bound up in a larger pattern of civilization that stressed discipline and reserve and work. The religion nurtured for generations in the slave quarters was as incomprehensible to women like Laura Towne as was the Yankee religion to the blacks. It was no exaggeration from either perspective when the one black man rose to say: "The Yankees preach nothing but cotton, cotton," and when Towne herself described the religious shout as "savage" and "a regular frolic." A conception of freedom that included both the material and spiritual world was evident time and again and was dominated in both areas by a spirit of productivity and discipline, by the subordination of other freedoms to the demands of the market and indeed to a market definition of man.

Source: Rupert S. Holland, ed., *Letters and Diary of Laura M. Towne Written from the Sea Islands of South Carolina 1862-1884* (Cambridge, Mass., 1912), pp. 18-20.

The blessed soldiers, with all their wrong doing, did this one good thing—they assured the negroes that they were free and must never again let their masters claim them, nor any masters. I think it is very touching to hear them begging Mr. Pierce to let them cultivate corn instead of cotton, of which they do not see the use, since they worked it last year for pay which has not come yet, while their corn has saved them from starvation. Next week they are to be paid a dollar an acre for cotton they have planted under Mr. Pierce. They do not understand being paid on account, and they think one dollar an acre for ploughing, listing, or furrowing and planting is very little, which of course it is. Mr. P. wants to make it their interest to tend the cotton after it is planted, and so he pays on it just as little as he can, until it is all ready for the market. Meanwhile, if the masters drive us off, no return will ever be made for their work, to the people who are planting for us. Nothing is paid for the cultivation of the corn, and yet it will be Government property. The negroes are so willing to work on that, that Mr. P. has made it a rule that till a certain quantity of cotton is planted they shall not hoe the corn. This they take as a great hardship, for the corn wants hoeing. Several boxes of clothing have lately come here for distribution, and from early morning till evening the negroes are flocking here to buy. I do not like the prices fixed on the goods at all. They are in some cases higher a good deal than the retail Philadelphia prices.

* * *

The church was in the midst of splended live-oak trees hanging with moss, and the services were impressive only because they were so unusual, especially the singing. The garments seen today were beyond all description. One man had a carpet, made like a poncho, and he stalked about in such grandeur. There was an old woman there who came from Africa in a steamship. Her face was tattooed a little. Mr. Horton, who was one of our fellow passengers on the Oriental, a Baptist minister, preached a sermon upon true freedom, and I think the negroes liked it. We heard of one old negro who got up in meeting, when one of the young superintendents was leading the services, and said, "The Yankees preach nothing but cotton, cotton." The fact is that every man has thought it his duty to inculcate the necessity of continuing to work, and the negro can see plainly enough that the proceeds of the cotton will never get into black pockets—judging from past experience.

Tonight I have been to a "shout," which seems to me certainly the remains of some old idol worship. The negroes sing a kind of chorus,—three standing apart to lead and clap,—and then all the others go shuffling round in a circle following one another with not much regularity, turning round occasionally and bending the knees, and stamping so that the whole floor swings. I never saw anything so savage. They call it a religious ceremony, but it seems more like a regular frolic to me, and instead of attending the shout, the better persons go to the "Praise House." This is always the cabin of the oldest person in the little village of negro houses, and they meet there to read and pray; generally one of the ladies goes there to read to them and they pray.

60 The Catechism of Citizenship

Edward L. Pierce, another of those who went to the Sea Islands to teach and organize the freedmen, described some of his frustrations and successes in 1863 in the *Atlantic Monthly*. Familiar themes and issues of cultural contact emerge again, but Pierce showed pride in the successful efforts undertaken to inculcate proper ideas and habits. Again, the content of the values taught and the lessons prescribed focused largely upon productivity as the catechism he employed in his examination of school children demonstrated. After that experience he had no doubt about the ability of this race to "acquire with maturity of years the ideas and habits of good citizens." So important was this teaching mission that school itself sometimes interfered with the real substance of what was being taught; it should not be allowed "to interfere in any way with industrious habits." Thus the school children went into the fields, to tasks more important than those associated with the schoolhouse. Perhaps Pierce's greatest pride is evident in his boast that these people had gained acquisitive habits of ownership and desires for material comforts that would both generate and be served by a market system. With such habits freedmen had finally recognized the difference between slavery and wage-labor, although the precise difference is never made entirely clear by Pierce. One final duty and habit of citizenship enters the scene obliquely: the draft had taken the men and in that way permitted the women to learn the virtues of honest work by laboring in the fields.

Source: Edward L. Pierce, "The Freedmen at Port Royal," *Atlantic Monthly*, 12 (September 1863), 306-7, 308-9, 310-11.

Though I have never been on the school-committee, I accepted invitations to address the schools on these visits, and particularly plied the pupils with questions, so as to catch the tone of their minds; and I have rarely heard children answer with more readiness and spirit. We had a dialogue substantially as follows: -

"Children, what are you going to do when you grow up?"

"Going to work, Sir."

"On what?"

"Cotton and corn, Sir."

"What are you going to do with the corn?"

"Eat it."

"What are you going to do with the cotton?"

"Sell it."

"What are you going to do with the money you get for it?"

One boy answered in advance of the rest,—

"Put it in my pocket, Sir."

"That won't do. What's better than that?"

"Buy clothes, Sir."

"What else will you buy?"

"Shoes, Sir."

"What else are you going to do with your money?"

There was some hesitation at this point. Then the question was put,—

"What are you going to do Sundays?"

"Going to meeting."

"What are you going to do there?"

"Going to sing."

"What else?"

"Hear the parson."

"Who's going to pay him?"

One boy said,—"Government pays him"; but the rest answered,—

"We pays him."

"Well, when you grow up, you'll probably get married, as other people do, and you'll have your little children; now, what will you do with them?"

There was a titter at this question; but the general response came,—

"Send'em to school, Sir."

"Well, who'll pay the teacher?"

"We's pays him."

One who listens to such answers can hardly think that there is any natural incapacity in these children to acquire with maturity of years the ideas and habits of good citizens.

The children are cheerful, and, in most of the schools, well-behaved, except that it is not easy to keep them from whispering and talking. They are joyous, and you can see the boys after school playing the soldier, with corn-stalks for guns. The memory is very susceptible in them,—too much so, perhaps, as it is ahead of the reasoning faculty.

The labor of the season has interrupted attendance on the schools, the parents being desirous of having the children aid them in planting and cultivating their crops, and it not being thought best to allow the teaching to interfere in any way with industrious habits.

* * *

Next as to *industry*. The laborers, during their first year under the new system, have acquired the idea of ownership, and of the security of wages, and have come to see that labor and slavery are not the same thing. The notion that they were to raise no more cotton has passed away, since work upon it is found to be remunerative, and connected with the proprietorship of land. House-servants, who were at first particularly set against it, now generally prefer it. The laborers have collected the pieces of the gins which they destroyed on the flight of their masters, the ginning being obnoxious work, repaired them, and ginned the cotton on the promise of wages. Except upon plantations in the vicinity of camps, where other labor is more immediately remunerative, and an unhealthy excitement prevails, there is a general disposition to cultivate it. The culture of the cotton is voluntary, the only penalty for not engaging in it being the imposition of a rent for the tenement and land adjacent thereto occupied by the negro, not exceeding two dollars per month. Both the Government and private individuals, who have become owners of one-fourth of the land by the recent tax-sales, pay twenty-five cents for a standard day's-work, which may, by beginning early, be performed by a healthy and active hand by noon; and the same was the case with the tasks under the slave-system on very many of the plantations.

* * *

The laborers do less work, perhaps, than a Yankee would think they might do, but they do about as much as he himself would do, after a residence of a few years in the same climate, and when he had ceased to work under the influence of Northern habits. Northern men have sometimes been unjust to the South, when comparing the results of labor in the different sections. God never intended that a man should toil under a tropical sun with the same energy and constancy as in our bracing latitude. There has been less complaint this year than last of "a pain in the small of the back," or of "a fever in the head,"—in other words, less shamming. The work has been greatly deranged by the draft, some features of which have not been very skilfully arranged, and by the fitfulness with which the laborers have been treated by the military authorities. The work both upon the cotton and the corn is done only by the women, children, and disabled men. It has been suggested that field-work does not become women in the new condition; and so it may seem to some persons of just sympathies who have not yet learned that no honest work is dishonorable in man or woman. But this matter may be left to regulate itself. Field-work, as an occupation, may not be consistent with the finest feminine culture or the most complete womanliness; but it in no way conflicts with virtue, self-respect, and social development. Women work in the field in Switzerland the freest country of Europe; and we may look with pride on the triumphs of this generation, when the American negroes become the peers of the Swiss peasantry. Better a woman with the hoe than without it, when she is not yet fitted for the needle or the book.

* * *

Another evidence of developing manhood appears in their desire for the comforts and conveniences of household life. The Philadelphia society, for the purpose of maintaining reasonable prices, has a store on St. Helena Island, which is under the charge of Friend Hunn, of the good fellowship of William Penn. He was once fined in Delaware three thousand dollars for harboring and assisting fugitive slaves; but he now harbors and assists them at a much cheaper rate. Though belonging to a society which is the advocate of peace, his tone is quite as warlike as that of the world's people. In this store alone—and there are others on the island, carried on by private enterprise—two thousand dollars' worth of goods are sold monthly. To be sure, a rather large proportion of these consists of molasses and sugar, "sweetening," as the negroes call it, being in great demand, and four barrels of molasses having been sold the day of my visit. But there is also a great demand for plates, knives, forks, tin ware, and better clothing, including even hoopskirts. Negro-cloth, as it is called, osnaburgs, russet-colored shoes,—in short, the distinctive apparel formerly dealt out to them, as a uniform allowance,—are very generally rejected. But there is no article of household-furniture or wearing apparel, used by persons of moderate means among us, which they will not purchase, when they are allowed the opportunity of labor and earning wages. What a market the South would open under the new system! It would set all the mills and workshops astir. Four millions of people would become purchasers of all the various articles of manufacture and commerce, in place of the few coarse, simple necessaries, laid in for them in gross by the planters. Here is the solution of the vexed industrial question. The indisposition to labor is overcome in a healthy nature by instincts and motives of superior force, such as the love of life, the desire to be well clothed and fed, the sense of security derived from provision for the future, the feeling of self-respect, the love of family and children, and the convictions of duty. These all exist in the negro, in a state of greater or less development. To give one or two examples. One man brought Captain Hooper seventy dollars in silver, to keep for him, which he had obtained from selling pigs and chickens,—thus providing for the future. Soldiers of Colonel Higginson's regiment, having confidence in the same officer, intrusted him, when they were paid off, with seven hundred dollars, to be transmitted by him to their wives, and this besides what they had sent home in other ways,—showing the family-feeling to be active and strong in them. They have also the social and religious inspirations to labor. Thus, early in our occupation of Hilton Head, they took up, of their own accord, a collection to pay for the candles for their evening meetings, feeling that it was not right for the Government longer to provide them. The result was a contribution of two dollars and forty-eight cents. They had just fled from their masters, and had received only a small pittance of wages, and this little sum was not unlike the two mites which the widow cast into the treasury. Another collection was taken, last June, in the church on St. Helena Island, upon the suggestion of the pastor that they should share in the expenses of worship. Fifty-two dollars was the result,—not a bad collection for some of our Northern churches. I have seen these people where they are said to be lowest, and sad indeed are some features of their lot, yet with all earnestness and confidence I enter my protest against the wicked satire of Carlyle.

Is there not here some solution of the question of prejudice or caste which has troubled so many good minds? When these people can no longer be used as slaves, men will try to see how they can make the most out of them as freemen. Your Irishman, who now works as a day-laborer, honestly thinks that he hates the negro; but when the war is over, he will have no objection to going South and selling him groceries and household-implements at fifty per cent advance on New York prices, or to hiring him to raise cotton for twenty-five or fifty cents a day. Our prejudices under any reasonable adjustment of the social system, readily accommodate themselves to our interests, even without much aid from the moral sentiments.

Let those who would study well this social question, or who in public trusts are charged with its solution, be most careful here. Every motive in the minds of these people, whether of instinct, desire, or duty, must be addressed. All the elements of human nature must be appealed to, physical, moral, intellectual, social, and religious. Imperfect indeed is any system which, like that at New Orleans, offers wages, but does not welcome the teacher. It is of little moment whether three dollars or thirty per month be paid the laborer, so long as there is no school to bind both parent and child to civil society with new hopes and duties.

61 A Persistent Culture

Despite missionary instruction to the freedmen on the Sea Islands, many of the cultural habits of the blacks persisted, although some of them were practiced more discreetly. In 1862 Laura Towne (Document No. 59) attended such a religious shout as Charlotte Forten describes below in 1864. Forten did not know with certainty that the ceremony was a religious one; some blacks indeed denied that it was religious. Given the assumption of these missionaries that the shout was "destined to pass away under the influence of Christian teachings," there was good reason for the denials. Forten was glad that finally former slaves were allowed to be legally married, even though some couples had already grown old together and had families. Still the decorous legal ceremony helped them to lead "right and virtuous lives." Little of the freedmen's culture could be approved by the missionaries as they found it.

Source: Charlotte Forten, "Life on the Sea Islands," *Atlantic Monthly*, 8 (May 1864), 593-94.

In the evenings, the children frequently came in to sing and shout for us. These "shouts" are very strange,—in truth, almost indescribable. It is necessary to hear and see in order to have any clear idea of them. The children form a ring, and move around in a kind of shuffling dance, singing all the time. Four or five stand apart, and sing very energetically, clapping their hands, stamping their feet, and rocking their bodies to and fro. These are the musicians, to whose performance the shouters keep perfect time. The grown people on this plantation did not shout, but they do on some of the other plantations. It is very comical to see little children, not more than three or four years old, entering into the performance with all their might. But the shouting of the grown people is rather solemn and impressive than otherwise. We cannot determine whether it has a religious character or not. Some of the people tell us that it has, others that it has not. But as the shouts of the grown people are always in connection with their religious meetings, it is probable that they are the barbarous expression of religion, handed down to them from their African ancestors, and destined to pass away under the influence of Christian teachings. The people on this island have no songs. They sing only hymns, and most of these are sad. Prince, a large black boy from a neighboring plantation, was the principal shouter among the children. It seemed impossible for him to keep still for a moment. His performances were most amusing specimens of Ethiopian gymnastics.

* * *

After the service, there were six couples married. Some of the dresses were unique. One was particularly fine,—doubtless a cast-off dress of the bride's former mistress. The silk and lace, ribbons, feathers and flowers, were in a rather faded and decayed condition. But, comical as the costumes were, we were not disposed to laugh at them. We were too glad to see the poor creatures trying to lead right and virtuous lives. The legal ceremony, which was formerly scarcely known among them, is now everywhere consecrated. The constant and earnest advice of the minister and teachers has not been given in vain; nearly every Sunday there are several couples married in church. Some of them are people who have grown old together.

62 Toward a New System

In the postwar South it was not inevitable for any specific system of organization of the economy and society to emerge. However, the new agricultural system that did emerge focused upon the devices of the marketplace: (1) the contract as the connection between workers and owners, (2) government officials serving as enforcers of the terms of the contract, (3) the withholding of payment for work until the crop was harvested and in the interim charging farm laborers interest on the provisions they purchased. While the parties to the contract would change before too long to farm workers and commercial operators, the following letters make clear that in the years immediately following the war the owners of the land, though clearly beset by a lack of capital and a change in social relations, still commanded power over their plantations. The need for money through loans from Charleston indicates a dependence on a commercial class even at this point. Of course, it would then be the croppers at the bottom who payed the final interest on that money. The first letter printed below carries with it the recurrent theme of a labor shortage, and it is clear that only the doling out of rations by the government kept the freedmen from all going to the planters who were more capable of paying them. The rations seem to have saved the planters by averting the natural force of labor upon the marketplace. The labor situation itself is also curious. The blacks were unacquisitive; they were content having planted only small patches; they were at best reluctant to contract. Part of that reluctance may have been due to the actual terms of the contract as spelled out in the letter. With the itemized deductions from their share the workers would do well to receive a third of the value of the crop that they planted and harvested. The second letter confirms that their living expenses were exorbitant. Indeed, both letters reveal a changing social system in which the economics of the market de-

termine the relations between the races in a most material way. The
new system of sharecropping replaces slavery, and the chief difference between the two systems appears ever so discreetly. The responsibility for the bottommost place of the blacks in the sharecropping system is viewed as due not to the market system into
which they were born but to their individual and collective laziness.

Source: William Elliott to his mother, March 25, 1866, and Mrs. (Hattie) A.J.G. to her
mother, May 3, 1868, Elliott-Gonzales Papers, No. 1009, Southern Historical Collection,
The University of North Carolina at Chapel Hill. Printed with the permission of the Director
of the Southern Historical Collection.

"The Ruins" March 25th 66

My Dearest Mother
    Your letter reached me in Charleston; too late, however, to undo what had
already been done, for I had already contracted with the hands at Cheeka. To
have asked your opinion first would have lost too much time.—I will briefly
state the circumstances which you could not know or judge of at such a distance.
1st I found it extremely hazardous to plant here, from cattle being every where.
If kept out of the home field they would most certainly destroy town hill & the
two Cypress fields. The poor people own them *and in spite of any law* cannot if
they would inclose them for *want of the labor.* That they have no intention of
attempting it even is indicated by their burning of all the pine barrens in the
neighborhood. That Major King & Clement have no faith in their ability or
intention to enclose them is shown by the fencing they are putting up. Now
even with hands t'would be too late for me to make fences. But I have been
unable to get them. One promised to come with two others & failed. When Dick
came on the 15th, I sent Jacob on a mule to try & procure them. He failed. All
the labor of the neighborhood except disbanded soldiers has been absorbed.
Jacobs six or seven relatives have not appeared and he, I am compelled to think
is indifferent in the matter. He wishes to squat on the place and have lions share
of everything he may make. I offered him half of everything if with Rose he
would plant 5 or 6 acres of Sea Island Cotton. He prefers planting two & having
all the provisions he may make for himself—this in consideration of his past
important services to the family. I told him I thought the obligation lay the other
way. He is eaten up with self esteem & selfishness. He thinks it hard provisions
are not to be advanced him. This I'll not make a stumbling block if funds are
furnished. I say to him—"get two or three hands & you can plant the home
field so your mistress have some income from the place." He insists they cannot
be got.—"The place has no houses, no mill." Everybody of course has got the
start of me by several weeks & by first supplying themselves with provisions
attracted labor.
    I was very loth to give up what I should have been proud to accomplish. I
have sacrificed thereby comfort-convenience & inclination but it was not time
to stand still. I must try Cheeka where the hands already were. Accordingly on

Sunday last I rode over on mule back carrying Jacob. The Negroes were civil but would not come over having already planted their patches. They had also listed several Acres of Cotton land. I must therefore plant there or not at all. Now the idea that you would [receive] anything from their crop will vanish, when you know that the Bureau had issued them only two weeks rations—that rations were then ordered to be discontinued to all able bodied negroes, by the govmt—and the negroes were [receiving] a scanty & uncertain subsistence by working sometimes for people in the neighborhood. This labor then would not have been devoted to the "Bluff" but absorbed by the Rhetts & others capable of feeding them, and sadly in want of hands. They had no cotton seed & no money (as far as I could learn) to buy it. They meant to squat on patches. Would the Est get anything think you? I thought (as others tell me) there was a far *better* chance for a crop there even if the impossibility of getting hands for this place did not exist. Passing through Wm Mears. Lt. Rhett only was there & told me of the terms of contract adopted by the neighborhood. Well they give half the crop & advance the provisions, the percentage charged the negroes on which is enormous. I spent a day and a half explaining to them the advantages of a contract. They objected to nothing but that they could not have Saturday. I put my foot down against that & sent for the Lieut at Corn bakes who sent a letter he desired I should read them & which stated he allowed no such squandering of time in any contract that "they must sign it "t'was best for them"&&. It had the desired effect—and your letter found me in Charleston getting corn imple- ments (the last I could not get before) and *a loan* of $200 'til 23d April from Willis & Chisolm, part of which I retain & the rest has been bestowed in a way to be accounted for. You have purchased the seed (tho it has not yet arrived) was I to throw it away? Nearly everybody here is planting Friff seed. Now the money for Oak Lawn would plant the Bluff with better results. Even with another mule the cost would scarcely be over $800,—I'd undertake it with $500. There is no danger of your having to part with Oak Lawn my dear mother. All this may be a great error or folly on my part but it is too late to recede. To go backward would be ruinous. Tis not so clear that the opposite course would. I've under- gone great fatigue but no exposure & the change of air has much benefitted my cough. My plan is not fully developed as yet but I expect to be there during April—until the crop is sown. I may then return to Adams Run for the summer— going over once a fortnight & making Johnson (negro with the pleasant coun- tenance) the foreman—report to me here every other week. Or if neighbours are found Chisolmville may do for part of the summer. Dick left this morning with wagon and provisions & I go by train far as Ashepo [?] Ferry on Tuesday. There are many Neighbours at the Bluff all planting & no cattle near—land looks fresh—not requiring manure or very little—some could be planted today if the seed had come. The gang eleven & expecting two more—small but prime. I'll turn over Myrtle Bank to the Est before you shall lose Oak Lawn. Dick will put me up a shantie over there. I consulted with that ingenious mechanic about this outhouse—and agreed with him that for $150.00 it could be put in excellent order. The upper rooms are quite comfortable & both stories have good fire- places. Now with repairs of Boards paint & papering and thorough refitting & cleaning it would be good enough for a small white family to live in twice as good as Balls used to be. This in case there were not time or means to build a cottage next winter. I will do what I can to make a crop for that end, feeling an interest in the place & being very grateful for your and my sisters kindness to me & wish Gods blessing I may succeed. I expect to make 4 bags to the hand which at 20 cts will give 44 bales multiplied by 80 = $3250. Divide by two = $1760, half the crop. Now at least $230 will come out of the other half from percentage, sickness, paying for 1/2 mule feed, injury to tools & & all deducted from their share. You have there $2000, clear—added to prime cost of provisions of course much more from the lowest probable price next year. I beg then if you get the loan you will help instead of blaming me. Everybody is at work and more despondent. I've done what I believe best for your interests—I would not see you dependent without a cent of income from three (4) plantations. Others perhaps may see their interest in this and take an especial pleasure in seeing the tables turned & prey upon your necessities. Humiliating twould be to be assisted now—far deeper & more grinding another year.———

* * *

Social Hall May 3d [1868]
Dearest Mama
   We are not quite as energetic as you are & seldom finish breakfast before half past seven—but then we are busy quite late every evening, hands coming for rations & buying provisions, all the workman at the farm but one are paid in provisions or cloth—I determine the prices of the last—the Gen thinks I am too exorbitant but I tell him I *am sure* the nigs do not do 'full work'—a piece of nice blue check which cost 22 cts by the piece, your Jewess' of a daughter gets 60 cts for—& the freedmen get 12 yds at a time—& I have now a box of assorted candy to tempt them—but as these articles are paid for in work of course my satisfaction at getting high prices is greatly diminished. Dont imagine that I allow my children to be with negroes out of my presence—on one occasion only have they been so with my knowledge—I was too glad to get the boys out of Charleston—the boys there are so profane & vulgar—Good by dear Mama
                                                                                          Hattie

63 Up from Slavery?

That freedom did not come as an unmixed blessing is clear from the following letter to a former master by his ex-slave. The dire circumstances that must have prompted the request to return can only be imagined. While this free woman seems to reflect on some kind of paternalism when she laments that "no one ceares for me heare," it is clear that the request says less about the benevolence of slavery than about the severity of freedom as manifest in the new system of society following the war. Or put another way, perhaps it was true as has been suggested, that the only freedom available now was the freedom to starve.

Source: Isabella L. Sousten to Master Manual, July 10, 1865, in Edward Coles Collection, University of Virginia Library.

Liberty, Va. July 10th/65

Master Manual

I have the honor to appeal to you on[c]e more for assistance. Master, I am cramped hear nearly to death and no one ceares for me heare, and I want you if you please Sir, to Send for me. I dont care if I am free; I had rather live with you I was as free while with you as I wanted to be. Mas. Manual you know I was as well satisfied with you as I wanted to be. Now Affectionatee Master pleas, oh, please come or Sind for me. John is still hired out at the same and doing Well and well Satisfied only grieving about home. he want to go home as bad as I do. if you ever Send for me I will Send for him immediately and take him home to our kind Master. Mas. Manual pleas to give my love to all of my friends, and especially to my young mistress. dont forget to reserve a double

portion for yourself. I will close at present, hoping to bee at your Service Soon—
yes before yonders Sun Shal rise and Set any more.

May I Subscribe
myself your most affectionate
humble friend and Servt—,
Isabella. L. Sousten.

64 Military Authority and Social Tensions in Reconstruction

The emerging system in the postwar South was of course much more than economic. The federal troops stationed there with a design to "Reconstruct" the South and to protect the freedmen in the exercise of their rights were also fostering a system of authority and law and order. That this system was not one which guaranteed equity or actually facilitated, a form of black rule, as sometimes alleged, is clear from the following statement from a Mississippi white man about an incident in 1868. Indeed, if anything, it may be that the military authorities in this case actually proved counterproductive by encouraging the freedman charged with the crime to return to his work where he would be protected. Of course he returned, was arrested and hastily tried, convicted, and hanged, thanks in part to the inaction of the military. In his final statements the writer's salutary approval of this action suggests most eloquently the fear that must have plagued the blacks. If protection were not coming from federal troops, who would dispense real justice? But other qualities are also evident in the incident: the change to a new contract-based system of agriculture was as difficult for old Judge Calhoon to appreciate as for anyone who apparently attempted to maintain the precise system of authority and supervision that had existed under slavery. When the freedman resisted and threw back at the judge the terms of his contract, the judge "was indignant at the negro's insolence and especially his manner." That finally the authorities failed to intercede on the part of the black man indicated how much the system was going to remain the same.

Source: W. H. Hardy, "Recollections of Reconstruction in East and Southeast Mississippi," *Publications of the Mississippi Historical Society,* 7 (1903), 199-203.

I recall one of the saddest occurrences of the reconstruction period which occurred in Jasper county in the spring of 1868. Judge Henry Calhoon had amassed a handsome estate before the war, and had retired from the practice of the law to his plantation, near the town of Paulding. He had a distinguished appearance, tall, broad shoulders, florid complexion, iron gray hair, with courtly manners. He had an ideal country home, a charming family of three accomplished daughters and two sons. It was a happy home, with books, paintings, music and flowers. George, the elder son, was about 20 years old, handsome and intelligent. He possessed a magnetism that made him exceedingly popular with those who came in contact with him, and the idol of his parents and his sisters. He had nearly completed a law course under the tutelage of his father, and expected at the next succeeding term of court to stand examination for license to practice his chosen profession. He assisted his father in the management of the plantation, and really managed the freedmen better than his father. It might be well to state here as a historical fact that the old slave owners generally could not manage successfully free negroes. Having all their lives been accustomed to command, and to be obeyed, they lacked the tact and discretion that was necessary to be exercised in controlling freedmen. The old judge, as was his custom, made the rounds of his plantation on horseback, visiting the different squads of laborers, and had occasion to reprimand a negro man, a big, strong, stalwart, surly fellow, for the manner in which he was doing his work. The negro stopped and, leaning on his hoe, told him that he was doing his work properly; so good as any of the rest, and he did not intend to change, and that he was a free man now, and that he did not intend that any white man should ever "oversee" him again. The judge was indignant at the negro's insolence and especially his manner, and started towards him on his horse, raising his riding switch, and uttering some imprecation, when the negro promptly threatened to use his hoe on him. He desisted, but ordered him to leave the place at once. The negro told him very cooly he would not do it; that he had a contract with him for the year, that he was going to stay and that he could not drive him off. The judge on his return to his house told his son what had occurred, and suggested that he might be able to adjust the matter with the negro and get rid of him without trouble; that he was a vicious fellow, and he was really afraid that he would appeal to the military authorities, and they would interpose and cause them a great deal of trouble.

Young George Calhoon put a pistol in his pocket, mounted a horse and rode to the field where the negro was at work; told him about how he treated his father and that he had come to tell him that he must leave; that he must come to the house and he would go over the books and see what was due him, if anything, and he would pay it, and that he must get off the place and never come back. The negro said to him flatly that he was not going to do it; that he had a contract and he was going to stay there, and dared him to send him off. George Calhoon drew his pistol, told him to drop his hoe and leave instantly and never to come back; if he did, it would be at his peril.

The negro obeyed promptly, left the field, going towards the "quarters," and young Calhoon returned to the house. It happened that the night following this occurrence was the night on which weekly rations were issued to the "field hands"—usually three pounds of bacon and a peck of cornmeal for each hand.

Young Calhoon, who attended to this business, had finished weighing and measuring the meat and meal, locked the smokehouse and turned to go back to his room, having a lantern in his hand. When he was about twenty feet from the smokehouse he was shot in the back with a load of buckshot. He fell to the earth and died almost instantly. The family rushed out and bore the dead body of the idol of that home into the house. Not a negro who heard that shot came to their relief, and the female members of the family were alarmed lest the negroes would come and murder the old gentleman. The younger brother, Henry, a lad of 15 years, went through the darkness of the night to a neighbor's house and carried the information of his brother's assassination and at once messengers were dispatched to other neighbors and also to the sheriff at Paulding, and by daylight the white male population of the whole country were aroused and on the hunt for the assassin—the negro who had been discharged. Men were sent in every direction, but no tiding were had of him. This hunt continued for a week. The mails were freely used, a description of the assassin being sent to various parts of the State. This went on for a week or ten days, when the people engaged in it gave it up and returned to their usual vocations, except a few who had been employed to keep on the lookout. Mr. John H. Cook, a neighbor of Judge Calhoon's, was riding into Paulding one afternoon and met the assassin in the public road, recognized him and stopped and spoke to him. The negro stopped and Cook engaged him in conversation in a friendly tone and manner, and asked him where he was going; he said he was going back to Judge Calhoon's and was going back to work. He said that George Calhoon had run him off the place, and he had been to Meridian to see the officer in command, and that he told him all about being run off of the place without being paid; that the officer told him to go back and go to work and he would see that he was not interfered with. Not a word was said by either of them about George Calhoon's assassination. Cook was unarmed and afraid to undertake the negro's arrest alone, and was about to ride on, when he saw two men riding along the road, coming from towards Paulding. He asked the negro about his trip to Meridian, what he saw, and so detained him until the men came up. They each recognized the negro, and one of them having a pistol promptly covered him and he submitted to arrest. They told him they arrested him for killing George Calhoon. He said that he killed him and would do it again if it were to do over; that Calhoon had drawn a pistol on him and run him off of his place; that he killed him and started the same night on foot through the country to Meridian and reported the case to the officer in command of the Yankee troops, and the officer took down his statement and told him to go back and go to work, and if he was molested he would have the Calhoons arrested and punished.

When the circuit court convened he was indicted for murder, arraigned, tried and convicted. The writer assisted the district attorney in the prosecution. He was defended by able counsel appointed by the court. Immediately after his conviction a petition addressed to the military governor of the State, alleging that he had not had a fair trial; that the confession was extorted from him and prayed that the conviction be set aside and that he be tried by a military court. This was signed by a great many negroes from every part of the county, and by one white man, McKnight, a native of the county. It was sent to the commandant of the military post at Meridian. He forwarded it to the judge and district attorney with the request that they endorse on it the true facts and return it to him. They endorsed on it the statement that the negro had a fair trial, able counsel appointed to defend him; that his guilt had been clearly established by testimony other than his voluntary confession.

The negro was publicly hanged by the sheriff of the county on the day fixed by the court in the sentence, and a few days after his execution the petition was returned from the military headquarters with the endorsement on it that it was not received until after the execution of the condemned man.

This was the first rebuff the negroes had received from the military power in the State, and it had a most salutary effect upon them. For the first time it had dawned upon their deluded minds that they could not rely implicitly upon the military authorities to uphold them in the commission of crimes against the white people.

65 The Ku Klux Conspiracy

That the caste system of the South was not dismantled upon emancipation is clear from the testimony of the following individuals taken in 1871. While federal laws and troops ostensibly protected the freedmen, new forms of subjugation that proceeded under cover of darkness and in disguise came to plague blacks for a variety of reasons. Among the transgressions punished by Ku Klux Klansmen and others (as related in Congressional hearings, from which the following item was extracted) were teaching a school for black children, voting the Republican ticket, testifying before a Congressional committee, practicing the trade of gunsmith, suspected murder, speaking out against the Klan, having a good crop and being able to pay debts, and having a bad crop and being unable to pay debts. These "crimes" suggest that the "anarchy" perceived by some whites was mainly the erosion of a traditional power structure in which both blacks and whites knew well their respective places—they had inherited them. It is much the same spirit evident in the Memphis riot and in others: nothing less than a counter-revolution against the potential of the new market system. All the while, of course, the one accepted component of the market was its ability to grind blacks back into the same oppression. Beyond that, white Southerners defensively mobilized to subjugate the freedmen who exercised their freedoms. As much as anything it was a concerted effort to hold onto the past as they knew it. The following testimony reflects the typical intimidation process. The provocation seems to have been voting Republican and having a good crop.

Source: *The Ku Klux Conspiracy*: Testimony Taken by the Joint Select Committee to Inquire Into the Conditions of Affairs in the Late Insurrectionary States. *Georgia*, Vol. 1, 42d Congress, 2d Session, Senate Report No. 41, Part 6 (Washington, 1872), 308-12.

SIMON ELDER (colored) sworn and examined.   Atlanta, Georgia,
                                                             October 28, 1871.

By the CHAIRMAN

Question. What is your age, where were you born, and where do you now live?

Answer.   I am fifty-six years old, going on fifty-seven; I will be fifty-seven next
          cotton-planting time; I was born in Clarke County; and I now live in
          DeKalb County.

Question. When did you leave Clarke County?

Answer.   This very next month, about the middle of the month, will be two
          years ago.

Question. Why did you leave?

Answer.   Because I was compelled to leave by the Ku-Klux, or what they call
          Ku-Klux, anyhow; I do not know what they were, but they were ill-
          advised men. They came to my house on Saturday night about 11
          o'clock in the night. There was no one there but me and my wife,
          and we were sitting down laughing and talking just before they came
          in. It was a mighty cold night. She observed to me, "Come, old man,
          let's go to bed." Said I, "Old lady, you can go on and lay down, and
          I will come directly." The fire was very warm, and I was lying down
          before the fire, for I was tired. I dropped off a little dose of sleep.
          But as near as I can recollect it was about 11 o'clock when they carried
          me out of the house. When I waked up they were knocking at the
          door. It was just like a whole gang of rocks coming against the door.
          I jumped up and said, "Halloo!" By that time they flung the door
          down, and fell against me. When they did that my wife says that
          four of them jumped on me at once and commenced beating me over
          the head with clubs that they had. One of them said, "You damned
          radical son of a bitch, we intend to put an end to you." Said I, "Lord,
          have mercy!"—just so; I recollect saying that. The man who was
          beating me over the head sort of stopped beating me then, and asked
          me if I had a pistol in the house. I said, "The pistol is not here; I
          bought it for my son, and he is now either in Atlanta or in Augusta,
          I do not know which. He has an uncle living in Augusta, and he may
          be there. He carried it off with him." He said, "You are a damned
          liar; that pistol is in this house, and we intend to have it this night
          or kill you." Now, gentlemen, I told them the truth; the pistol was
          not in the house; my son had carried it off. One of the men who was
          out of doors—I knew his voice very well—said "God damn him, fetch
          him out here." They then dragged me out of the house and carried
          me off. When they did that, I asked them if they pleased to let me
          put on my shoes; it was mighty cold. Said he, "No, God damn you,
          you need not put your shoes on; we are Yankees from the Federal
          City, and we will have you in hell before to-morrow night this time."
          They took me out, and dragged me over the fence, and got me into
          the big road. They asked me if I could run. They had been beating
          me, so they wanted to see if I could run or not. They beat me over

the head; as God would have it, they did not beat my legs. I went blundering along making out that I could not run. They ran along by the side of me. When I got along down by my patch fence I struck the woods, and one came out from there and said something that I could not understand. The others were dressed in white; I did not see how he was dressed. They made me go into the thicket of woods, and there it looked almost like a judgment to me. I thought my wife was in the house, but there she was up in the woods. They had tied their horses out there when they went to the house. When they got me out there they got around me and ordered me to strip myself as naked as ever I came into the world. I was qualified of their voices, but they had their faces in disguise, and all had uniforms on. I thought I would as quick die with a quick pain as a slow fever, and I made a spring and ran off. They shot the third time at me, and put one bullet through an old pair of breeches, but I got away from them, clear. One of them said, "God damn him, he dodged down here." This is what my wife told me when I got back. They said, "Hunt about; hunt about!" but I had run clear away from them. One said, "Now, gentlemen, isn't that a damned shame for one damned old nigger to get away from as many men as we are here?" That is what my wife said she heard them say. They thought that I had a pistol, and I reckon they expected that the pistol was out somewhere there, and that probably I would run for it and come back and shoot some of them. They went to her and said, "Where is he?" She said, "I don't know; I have not seen him since you all had him." They said, "That's a damned lie; you know where he is; if you don't tell I will blow your brains out." They had my wife out there in the woods, and one said, "Aunty, I expect you can get back to house; and men, you had better get away from here." I saw them as they all came up the lane before me. I was in the brier patch. There was a long row of them, two at a time, as long as from here to that white house. [Pointing through the window at a house.]

Question. How many do you suppose there were in all?

Answer.   I thought there were about thirty. There were two who beat me, and I am qualified of one who beat me, for he could not alter his voice so I could not catch it.

Question. Who was that?

Answer.   Jourdan Elder.

Question. What had they against you?

Answer.   Nothing on God's earth, only they told me that it was because I was getting too much for them. I paid this very man who beat me over my head. I rented land, and I and my wife and son and daughter paid the taxes. I paid that man for thrashing 223 bushels of wheat for me; I paid the toll on it; I paid nobody else about there.

Question. What did they say to you about a radical?

Answer.   They said I was a damned old radical, any how, and that they would
           have me in hell betwixt then and to-morrow night at that time.

Question. What did they mean by calling you a radical?

Answer.   Because I voted the republican ticket; that is what they meant. They
           could not turn me in any other way; I would vote that way.

Question. Do they call republicans radicals in your country?

Answer.   Yes, sir; they call them radicals there.

Question. Did they hurt your wife at all?

Answer.   She can give her evidence about what they did.

Question. Have they troubled you since?

Answer.   No, sir. I staid there that night; I kept traveling from one place to
           another all that night. I concluded I would go to the house of the
           man I rented land from. After I got shut of them, and they were all
           gone, I put out to his house, about a mile and a half. He and his
           wife were sitting up by the fire when I got there, about midnight, I
           reckon. His son, that was always there with us, I rented a little quarter
           from. His son was there and in the room, and when I was showing
           them, and his wife was pouring stuff over the wounds on my head;
           he came out of the room and claimed to be sick. I found him at home
           when I got there. He might have been there.

Question. Were those men all disguised?

Answer.   Every one.

Question. What do they call that kind of men in your country?

Answer.   They call them the Ku-Klux men.

Question. Have you ever heard of their being out at any other time?

Answer.   I did not finish telling how long I staid there. I staid there the balance
           of Saturday night, Sunday, and Sunday night, and part of the day
           Monday. I started from there; I hired a wagon to carry me to Madison
           depot, and then I got on the train and left and came to Decatur, in
           De Kalb County, and I have lived there ever since.

Question. When did you come to Atlanta?

Answer.   I came here Monday morning, I and my wife both.

Question. What brought you here?

Answer.   I did not know anything about this committee, but there was a colored
           man up here on Saturday that found out it was here, and he came
           down and told me about it. I have always been wanting to report
           these men to somebody or other that I could depend upon, and I
           trust in God you are men I can depend upon. I have come here and
           I have been here ever since, I and my wife both. I had $5 Monday
           morning, and I paid it all away last night to go backward and forward
           on the train, and this morning me and her took it afoot and walked
           here.

Question. Had you heard of the Ku-Klux around in that country before?

Answer.   Yes, sir; over and often and divers of times since.

Question. What are they doing?

Answer.   Going about destroying and disturbing everything they can of the Union party. Well, this man's son told me, they very day I finished cutting my wheat, "I ought not to begrudge it, but I do; you will never have another chance." I do not know that he was there; I will not say that.

Question. Do you know of any that were there besides the one you have told about?

Answer.   Yes, sir; I would qualify to the two that ran beside me.

Question. Who were they?

Answer.   One was James Dillon and the other was Louis Anderson. There were two more, but I would not qualify to them; but there have come some little points since that tell me of the fact that those two were Bill Marshall and John Marshall.

Question. Did you make any attempt to have them arrested and punished?

Answer.   My God! I was for getting away and saving myself; I did not stay there long enough. They met a colored man and told him, "By God! we did not get him to-night, but we will see him again in a short time." I could not rest there; I expected that they aimed to kill me and my wife too. They went all over the house. They pulled my wife out of bed. She had on her dirty clothes, that she had been trying up a little lard in. When she lay down she took my pocket-book and put it in her dirty clothes, and they walked all over it and did not find it.

66 Toward a One-Party South: Yazoo, Mississippi, 1875

The intimidation of black voters reached major proportions as whites moved to establish governments in their states friendly to the old regime. In Mississippi in 1875 the coercion was so notorious that Congress dispatched a committee to investigate election frauds. The letters below from persons describing the situation in Yazoo County reveal the deliberateness and the desperation with which the "White League" prevented blacks from voting and the Republican Party from organizing or distributing its tickets. It was, as one letter described it, a complete "reign of terror."

Source: *Mississippi in 1875*. Report of the Select Committee to Inquire into the Mississippi Election of 1875 with the Testimony and Documentary Evidence, Vol. 2, 44th Congress, 2d Session, Senate Report 527, Part 2 (Washington, 1876), 97-98, 101, 103-4, 106-7.

YOUR EXCELLENCY: Eight days have now passed since the assault of the "White League" on our club and their occupation & possession of the town and seizure of authority. I have caused letters to be written to you, telegrams sent you, and, by every means in my power, sought to reach you that we might get help from some quarter. I have been unable to get further word from you or from Jackson than was brought by my brother's wife on her return.

Can *nothing* be done? I am in great danger of losing my life. Not only that, all the leading republicans, who have not ran away, in danger. They are all secreted like myself; not with me, however. I get word from them occasionally. The town is so strongly guarded by pickets, police, & men, women, & children from every door-step, porch, & window, besides armed men who patroll the streets at night, that none can get away if they would. The league here have adopted a new policy, which is to kill the leaders and spare the colored people, unless they "rise." A certain element here headed by Dixon, H. M., and men like him who have been and are still doing all they can to drive, provoke the colored people to show fight. They seem anxious to "distinguish" themselves.

The larger, and so far stronger, class are doing all they can to prevent this, but all seem to dread the Dixon men. At the same time Dixon is the lion of the hour. Lawyers and others tell him he has won a victory he deserves great credit for. Halder openly boasts on the street that he killed Dick Mitchell. He took his pistol. The colored people—I have been speaking only of whites—in the country are very much excited. They have acted discretely so far. They have no arms, save occasionally a shot-gun, and cannot get ammunition even for these. I have done all in my power to prevent them coming to town. I could not do much in my position, of course. They have exhibited no bad blood so far as I have been able to learn. The patrolls have been to the country and warned some of the country leaders to leave. During the first few days the town was filled with all sorts of rumors of the "niggers rising." I am satisfied they are mainly hatched by the Dixon men. Every time any such story was started the citizens would be called together and patroles sent out to warn or drive them off. These means seem to be used to "rouse" the "indignant" whites to action as whiskey is given to soldiers just before a battle, or to approval or acquiescence in the conduct of the leaguers in killing republican leaders and driving off others. Last night they were called together—the white citizens again. Within twenty yards of my hiding place, on either side, were stationed two pickets. Men were passing & repassing all night. I heard one man say to another as they passed by, "if they catch him they will hang him." I can see & hear a great deal that goes on. Much comes to me by messengers which is exaggerated. I am giving you what I see & hear, and the messages I get after sifting & comparing them. I do not feel like running away from here, even if I could. I might get shot in the back, or more roughly handled, even, than that.

My friend, I fought four years; was wounded several times; suffered in hospitals, and as a prisoner; was in twenty-seven different engagements to free the slave and save our glorious Union—to save such a country as this! I have some love left for my country, but what is country without it protects its defenders? I have had a letter from my wife. She takes it bravely, but her condition is such I fear the consequences. I know how you are situated. I do not blame you. I would not give you more pain than you already feel at your inability to help; but can't you get an officer to come here? Is there no protection for me? Can't an officer of the camp there be sent here? I don't want troops if Ohio is to be lost by it; I prefer to die first. Indeed, I am ready to die, if it is necessary, and good result from it; but to be butchered here by this mob after all I have done here is too cruel.

Respectfully, yours, &c.,

A. T. MORGAN.
[Sheriff]

YAZOO CITY, September 9th, 187[5]

* * *

During a stay of two days at Yazoo City, Yazoo County, State Miss., I found the community very much excited about the political situation. I am convinced that free speech is not tolerated in that city at the present time; that is if a republican should attempt to utter republican sentiments on the streets of said city he would do so at the peril of his life. The colored element is thoroughly intimidated, and will not vote at the ensuing election for fear of their lives. This intimidating business has been carried to this extent, that the republican party has failed, through fear, to put a county ticket in the field. During my visit I heard several parties, whom I judged from their appearance to represent the better class of citizens, speak in the most contemptuous terms of the peace arrangements agreed upon between Gov'r Ames and Gen. George. They will not carry out this arrangement. They, the democrats, are thoroughly armed and equipped. I saw armed men round about town, and know they drill regularly. I saw a company of men armed and mounted leave the town shortly after night, for the purpose, as I heard one of their number say, "on a little scouting business." The life of a republican in that county and city is not safe, that's if he should see fit to exercise his right as an American citizen and give utterance to his sentiments. This county has a republican majority of at least 1,500, still they, the republicans, dare not put a ticket in the field. From what I heard I am satisfied that if A. T. Morgan should return to the county and attempt to assume the functions of his office he would be killed. There is no doubt of this in my mind. I do not believe it would be prudent for any republican to attempt to make a speech in that city at the present time.

O. A. ESQUIROL.

Sworn and subscribed to before me this 28th day of October, 1875.

N. HODGE, Ct. Clerk.

V. BENTHIEN, D.C.,

Depy Circuit Clerk, Hinds County.

67 Toward a One-Party South: Edgefield County, South Carolina, 1876

The process of disfranchisement took many forms, limited only by the imagination of the perpetrators. This official deposition describes the process of denying blacks the vote in one county of South Carolina. While the two parties tended to project nearly sacred images of themselves as saviors of certain principles or factions, a characteristic of late nineteenth-century national politics, much more was at stake than the fate of either the Democratic or Republican parties. What was involved, as the denial of the vote by threat and violence in Yazoo County, Mississippi, and by turning the election into a sham in Edgefield County, South Carolina, made clear, is the elimination of any potential system for redress of grievances. Not only did disfranchisement close the door to the possibility of social change through democratic devices, but it actually generated a system of social control. And that system of social control functioned on two different levels. One was simply that of subjugation through denial of representation and participation in the governmental processes. The other, however, was more discreet and perhaps more devastating. It provided a basis for political unity based not on class or principle, but on color. Thus the South's political system would for generations to come enshrine the Democratic Party not with a particular set of principles, but for its appeal to race as a unifying agent and hence the subordination of social issues that could bind blacks and whites together. Any issue that could divide whites would thereafter be a threat to the one-party political system and to white domination.

Source: Martin Witherspoon Gary Papers, William R. Perkins Library, Duke University. Used by permission of the Curator of Manuscripts, Duke University Library.

South Carolina

Edgefield County   Personally appeared before me Wiley J. Williams and Abraham Landrum two of the managers of Box No 1 Edgefield C[ourt] H[ouse] and D.B. Cotton clerk for said Box and made oath that on the morning of the election they appeared to the C.H. as managers to conduct the election. That according to the instructions given by the commissioners of election, they intending to hold the election under the arch of the C.H. steps, that H. H. Glover one of the managers took the Box contrary to the desire of these two managers, and the directions of the commissioner of election, and carried it up into the C.H. That at the time the C.H. was crowded with armed white men, and that there were some arms stacked away in the C.H. That the C.H. was packed with white men and [had] been all night. That after these men voted they remained in the C.H. and on the C.H. steps, and so crowded the polling place that colored men were not allowed to vote. That about 9 oclock this crowd had all voted yet they remained in the C.H. and on the C.H. steps several hundred horsemen were crowded around the C.H. steps in such a manner that colored men could not approach the C.H. That during the day many of these parties voted 4 or 5 times and when we protested against such a proceeding we were told that it was none of our business. That Wm. T. Gary of Augusta Ga told these managers that he had several boys here today from Georgia that no on Know. That when these deponents would protest against this repeating and would ask the repeaters where they lived they were told by James M. Cobb and J. C. Sheppard that it was none their business where they lived and hence these repeaters would not answer the questions. That these deponents finding that they could not carry out the election according to law were anxious to abandon the poll, but were told they would not be allowed to leave. That all of these white men around them were armed and that these deponents were compelled to yield to anything they demanded. That in the evening about 4 oclock the steps of the C.H. were taken possession of by Butler Gary and J. C. Sheppard who delivered speaches to the horsemen who were crowded around the C.H. steps. That the managers wanted to write the names of colard men under the column fixed for colard men and the names of white men under the column fixed for white men, but were not allowed to have it so done. That not more than 35 or 40 colard men voted at this Box during the entire day, and that most of these voted late in the evening when the men were accompanied to the Box by U.S. Marshall. That when the poll was closed after six oclock the Box was taken possession of by Wm. T. Gary of Augusta Ga J. M. Cobb and J. C. Sheppard of Edgefield C.H. who assisted without authority in the counting of the votes. That when the votes were counted in several cases 4 or 5 democratic votes were folded together.

That in the face of all these facts Knowing them to be true these deponents declare that the whole affair was unfair and contrary to law and enter their solemn protest against the counting of said votes for or against any of the candidates.

Sworn to before me

this 9th day of Nov. 1876   Wiley J. Williams

                                                                          his

    Jesse Jones   Abram X Landrum

                                                                          mark

    C.C.C.P.   D. B. Cottier

68 The Crop Lien

A subtle shift in Southern agriculture became apparent in the 1870s. The emergence of the crop-lien system would have enormous implications for the system of production as well as for race relations. The first freedmen to work on the plantations usually did so under some form of a wage system, paid either actual wages or a share of the crop they raised as their wage. In return the planter provided the land and some provisions (seed, tools, and such), and the freedmen would often work under the supervision of the planter or his agent in some kind of crew. Yet there was also an inclination for these freedmen to become tenants, that is, to rent parcels of land that they might farm themselves owing only a certain amount or share of the crop to the landlord. While offering potential independence, the sharecropping system kept the tenant subservient both to his landlord, who could dictate to some degree what was to be produced, and to the market which ensured that single-crop, or a subsistence pattern of agricultural production. And the landlord himself, as in Document 62, was dependent upon others for the working capital to keep the plantation running. This source of capital was the merchant who then received his money ultimately from Northern investors or from commercial investments within the South. And it was this merchant upon whom the cropper or tenant would often come to depend for his provisions and credit. The outgrowth of these forces was the crop-lien system whereby the tenant would borrow the rent money from the merchant. The collateral for the advance loaned would then be all the farmers' crops plus, as in the following contract, other possessions such as horses, mules, and cattle. In fact, in the following case, one of the individuals signing the agreement, Doc Harrington, was not able to produce the necessary 1,900 pounds of cotton and as a consequence forfeited ownership of a yoke of oxen to the lender, James B. Richardson (Joel Williamson, *After Slavery: The Negro in South Carolina during Recon-*

struction, 1861-1877 [Chapel Hill, 1965], 172). Richardson was a member of an old plantation family that was forced to sell and rent the land and also a school teacher who "made constant effort to obtain a more remunerative position." The crop-lien system helped to perpetuate a single-crop economy, cotton. But the system also fostered debt-peonage and virtually tied the freedmen to the person with the money indefinitely. With exorbitant prices for provisions and outrageous interest rates for credit needed, the freedman was less and less able to get out of debt, especially in years of poor harvests. The planter sensed control slipping away in favor of the merchant when he exacted interest or restricted markets. Or the planter himself became a merchant. Moreover, white tenants and croppers became engulfed in the same system. When powerlessness and subjection intensified, so too did the possibilities of racial friction or class war.

Source: James Burchell Richardson Papers, William R. Perkins Library, Duke University. Used by permission of the Curator of Manuscripts, Duke University Library. I am especially grateful to Robert L. Byrd for helping to locate this document and for providing information concerning Richardson.

State of South Carolina
    Clarendon County

On or before the First day of October 1874, We promise to pay James B. Richardson, on order 1900 lbs. good White Lint Cotton in Bales for value received, advanced and furnished to us by the said James B. Richardson of county and State aforesaid for use in the cultivation of crops on the Plantation or farms now being cultivated or about to be cultivated by us in Clarendon County, South Carolina during the year 1874.

And, in consideration of the said advance made us, We covenant and agree to, and do hereby give, make & grant, to the said James B. Richardson—a lien to the extent of said advance on all crops which may be grown on the said plantations or farms during the year 1874 wherever said crops, or part or parts of them are to be farmed.

This lien hereby is executed and is to be inforced in accordance with the provisions of the statute of the State of South Carolina approved September twentieth A.D. Eighteen hundred and sixty six.

In consideration of the said amount having been furnished us, and of One Dollar paid us of which we acknowledge receipt, and in order further to secure the payment of the above stated amount unto the said James B. Richardson We do hereby Mortgage, pleadge, assign and convey to the said James B. Richardson all our Horses, Mules and Stock which at the date of these present we have, hold, own or possess.

This deed of Mortgage to be void only upon the payment of said 1900 lbs. good white Linte cotton in Bales, otherwise to remain in full force, with right to said James B. Richardson to foreclose and sell according to the provisions of the Statute.

We further agree that in case legal measures are taken towards the enforcement of the lien, foreclosure of Mortgage, or collection of note herein given, that all costs and expenses incident thereto including attorneys fees shall be due and collectable as if they were a part of the same.

And we certify that no other lien or Mortgage on said crop or property have been given by us.

Witness our hand and seal this 14th day of February eighteen hundred and seventy four.

Signed, sealed and delivered in presence of

his
Henry X Thomas
mark

Witness
Robert Mathes
Smart Thomas
Thos Covenel

his
Thomas X Henry
mark

his
Doc X Harrington
mark

his
Ned X Johnson
mark

his
Henry X ——
mark

his
Wash X ——
mark

69 The Evolution of Farm Tenancy

The following account of the partition of a large plantation into a number of tenant farms is as important for what it does not say as for what it reveals. A kindly view of the whole operation of the Barrow plantation (probably written by David Barrow, Jr., who was then a professor at the University of Georgia), it notes how the freedman actually had more freedom in this system than in the previous wage or crop sharing systems. It is a description of what the author calls a "solution of the dreaded 'negro problem' in a practical way," by an adjustment of both races to economic forces. The freedom of the black man, according to the author, "fits him as if it had been cut out and made for him." And indeed it had been cut and made just exactly for him, not something he had made for himself but something narrowly defined and imposed. The concluding sentiment of Lem Bryant, particularly defiant and uncontrollable as a slave, suggests the subtle restraints of the new system: "Ah, master! [some relations appear not to have changed] I'm free now; I *have* to do right." The compulsions in freedom were evidently more powerful than in slavery. The nature of those compulsions enters the following narrative only obliquely.

However, despite their efforts to grow their own food, clearly the tenants must still purchase some meat. The price of food and interest on money advanced is not recorded below. The written agreements entered into between the Negro and the landlord are not "required" by the tenants, according to the author, but in light of possible abuses, one can only speculate how much free choice is permitted. There is wide variance between this contract and those in nearby South Carolina. Whereas James Burchell Richardson's tenants in the contract in Document 68 were required to provide 1,900 lbs. of cotton, the Barrow plantation required only 500 lbs. This may be attributed to different situations; the Barrow rent is based upon a one-horse farm. Is the rent higher if the tenant owns more stock and thus can be more productive? Viewing the author's pride that no one had left and joined the exodus to other parts of the country, one wonders again how free that choice was. Just as the tenancy system might allow the former slave the opportunity to manage his own affairs, so too might it tie the freedman to the land through debts that were as powerful as the chains of slavery. At best the author finds them to possess the freedom of tenancy, as opposed to gang labor. The real condition of freedom, that of ownership of the land, appears out of the question and never enters the discussion. Without that material base for freedom the prime freedom available to these freedmen would be to bear the responsibility for adversity, and that adversity was built into the system.

Source: "A Georgia Plantation," *Scribners's Monthly*, 21 (April 1881), 830-36.

That in many parts of the South (and notably the State of Georgia) the labor-relations of the two races are adjusting themselves and working out a solution of the dreaded "negro problem" in a practical way, has been known to all observant residents or visitors. The confident prophecies of the croakers that Southern plantations would go to waste, and that nothing but ruin lay before us, have proved the merest bosh. The enormous increase in the cotton crop of the South alone shows that the colored people, as free laborers, have done well, for it is not to be disputed that they form very nearly the same proportion of the laborers in the cotton fields that they did when they were slaves. I do not wish to be understood as stating a proportion in which free labor is to slave labor as the cotton crop since the war is to the cotton crop before the war. This is not true; the yield of cotton has been increased by other causes. But I do say that under no circumstances could worthless labor have produced the enormous increase in that crop.

In Georgia, the negro has adapted himself to his new circumstance and freedom fits him as if it had been cut out and made for him. It is not true that the negroes have formed a restless, troublesome population, nor is it true that they are like a herd of huddled sheep, frightened at the approach of strange white men, in dread of the terror of Ku-klux. As far as I know, our philosophers have presented them in one or the other of these phases, according as the writer wished to show the dread which is felt by the country of the negro, or the terror which his surroundings inspire in him. Nothing can be further from either of these ideas than the facts of the case; and when we come to look at these, we find the solution to the whole difficulty at our very doors.

To make this plain, I shall endeavor to give some ideas of the home life of our colored people as it really exists, and shall, for my purpose, take a Middle Georgia plantation, and tell what the negroes are doing on it, and how they live. I shall confine myself to the colored man as a farmer, for the reason that the mass of colored people of whom little is known are farmers.

In most cases there has been an entire change in the plan upon which our

Georgia lands are worked, the change being entirely in favor of "local self-government as opposed to centralization of power." It is true that in some rare instances large plantations are still worked under the direction of overseers, with labor hired for yearly, monthly, and daily wages, but, generally speaking, a tenant system prevails.

One of the first planters in Middle Georgia to divide his plantations into farms was Mr. Barrow, of Oglethorpe. The plantation upon which he now lives is the one which I wish to present as a fair exponent of negro tenant life in Georgia. This place contains about two thousand acres of land, and with the exception of a single acre, which Mr. Barrow has given to his tenants for church and school purposes, is the same size it was before the war. Here, however, the similarity ceases. Before the war everything on the place was under the absolute rule of an overseer (Mr. Barrow living then on another place). He it was who directed the laborers each day as to their work, and to him the owner looked for the well-being of everything on the place. Under him, and subject to his direction, the most intelligent and authoritative negroes were selected, whose duty it was to see that the overseer's orders were carried into effect. These head men, with us, were called foremen, and not drivers; in fact, though I was raised here in Georgia, my first acquaintance with the word driver, and the character which it presents in this connection, was had from one of Mayne Reid's tales. As will be seen by looking at the plot of the plantation, "as it was," all the negro houses were close together, forming "the quarter." The house in which the overseer lived was close to the quarter, lying between the quarter and the stables. This was always distinguished as "the house," and I have so marked it on the plot. It will appear that this arrangement of the building was the best that could be made, giving, as it did, the overseer the best opportunity for overlooking the property under his control. This has all been so changed that the place would now hardly be recognized by one who had not seen it during the past sixteen years.

The transformation has been so gradual that almost imperceptibly a radical change has been effected. For several years after the war, the force on the plantation was divided into two squads, the arrangement and method of working of each being about the same as they had always been used to. Each of these squads was under the control of the foreman, who was in the nature of a general of volunteers. The plantation was divided into two equal parts, and by offering a reward for the most successful planting, and thus exciting a spirit of emulation, good work was done, and the yield was about as great as it had ever been. Then, too, the laborers were paid a portion of the crop as their wages, which did much toward making them feel interested in it. There was no overseer, in the old sense of the word, and in his place a young man lived on the plantation, who kept the accounts and exercised a protecting influence over his employer's property, but was not expected to direct the hands in their work. The negroes used to call him "supertender," in order to express their sense of the change.

This was the first change made, and for several years it produced good results. After a while, however, even the liberal control of the foremen grew irksome, each man feeling the very natural desire to be his own "boss," and to farm to himself. As a consequence of this feeling, the two squads split up into smaller and then still smaller squads, still working for part of the crop, and using the

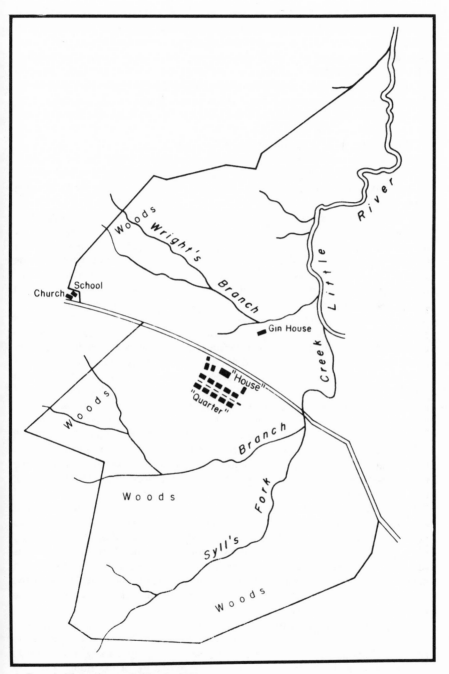

A Georgia Plantation as It Was in 1860.

owner's teams, until this method of farming came to involve great trouble and loss. The mules were ill-treated, the crop was frequently badly worked, and in many cases was divided in a way that did not accord with the contract. I have been told an amusing incident which occurred on a neighboring plantation: A tenant worked a piece of land, for which he was to pay one-fourth of the crop produced. When he gathered his crop, he hauled three loads to his own house, thereby exhausting the supply in the field. When, soon after, he came to return his landlord's wagon, which he had used in the hauling, the latter asked, suggestively:

"Well, William, where's my share of the corn?"

"You aint got none, sah," said William.

"Haven't got any! Why, wasn't I to have the fourth of all you made?"

"Yes, sah; but hit never made no fourth; dere wasn't but dess my three loads made."

Now, of course, this was an honest mistake, and while many equally honest and vexatious constantly occurred, I am constrained to say the tendency to divide on the same plan was frequent when there was no mistake. These and other troubles led to the present arrangement, which, while it had difficulties in the way of its inception, has been found to work thoroughly well. Under it our colored farmers are tenants, who are responsible only for damage to the farm they work and for the prompt payment of their rent. On the plantation about which I am writing, all of the tenants are colored men, who farm on a small scale, only two of them having more than one mule. Indeed, the first trouble in the way of dividing up the plantation into farms was to provide the new-made tenants with mules. Up to this time their contracts had been such that they plowed with mules belonging to Mr. Barrow, and very few had bought mules of their own. This trouble was met by selling them mules on credit, and though the experiment looked risky at the time, the mules were paid for in almost every case. After this, the location of the houses caused considerable inconvenience, and so it was determined to scatter them. When the hands all worked together, it was desirable to have all of the houses in a central location, but after the division into farms, some of them had to walk more than a mile to reach their work; then, too, they began to "want more elbow-room," and so, one by one, they moved their houses on to their farms. I have made a plot of the place "as it is," showing how the houses are distributed. Wherever there is a spring, there they settle, generally two or three near together, who have farms hard by. When no spring is convenient, they dig wells, though they greatly prefer the spring. A little bit of a darky, not much taller than the vessel he is carrying, will surprise you by the amount of water he can tote on his head. I have seen a mother and three or four children pulling along uphill from the spring, their vessels diminishing in size as the children do, until the last little fellow would carry hardly more than two or three cupfuls.

I suppose nothing like one of these settlements is to be found elsewhere in Georgia. The dwelling-house is an ordinary log-cabin, twenty feet square, the chimney built of sticks and dabbed over with mud; then there is a separate kitchen, which, in architectural design, is a miniature of the house,—in size approaches a chicken-coop, and is really ridiculous in its pretentiousness. Off to one side are the out-houses consisting of a diminutive stable, barely large

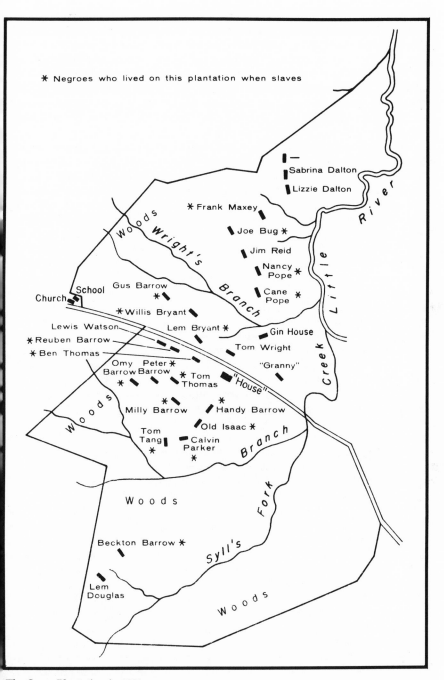

The Same Plantation in 1881.

enough to pack a small mule in, and a corn-crib and fodder-house, equally imposing. Every tenant has a cow—most of them several; and there is one old man—Lem Bryant—who is quite a Job in this respect. There is no law requiring stock to be kept up, and there is a large quantity of uncultivated land for pasture, so that the only cost connected with cattle is ten or fifteen dollars purchase money. An open pen, called the "cuppen," in this mild climate serves in place of cow-stables. On the opposite side from the lot, the house is flanked by the garden, surrounded by what is known as a "wattle" fence. This fence is made of split pine boards, "wattled" around three horizontal rails, fastened to posts, the first at the ground and the others respectively two and four feet above. Inseparable from this garden is a patch of "collord greens." The negroes think "collord greens, biled with plenty fat meat, hard to beat," when you are considering table delicacies. The only other noteworthy feature in connection with this home is the 'possum dog, who is the first to greet your approach. You will know him by the leanness of his body, the fierceness of his bark, and the rapidity of his retreat.

The labor of the farm is performed by the man, who usually does the plowing, and his wife and children, who do the hoeing, under his direction. Whenever they have heavy work to do they call on their neighbors, and receive willing aid. Their crops are principally corn and cotton, but they have patches of such things as potatoes, melons, and sorghum-cane, from which they make their sirup. They plant whatever they please, and their landlord interferes only far enough to see that sufficient cotton is made to pay the rent, which is seven hundred and fifty pounds of lint-cotton to each one-horse farm. The usual quantity of land planted is between twenty-five and thirty acres, about half of which is in cotton and the rest in corn and patches. An industrious man will raise three times the amount of his rent-cotton, besides making a full supply of corn, sirup, and other provisions, while really good farming would require about five times the rent to be raised in addition to the supply of provisions. Candor compels the admission that only a few tenants reach this standard of good farming; the others work sufficiently well to pay the rent, and make money enough to buy their clothes and spend at Christmas, and let the rainy days of the future take care of themselves. It is a point of honor with them to pay their rent, even if they find it necessary to mistake whose cotton they pay it with.

There is one misfortune which, to our Georgia tenant, dwarfs all others, and this comes when his mule dies. Thanks to mulish endurance, this does not often happen, but when it does, the owner invariably expresses himself "broke up." He has to buy another on time, and work hard and live close the next year in order to pay for him, or else make his crop with a steer. An enterprising colored man will buy the mule, but I have frequently known tenants to resort to the steer. Whenever they get into trouble of this kind, they remind their landlord in pathetic terms that he is their old master, and generally get off with the payment of half the rent.

The slight supervision which is exercised over these tenants may surprise those ignorant of how competely the relations between the races at the South have changed. Mr. Barrow lives on his plantation, and yet there are some of his tenants' farms which he does not visit as often as once a month, and this, too, because they do not need overlooking. Very many negro farmers are capable of directing the working of their own crops, and not a few object to directions. There are, on the other hand, many, in fact a large majority, who, while they know how their crops should be worked, are slow to think and act for themselves and an occasional visit from the landlord does them much good.

One of the most intelligent colored men I know is Ben Thomas, the old foreman on this plantation, and the best farmer among the negroes on the place. I have secured Ben's contract for the past year, which reads as follows:

"By or before the 15th November, 1880, I promise to pay to David C. Barrow, 500 lbs. of white lint cotton, 40 bushels of cottonseed, 25 bushels of corn and the shucks therefrom, and 500 lbs. of good fodder, as rent for land on Syll's Fork, during year 1880.

			his
1st Jan., 1880.			Ben X Thomas.
			mark

Witness: O. C. WATSON.

It will be seen that this contract is nothing more than a memorandum of the amounts to be paid, expressed in the form of a promissory note. Very few of the negroes require any copy, or any written agreement; they have the land, they say. Ben's contract last year was exactly the same as this, and his crop, as near as I have been able to ascertain, was as follows:

5 bales	Cotton,	2500 lbs.	@ 11 cts.	$275.00
	Corn,	160 bush.	@ 75 cts.	120.00
	Fodder,	3000 lbs.	@ $1.00 per hun.	30.00
	Wheat,	30 bush.	@ $1.00.	30.00
	Total			$455.00

This crop was raised by himself, his wife, a son and a daughter.

As one of the class who work not so wisely as well, Beckton Barrow is a good specimen. When the mules were divided out, upon the inauguration of the tenant system, Beck bought a large, fine young mule, promising to pay two hundred dollars for him. This was a big debt for a man whose earthly possessions consisted of a wife, two daughters, and a limited supply of provisions, but he paid it all off in two years, and since then he has been "well off," not to say rich. As soon as his mule was paid for, Beck seemed to dismiss further thought of economy and if he knew what it meant, I have no doubt his motto would be *dum vivimus vivamus*. His contract is the same as Ben Thomas's, except that he pays one-fourth of his corn and fodder, instead of a stated amount. Under that contract, his last year's crop was as follows

3 bales	Cotton,	1500 lbs.	@ 11 cts.	$165.00
	Corn,	200 bush.	@ 75 cts	150.00
	Fodder,	3500 lbs.	@ $1.00 per hun.	35.00
	Total			$350.00

As the risk of growing monotonous, I present one more crop, on account of some differences between it and the others. Handy Barrow pays as rent 750 pounds of cotton and sixty bushels cotton-seed, an increased amount of cotton, instead of corn. He is not so good a farmer as Ben Thomas, but his force is stronger, his father and mother assisting him. His crop was:

5 bales	Cotton,	200 lbs.	@ 11 cts $275.00
	Corn,	180 bush.	@ 75 cts. 135.00
	Fodder	3000 lbs.	@$1.00 per hun........... 30.00
	Wheat,	25 bush.	@$1.00 .... 25.00
	Sirup,	50 gals.	@ 40 cts. 20.00
	Total $485.00		

The cane from which the sirup is made is very exhausting to land, and while landowners do not prohibit its cultivation, because it is such an important food crop, they discourage the negroes from raising it for sale, and for this reason Mr. Barrow charges one-fourth of the sirup extra, whenever it is made.

These estimates are as exact as can be had, for the reason that, as soon as the rent is paid, the tenant gives no further account of his crop; they are none of them very exact. The figures I have given are within the actual value of the crops, the prices being low, except for cotton, which is nearly correct, and several important items, cottonseed for one, being omitted. The number of bales of cotton is correct, but the tenants frequently sell a part of their crop in the seed, and have what they call "remjents" left over, which are sold as loose cotton.

Handy and Ben are among the best farmers on the plantation, and Beck is an average specimen.

I have a letter from Mr. Barrow, in which he says: "They make per annum, on a farm plowed with one horse, from eighty to two hundred and twenty bushels of corn, two to six bales of cotton, some of them as much as forty bushels of wheat; with oats, peas, potatoes, and other smaller crops."

All of these negroes raise hogs, and these, with chickens, of which they raise great numbers, constitute a large portion of their meat food. They generally have to buy some meat during the year, however, for which they pay in the fall.

The land of this plantation is rich, and the tenants are, perhaps, better off than in some other places, but an industrious negro will pay good rent for land and make money for himself almost anywhere in Middle Georgia.

The last census showed three white and one hundred and sixty-two colored people on this plantation. I mention this to show that there must be many children among our country negroes. The adage, "poor folks for children," finds no exception here. There is one woman on the place who has three babies, Shadrach, Meshach, and Abednego, and fine children they are, too, and well cared for in spite of the number. It was commonly thought that the negroes, when freed, would care very little for their children, and would let them die for want of attention, but experience has proved this surmise unfounded. On the contrary, I suppose they take as good care of them as do the same class of people anywhere.

It will be seen by reference to plot of the place "as it is," that one corner has been cut off, and a church and school-house built on it. This has been given to them so long as they use it for church and school purposes. The church building is forty by fifty feet, and is a frame house, the Lord's house being here, if not elsewhere, better than the people's. They have a membership of about two hundred, from the plantation and the country around, which is in charge of the Rev. Derry Merton, a colored man, who preaches there twice a month. He has had charge of this church nine or ten years, and has other churches under his care. For its support, the male members pay fifty cents and the females twenty-five cents per annum. In addition to their regular church services, they have a Sunday-school, with a membership of one hundred and fifty or more, which has a regular superintendent, one of the tenants on the place. They use regular lesson-papers and singing-books, and especially delight in singing. I believe, generally speaking, negroes in the country are Baptists; at any rate, those on this place are. To go under the water is far more necessary to salvation, in their eyes, than anything else. There is a great tendency among them to become preachers, which, I fear, is induced as much by the desire to display their oratorical powers as by excess of piety. Once a year, during August, there is a big meeting at Spring Hill church. From far and near friends come in, and all the houses of all the members are thrown open. They kill their pigs, kids, lambs, chickens, everything, by wholesale, and for three or four days they do little else but preach, sing, and eat. Fortunately their meeting comes at a time when very little work is to be done, so that the crops do not suffer. This August meeting, and the necessity of going under the water, are the bulwarks of their church.

Too great praise cannot be bestowed upon the earnestness which all negroes feel on the subject of education. Very soon after they were freed, these hands manifested a desire to establish a school, and Mr. Barrow gave them a site upon which they promptly built a schoolhouse, and they have employed a teacher ever since. Free schools in Georgia last only about three months, but the negroes cheerfully pay their teacher the remainder of the year themselves. Quite a number who were grown when freed have since learned to read, and write, and they all send their children. It is a strange fact that, even while they desire their children to be educated, many of them have a great prejudice against the profession of teaching.

An old colored woman said to one of my sisters: "I tell you what, Miss Sallie, of all the lazy, good-for-nothin' trades, this here sittin' down in a cheer all day, with a book in your hand, hearing chillen say lessons, is the laziest." The latest romance of the plantation was the elopement of the schoolteacher and the daughter of one of the old foremen. "Mr. Map" (so-called, I suppose, on account of his knowledge of geography) won the heart of "Ben's Mary," and sued for her hand. Very much to his surprise, the father not only refused, but it is said declared his intention of giving them both a good whipping the first time he caught them together, adding his opinion of the laziness and worthlessness of the suitor. As the old man would most likely have carried his threat into execution, the young couple had nothing left but a separation or an elopement. I think there was nothing against Map, except his occupation, and as he supported his wife, the old man soon relented and allowed them to return to the neighborhood.

I have thus briefly given some facts connected with the farm life of the colored people in Georgia. If I have made my descriptions true to life, they fit any place in this portion of the State, *mutatis mutandis*. They all live nearly the same way. Occasionally one is found who wishes to have more of this world's goods; such buy land and pay for it as they did for their mules, and work the same crops as these I have written about. As a people they are happy; they have become suited to their new estate, and it to them. I do not know of a single negro who has swelled the number of the "exodus." That they have improved, and continue to improve, seems beyond controversy. The one man on this plantation who, as a slave, gave most trouble, so much, in fact, that he was almost beyond control of the overseer, was Lem Bryant. Since he has been freed, he has grown honest, quiet, and industrious; he educates his children and pays his debts. Mr. Barrow asked him, one day, what had changed him so. "Ah, master!" he replied, "I'm free now; I *have* to do right."

70 A Preference for Black Labor

Many planters, when given any choice in the matter, decided in favor of black labor over white. Their reasons are explained fairly cogently in the statement below excerpted from a letter to the editor of a Mississippi newspaper. Hardly generous in its appraisal of black labor, the letter does suggest the greater racial identification of the labor source of Southern agriculture. It also hints at potential racial antagonism emerging from discrimination against white laborers who might be inclined to blame black competition rather than the market system itself for their plight. So long as whites blamed their problems on black competition, so long would fundamental criticism of the system hindering both blacks and whites be defused. The author of the letter also notes another product of the market so evident in 1886—the strike.

Source: Letter from a landowner near Terry, Mississippi, to the Raymond, Mississippi, *Gazette*, May 8, 1886, reprinted in Vernon Lane Wharton, *The Negro in Mississippi 1865-1890* (Chapel Hill, 1947), p. 121.

I do not say this to decry white labor, for I like it, when of the right kind, but if either must go, give me the nigger every time. The nigger will never "strike" as long as you give him plenty to eat and half clothe him: He will live on less and do more hard work, when properly managed, than any other class, or race of people. As Arp truthfully says "we can boss him" and that is what we southern folks like.... I have worked both kinds of labor, side by side, with varying results. The nigger will do the most work and do it according to personal instructions.... I record Experience against Theory.

71 Steps Toward Segregation

While a distinctive system of production was emerging in the post-war South, social relations were also in the process of change in a variety of areas of activity, revealing the origins of habits of race relations that would become entrenched in custom and later often written into law. It has already been noted that the races in the "free" North had been frequently separated before the Civil War; likewise the close proximity of the races, without any pretense of equality, in the South appears to have been the dominant pattern. The logic of the choices made at this time is often a curious one to the sensibilities of modern generations accustomed to the rantings of apartheid advocates. The following item is a case in point. This history of the Presbyterian Church in South Carolina notes that church officials after the Civil War attempted to halt the flight of blacks from the church. Blacks composed about half the membership but "were almost entirely dependent on our people for moral advancement and spiritual culture." For the part of the blacks: "The Gospel was offered them but they declined it as coming from us." In their effort to keep the freedmen in the congregation the whites were attempting in an honest and explicit way to exercise a form of social control which they recalled from days of slavery. The blacks initiated this separatism, in this area, precisely to avoid that social control. While this move may not have struck a blow for racial equality, it did repudiate paternalism, no matter the good intention in which it was clothed.

Source: F. D. Jones and W. H. Mills (eds.), History of the Presbyterian Church in South Carolina Since 1850 (Columbia, S.C., 1926), pp. 119-23.

Harmony Presbytery in October, 1865, sent to the General Assembly a memorial as to the duty of maintaining and perpetuating our present ecclesiastical organization. Some were ready to conclude that as the political bonds which formerly bound the South and North together were being reestablished, so the ecclesiastical bonds which had been severed should also be restored. But this was regarded as an unwarranted deduction.

One reunion was to be regarded as brought about by the providence of God, while the same providence stood directly in the way of the other reunion. The memorial recounts the actions of the Northern General Assembly in receiving private members. That Assembly was charged not only with excommunicating us from fellowship but with inaugurating measures which aimed at our overthrow, as a Christian Church. Another ground of complaint was found in the legislation of the Northern Church in regard to political matters. The best thing to be done was to stand in our lot, feeling assured that God would never forsake us. A very fine and earnest pastoral letter was issued by the Presbytery to its own churches. The difficulties of the situation were set forth, the desolating effects of war, the loss of members, the infidelity and immorality which threatened to invade us. Personal religion was to be guarded, the Church of God to be cared for, reclaiming the wandering, encouraging the doubting, supporting the feeble, stimulating attendance. The claim of the ministry for a support was to be urged and feeble churches and missionary stations were to be strengthened. The colored members, now intoxicated with their first experience of liberty, were to be dealt with gently, forbearingly and patiently. "Let us remember their infirmities and not be too hasty." The *Narrative* presented a report in which the shadows prevailed. Preaching had been regular, but the attendance had been interfered with by the ravages of war, the falling off of the colored members had been considerable. "The reaction from the restraints and excitement of war shows itself in some by the inactivity of despair, others resort to dishonest gains, while others seek relief in the frivolities and dissipations of the world." There was a call for liberality on the part of churches in supporting the ministers and a call for self-denial on the part of the latter. The *Narratives* of this period were written largely in Biblical language, and made free use of Biblical figures. This one concludes, "Finally, brethren, all that remains for us is to go down into the swelling of the floods of this Jordan, bearing the ark of Jehovah's covenant; doubtless we shall pass over and possess the fair land of our inheritance."

The Presbytery resolved that notwithstanding the change in the social and political condition of our colored people, "we regard our obligations to impart to them the blessings of the Gospel as unimpaired, and enjoin on ministers and churches to continue to instruct them by preaching, catechetical teaching, and all other means of improving their spiritual condition." About one-half the membership in the churches of this Presbytery was then composed of negroes, who were almost entirely dependent on our people for moral advancement and spiritual culture.

The churches were urged to impress upon the colored people that their obligations to God and the Church were not weakened by the change in their civil relations, that this change laid them under greater obligation to contribute to the support of the ministry. Their marriages were to be celebrated by regularly ordained ministers, and "Christian parents were to remember their duty to consecrate their infant children to God in baptism." The treasurer of Presbytery was to be freed from any obligations to pay out funds received in Confederate money, which had now become worthless. A good deal of calculation was necessary to adjust the debts incurred by the Presbytery to its evangelists and home missionaries, in accordance with the change of currency. The current "greenbacks" varied so much in value, owing to the high cost of gold, that the amount due in United States currency had to be ascertained.

The *Narrative* for October, 1868, was more hopeful. "The cloud is beginning to pass away." Worldly-mindedness and love of gain are still prevalent but some churches had been revived, and conversions had been made. A severe drought had cut off supplies. Some pastors, both old and young, had been removed or laid aside by illness and in the financial straits of the period, the support of the latter class was precarious. Attention had been given to the "Freedmen," a new term in phraseology! They were manifesting some disposition to return to our communion, after a temporary alienation from us. Several mission stations had been established for their benefit, and it was hoped that a regular missionary for them might be employed.*

The Home Mission Report mentioned the various stations which had been established for the Freedmen, six in all, supplied usually by the nearest white pastors and having an attendance of from eight to one hundred and fifty persons. At these stations, some white people had also attended, such as had rarely gone to any place of worship.

Three of these stations were afterwards given up to the colored people. "They were too unsettled, politically and religiously, to inaugurate any permanent plan of religious instruction among them, separate from the old plan. The pastors must still do all they can in the midst of manifold discouragements." The anomalous condition in which these people find themselves, the inducements held out to them to tear them away from their former relations by designing emissaries from abroad and designing persons at home make the fact that they are conducting themselves with any prudence or propriety at all more surprising than the excesses into which they have run. We can never forget the time when they crowded to our sanctuaries, when they listened to the Gospel as preached to their owners, and then to the additional discourse designed especially for themselves. We can never forget the communion table spread for master and servant; the bread and the wine administered to each by the same hand and from the same vessels and at the same table. These are all pleasant memories and they greatly comfort us amid the surrounding desolations, giving us the assurance that we had attempted to do something for this unfortunate race in their highest interests.

In October, 1867, the Presbytery had thirty-two ministers, thirty-nine churches, three licentiates, seven candidates, and 3,276 communicants. There had been received on profession 333, and by letter 45. To foreign missions had been given $541; to home missions, $591; to education, $426.

The *Narrative* for April, 1868, reported nothing very encouraging. Some pastors had been supported, others had been compelled to seek other fields of labor. Little had been done for the instruction of the colored people. Only one preaching station was now open for them. "The Gospel was offered them but they declined it as coming from us. They have turned to other teachers, and for the most part, to such of their own class as are utterly ignorant, some of them not being able even to read God's Word. When the blind leads the blind, the result is inevitable. We ought to be sure, however, that we leave no opening unoccupied, no proper means untried to gain access to them with the Gospel.''

*Probably no greater harm was done the Presbyterian Church than the loss of its influence over the colored people, arising from the estrangement and bitterness of the reconstruction period. It has been shown how conscientiously and affectionately the religious interests of the negroes had been looked after, and what testimonials were given as to their consistent lives. Politics came in to separate the races, to break up forever the old tie of personal affection between master and servant, to substitute a hireling spirit and a bitter prejudice, the results of which are still felt, after fifty years.
—THE AUTHOR.

72 "By Their Fruits Ye Shall Know Them"

Black people themselves were not unified in religious sentiments. In 1878 Bishop Daniel Alexander Payne of the African Methodist Episcopal Church noted the prevalence of forms of worship that deeply offended his religious sensibilities. In many ways it is the same conflict as that previously noted between worship in the slave quarters and the religious habits characterized by restraint and solemnity urged upon them by whites. The significance of the competition may be seen first in the persistence of long-standing religious customs that were less than orthodox. By the last quarter of the nineteenth century the division in this particular forum may signal the strains placed upon the black community, and even a fragmentation or at least a split in that community. One side, represented by people like Bishop Payne, may have viewed itself to be, as he put it, "the most thoughtful and intelligent," but it was more the acceptance of a narrow orthodoxy that emphasized discipline and restraint. The other side, derived possibly from Africa, associated with voodoo, not only focused upon salvation (through the rings) but demonstrated an emotional excitement that, as Payne tersely observed, left them the following day "unfit for labor." The religious issue was far more than worshipping beside whites; it indeed followed the same dialectic as the issue of freedom.

Source: Bishop Daniel Alexander Payne, *Recollections of Seventy Years* (Nashville, 1888), pp. 253-57.

In May it was my privilege to visit the Sunday-school of Old Bethel, in Philadelphia, and at a meeting of the Sunday-school teachers I conducted responsive reading of the First and Second Psalms of David. I showed them how England had become great by habitually making her people read the Scriptures on Sunday in the great congregation; and how the colored race, who had been oppressed for centuries through ignorance and superstition, might become intelligent, Christian, and powerful through the enlightening and sanctifying influences of the word of God. I also stated that thereafter, by my orders, every pastor occupying the pulpit of Bethel should make responsive readings of the Holy Scriptures a part of the public worship. Bethel Church about this time had set about furnishing the music-room at our university, which they completed by June.

I have mentioned the "Praying and Singing Bands" elsewhere. The strange delusion that many ignorant but well-meaning people labor under leads me to speak particularly of them. About this time I attended a "bush meeting," where I went to please the pastor whose circuit I was visiting. After the sermon they formed a ring, and with coats off sung, clapped their hands and stamped their feet in a most ridiculous and heathenish way. I requested the pastor to go and stop their dancing. At his request they stopped their dancing and clapping of hands, but remained singing and rocking their bodies to and fro. This they did for about fifteen minutes. I then went, and taking their leader by the arm requested him to desist and to sit down and sing in a rational manner. I told him also that it was a heathenish way to worship and disgraceful to themselves, the race, and the Christian name. In that instance they broke up their ring; but would not sit down, and walked sullenly away. After the sermon in the afternoon, having another opportunity of speaking alone to this young leader of the singing and clapping ring, he said: "Sinners won't get converted unless there is a ring." Said I: "You might sing till you fell down dead, and you would fail to convert a single sinner, because nothing but the Spirit of God and the word of God can convert sinners." He replied: "The Spirit of God works upon people in different ways. At camp-meeting there must be a ring here, a ring there, a ring over yonder, or sinners will not get converted." This was his idea, and it is also that of many others. These "Bands" I have had to encounter in many places, and, as I have stated in regard to my early labors in Baltimore, I have been strongly censured because of my efforts to change the mode of worship or modify the extravagances indulged in by the people. In some cases all that I could do was to teach and preach the right, fit, and proper way of serving God. To the most thoughtful and intelligent I usually succeeded in making the "Band" disgusting; but by the ignorant masses, as in the case mentioned, it was regarded as the essence of religion. So much so was this the case that, like this man, they believed no conversion could occur without their agency, nor outside of their own ring could any be a genuine one. Among some of the songs of these "Rings," or "Fist and Heel Worshipers," as they have been called, I find a note of two in my journal, which were used in the instance mentioned. As will be seen, they consisted chiefly of what are known as "corn-field ditties:"

"Ashes to ashes, dust to dust;
If God won't have us, the devil must.
"I was way over there where the coffin fell;
I heard that sinner as he screamed in hell."

To indulge in such songs from eight to ten and half-past ten at night was the chief employment of these "Bands." Prayer was only a secondary thing, and this was rude and extravagant to the last degree. The man who had the most powerful pair of lungs was the one who made the best prayer, and he could be heard a square off. He who could sing loudest and longest led the "Band," having his loins girded and a hankerchief in hand with which he kept time, while his feet resounded on the floor like the drumsticks of a bass drum. In some places it was the custom to begin these dances after every night service and keep it up till midnight, sometimes singing and dancing alternately—a short prayer and a long dance. Some one has even called it the "Voudoo Dance." I have remonstrated with a number of pastors for permitting these practices, which vary somewhat in different localities, but have been invariably met with the response that he could not succeed in restraining them, and an attempt to compel them to cease would simply drive them away from our Church. I suppose that with the most stupid and headstrong it is an incurable religious disease, but it is with me a question whether it would not be better to let such people go out of the Church than remain in it to perpetuate their evil practice and thus do two things: disgrace the Christian name and corrupt others. Any one who knows human nature must infer the result after such midnight practices to be that the day after they are unfit for labor, and that at the end of the dance their exhaustion would render them an easy prey to Satan. These meetings must always be more damaging physically, morally, and religiously than beneficial. How needful it is to have an intelligent ministry to teach these people who hold to this ignorant mode of worship the true method of serving God. And my observations lead me to the conclusion that we need more than an intelligent ministry to cure this religious fanaticism. We need a host of Christian reformers like St. Paul, who will not only speak against these evils, but who will also resist them, even if excommunication be necessary. The time is at hand when the ministry of the A.M.E. Church must drive out this heathenish mode of worship or drive out all the intelligence, refinement, and practical Christians who may be in her bosom.

So far from being in harmony with the religion of the Lord Jesus Christ, it antagonizes his holy religion. And what is most deplorable, some of our most popular and powerful preachers labor systematically to perpetuate this fanaticism. Such preachers never rest till they create an excitement that consists in shouting, jumping, and dancing. I say systematically do they preach to produce such results, and just as systematically do they avoid the trial of persons accused of swindling, drunkenness, embezzling, and the different forms of adultery. I deliberately record that which I know, and am prepared if necessary to prove.

To these sensational and recreant preachers I recommend the careful and prayerful study of the text: "To the unknown God, whom ye ignorantly worship, him declare I unto you." (Acts xvii. 23.) The preachers against whom I make this record are intensely religious, but grossly immoral. "By their fruits ye shall know them."

73 Early Integration: An Uneasy Truce

While federal law until 1883 prohibited racial discrimination in public accommodations, the pattern of acceptance, resistance, and enforcement is far from clear in the postwar South. The following account of a trip on a steamship from Charleston to Beaufort, South Carolina, indicates the difficulty in generalizing about the openness of race relations, or, for that matter, the rapid emergence of segregation. While blacks and whites were both present on this trip, ways could be found to subvert the spirit of equal treatment if sufficiently desired. And in such an apprehensive atmosphere ways could be found to interpret any action—or inaction—as hostile. Most likely the closest appreciation of the situation could be found in Elizabeth Hyde Botume's summary comment: "We seemed to be living over a volcano." And possibly the issue was one that could be resolved only at each point it was raised. Precedents abounded for either course.

Source: Elizabeth Hyde Botume, *First Days Amongst the Contrabands* (Boston, 1893), pp. 267-69.

As we were returning South in the fall of 1868, we heard disheartening stories about the freedmen. We were told in Washington they were becoming usurpers. They realized their power, and began to feel they could do without white influence. It was said they had taken the entire direction of their schools, putting into office colored trustees and a colored superintendent, and they had removed several white teachers and put inefficient colored teachers in their places.

Miss Amy Bradley, who was giving her life to help the "poor whites" in Wilmington, N.C., spoke to us of the arrogant assumption of the negroes around her as a serious evil.

In Charleston we heard of riots in different parts of the State, excited certainly by what Governor Andrew had already predicted, the unwillingness of the old slave-holders to recognize free labor. We feared there was a growing hostility between the two races, *as races*.

We took a small steamer from Charleston for Beaufort. Here we found a decided change since we went North. Then no colored person was allowed on the upper deck, now there were no restrictions,—there could be none, for a law had been passed in favor of the negroes. They were everywhere, choosing the best staterooms and best seats at the table. Two prominent colored members of the State Legislature were on board with their families. There were also several well-known Southerners, still uncompromising rebels. It was a curious scene and full of significance. An interesting study to watch the exultant faces of the negroes, and the scowling faces of the rebels,—rebels still against manifest destiny and the new dispensation. Until now we had but little understood these portentous changes, the meaning of which we must study out for ourselves.

We were summoned to dinner. When we reached the table we found there only colored people occupying more than half the seats on each side. They were doing the honors with something of an air that said, "Receive this from me or go without." In all respects, however, they were courteous and attentive. There was no loud talking or laughing.

The stewardess came behind us, and leaning over whispered we had better wait a little, as they were obliged to give the colored passengers the first table. The white passengers would come to the second. We thanked her, but preferred to keep our seats. A few Northerners joined us. One, who we know had been a first-class Democrat, and "down on the niggers," was obliged to leave us and sit next to a man as black as ink. He swallowed his prejudices and took his seat, and fraternized with this neighbor to the best of his ability; besides, it was no longer a question of inclination, it was business. This was the point in which our fears were most aroused. The freedmen, no longer slaves, were fast becoming tools.

The negro who sat not far from me was an immense fellow, seemingly an iron man, with powerful physique and indomitable will. He had made an incendiary speech in July, telling his people this was their government, and they no longer needed or had any use for white people. All the morning he had walked around scanning and apparently marking the passengers. His looks seemed to say, "If you are with us, well and good; if not, stand back." Whilst the scowling faces and muttered words of the Southerners implied, "If you stand back, well and good; if you fraternize with the niggers, be—."

The little group of Northerners noted and translated what they saw. Each one watched his neighbor. I now understood why we were so frequently asked in Charleston if we were not afraid to return to Beaufort just now. Some friends had earnestly urged us to wait until after election on Tuesday, but that was the time we wanted to be with the people in our own district. We had no fears for ourselves, but grave apprehensions for our friends. These were exciting times. We seemed to be living over a volcano.

74 Early Integration: An Amicable Conflict

Sometimes potentially explosive relations emerged where integration was the rule; sometimes friendly relations emerged where segregation was the rule. In the following document a black man joins whites on a railroad car which is by rule separate. In the very form of the encounter a pattern of race relations in the Gilded Age again proves elusive. But in the substance of the report several related points emerge. One concerns the conflict between theory and practice on the railroad. While the stated policy was segregation by race in separate cars, the actuality appeared to be more a class division. This was also the case in the theaters discussed: the policy was flexible, depending upon the specific circumstances. It is difficult to determine if the particular black traveler on the car at the beginning of the account is accepted because he is recognized or because of his education and attire. Still, in the discussion of the two whites and the one black, a certain ritual appears to emerge, one that would come to dominate discussions of race relations. After stating their positions on the race question facing the nation with fair candor, the friendly participants were on the brink of an abrupt termination or unfriendly confrontation and drifted closer to the consideration of possible solutions to the problems facing black people. Deftly the black spokesman placed the responsibility for change not on his white adversaries but on the blacks themselves; to secure morality and education for his people was the main task. After having recited the injustices done to blacks with exceptional vigor and wit, this was a curious turn. Yet, something can be said for the strategic, or in this case tactical, qualities evident in this traveler's demeanor and for the content of his argument. This stance may not have been such a turn against his own people after all. August Meier in his *Negro Thought in America 1880-1915* has probed the ambiguities of the apparently accommodating philosophy of Booker T. Washington and found a complex array of hopes and commitments that may help explain this particular incident. On one level the black man's audience no doubt felt more comfortable when he turned his attention to the foibles and shortcomings of his own race. The burden appeared to have been taken from the backs of white people. But that same shifting of the burden served another purpose, one possibly less benign had his listeners perceived it. It was a thorough rejection of white paternalism and an assertion that blacks could and would make it by themselves—without the aid of the white man. They would not beg. It must still be recognized, however, that this approach undeniably carried the unfortunate consequence of confirming in the white mind the lack of social responsibility for the fate of the blacks and also the possible sacrificing of the present generation for the future. In this brief encounter between the races the black protagonist made one further point that was fraught with implications: "Gentlemen, you do not care if we are degraded and worthless; but it's bad for you, too, if the negro is a brute." In this it was true that he had a "comprehension of the subtle bonds that unite men in their moral destiny, and make the strong and fortunate in some ways dependent on the fate of the lowly," but was this a subtle appeal to their self interest or was it possibly even a veiled threat? Oppress the black man further only at your own risk. In either case it offered a recognition that there was indeed a limit to the autonomy and self-help that could be effectively developed by any subjugated people. But the ambiguity of the message, racial autonomy reconciled with accommodation to white values, institutions, and relations and those of the market and social Darwinism at that, remains perhaps the intriguing puzzle of Gilded Age race relations.

Source: J. B. Harrison, "Studies in the South," *Atlantic Monthly*, 50 (November 1882), 625-27.

A negro came in, and was recognized by two gentlemen as having in his childhood belonged to some one whom they knew, and they bade him sit down and give an account of himself for the long time that had passed since their last meeting. They were all evidently glad to see each other, and the conversation that ensued reciprocal regard and respect. One gentleman was a merchant from Nashville; the other I understood to be a physician from Mississippi. Both showed good manners, wide information, and much interest in public affairs. They appeared to be business men of high character, energetic and practical. They were democrats; the negro was a republican.

They soon launched broadly into a discussion of the whole question of the character, capabilities, and interests of the negro race in this country, and of the various problems growing out of the relations between the negroes and the white people. There was the utmost courtesy on both sides, but I was astonished at the ability and the boldness of the negro. He seemed to know and remember every political blunder and fault of the party in power in Alabama since its first organization after the war, and every instance of injustice done to the people of his race. Several times the gentlemen thought him in error regarding matters of fact, but he took a ponderous memorandum book out of his pocket, filled with newspaper cuttings, notes, and references, and showed in each case that he knew what he was talking about. For more than two hours there was such an exhibition of argument, wit, apt reply, and incisive repartee as I have rarely heard anywhere. There was great fairness and entire good humor all around. The two white men were evidently delighted with the ability shown by their antagonist, and when he was too strong for them they "owned up" heartily. He was nearly always too strong for them. He had evidently given most of the points discussed far more attention than they. I have scarcely ever heard his readiness of reply equaled. Both his opponents together were no match for him. As they concluded, he said, "Gentlemen, we give you notice that we intend to have our rights, all that the law gives us, and that we are going to fight for them—not with our hands, but with our mouths and our brains—till we obtain them. Sooner or later we shall have them, and you might as well understand it first as last."

Both gentlemen said, "That's right. We don't blame you. We like your spirit. Of course we would do the same in your place." Then one added, and the other expressed hearty assent and approval, "But I'll be damned if I'll ever sit down to the table with a nigger." The negro laughed, and taunted them with the far more intimate relations which white men frequently form with negro girls. All this talk was open and public. There were no ladies in the car, and the men gathered around to hear. The negro's account of the condition of his own race was very depressing, and he plainly felt that the chief obstacles in the way of their advancement were to be found, not in the opposition or injustices of the white people, but in the low qualities and tendencies of the negroes. He did not seem to be hopeful, but was full of spirit, and was plainly resolved to make a gallant fight for the improvement of his people, whatever the odds against him. In the course of the talk he described his efforts to put down vice and disorder among the colored people in the town where he lived. He had on a certain occasion organized and supervised a picnic for his own people, and when some vicious colored girls had intruded upon the company, he had forcibly expelled them from the grounds. They made a charge of assault and battery against him, and the affair cost him many hundreds of dollars. He confessed that he had violated the law in kicking and striking those disorderly women, but he had done so in protecting his own wife and daughters from insult and violence.

He thought that disorderly and licentious white men incited the baser class of the negroes to invade and disturb his picnic, and that even the good white people did not give him any sympathy or moral support in his efforts to maintain order and suppress vice among the colored people. Said he, "Gentlemen, you do not care if we are degraded and worthless; but it's bad for you, too, if the negro is a brute." His comprehension of the subtle bonds that unite men in their moral destiny, and make the strong and fortunate in some ways dependent on the fate of the lowly, would have delighted the heart of Carlyle. He said,

"There are three hundred and sixty-two lewd colored girls in my town. It's a shame and a curse for us. Do you think it's nothin' for you?"

This negro seemed a born leader of men. He was fully alive to the faults and weaknesses of the negro character, and appeared to be less hopeful regarding the future of his race in this country than were his white antagonists; but he loves struggle and conflict, and will, no doubt, contend bravely to the end for what he regards as the rights of his people. I had some talk afterward with his friendly opponents. They spoke of him in terms of admiration, and said that he had the reputation of being one of the best public speakers in the State, and they had no doubt it was deserved. Then they added that if a hotel, theatre, or church, or any place of entertainment, amusement, or public resort in the South, should be conducted on the plan of really making no distinction on account of color or race, no white person of good character would attend it, or support it in any way whatever. This is doubtless true at present, in the main, at least.

Civil Rights

On most of the railroads in the South the negroes were expected and told to take a particular car in each train, and they usually did so, but the rule did not appear to be strictly enforced. (Indeed, I could not see that anything was done strictly in the South.) Well dressed negroes sometimes traveled in the same car with "first-class" white people, ladies and gentlemen; and there were usually some white people, poor whites or working folk, in the negro car. In Norfolk, Virginia, the colored people were directed to a particular gallery or part of the house at all lectures or public entertainment, but I do not think they had been, of late, forcibly prevented from taking seats in the body of the house. In Richmond, Virginia, at the time of my visit to that city, two young colored men bought tickets for a public lecture, and attempted to enter the main audience room. The usher very courteously suggested that they would find seats in the gallery. They objected, and asked, "Do you forbid us to go into the best part of the hall?" "Not at all, gentlemen," he replied; "on the contrary, I call every one present to witness that I do not forbid you to go there. At the same time, I think you would better go into the gallery." Just then the manager of the lecture course came in, and the usher appealed to him. He smiled, and passed the negroes into the principal auditorium, and they took seats at one side and in the rear, where there would be nobody near them.

If there had been a crowd, the manager would not have authorized them to go in; and if the negroes had insisted on seating themselves among the white people, everybody in that part of the hall would have left it. Similar conditions and feelings appeared to prevail everywhere in the South in regard to these matters. There was a universal disposition on the part of the white people to avoid difficulty and conflict with the colored people respecting their civil rights, and the negroes were, in general, not disposed to contend for them. But a few colored men are inclined to insist upon enjoying whatever rightly belongs to them under the law, because they believe that any concessions on the part of the black people, or surrender of their legal rights, would invite and produce new injuries and oppressions. It is likely that some degree of irritation will often result from the attitude of the two races regarding this matter of the civil rights of the negroes.

75 Separate But Equal Education?

From the beginning the notion of separate facilities for the races raised a variety of issues, but the central and most commonly argued point was the provision of equal support to those facilities. Whether conceived as a test of public commitment to equality (and quality education) or as opening up the opportunities of a capitalist society in which education was essential to effective competition (à la Horace Mann), whether viewed as a charade for inequality or as a deeply felt commitment the issue rested on a single assumption shared by both sides: the institutions of society in America had the same obligations for black people as for whites. The commitment was there but, as the following letters reveal, the fulfillment of that commitment was elusive. Written more than a century ago, the language in the controversy over the fair allocation of public resources remains uncannily current.

Source: The Nation, 19 (November 12, 1874), 316.

To The Editor of *The Nation*:

Sir: In your issue of October 29, you have an article on the Force Act, which is so broad in its scope that I dislike to criticise any part of it; but there is in it an unjust allusion to Virginia, which ought not to remain uncorrected. Whilst admitting that in the Southern States the negro is fairly dealt with, even in those States where he is in the minority, you make an exception in these words:

"In Virginia, we believe, he is not fairly dealt with in the matters of common schools."

May I not reasonably ask, Mr. Editor, that, having gone so far you go further, and give to the public the facts or reasons on which you base a declared belief so seriously reflecting on the fair dealing of this State?

You cannot, in that remark, have referred to our law, which makes the same provision for the two races in every particular, and which, whilst requiring them to be taught in separate schools, requires also that the schools for white and colored children shall be "under the same general regulations as to management, usefulness, and efficiency."

If unfairness exists anywhere, it must be in the administration of the school system. If I, the chief executive of the system, have been guilty of it, I deserve to be exposed. If any one of our four hundred and fifty local school-boards, or of our ninety-four superintendents, has been guilty of a single act of unfairness to the negro, and you have information thereof, I beg that you will name the offender in your paper, or to me privately, and I will immediately investigate the case; and I guaranty that if the fact be ascertained, the guilty party or parties shall be expelled from office instantly. I do not call upon you to prove anything. I will call for evidence on the trial. I only ask you, or any other responsible party, to name the schoolboard or the school-officer in Virginia whom you believe to have been guilty of unfairness as between the races, and I will do the rest. If you do not like to mention the names of men or of boards, only indicate the locality—the city, county, district, or village—where the unfairness has been perpetrated, and I will follow that clue until the truth is ascertained. Moreover, all the proceedings taken, and all the persons and papers in the case, shall be open to the public, and everybody be allowed to examine and cross-examine to his heart's content.

Mr. Editor, if anything of this sort is going on, I do not know it, but I want to know it; and for the sake of the negroes, and more particularly for the sake of the truth, I again beg that you will help me to ferret out these oppressors; and then we will tell the world all about it.

To some this may seem to be making a great deal of a small matter; but this is the very gist of the argument in favor of the Civil-Rights Bill. The advocates of that destructive measure have pressed their cause chiefly on the ground that the Southern whites do not, and will not, treat the negroes impartially in the matter of education. I know the aspersion to be unjust so far as Virginia is concerned. Our officers may not be free from every fault. Our schools may not be as numerous or as good as might be justly desired; but the schools are in respect to the races as nearly equal in number and privileges as circumstances admit of, and all will confess that what we have are a great deal better than none.

W. H. Ruffner,
Superintendent of Public Instruction.

Richmond, Va., Nov. 5.
[The editor's response:]

We are very glad for various reasons that Mr. Ruffner has thought proper to ask us for our authority for the imputation on the State of Virginia to which he refers, because, whether it be well or ill founded, investigation such as he promises cannot but do good. We are at liberty to say that the charge of un-fairness towards the colored people in the matter of education comes from Miss C. F. Putnam, a well-known and much-respected Northern lady, who has been for some years and is now laboring in the most self-sacrificing way as a teacher of a colored school at Lottsburg, Northumberland County. What she says, in a letter dated July 26, 1874, is this:

"While the State professes to provide schools (separate schools) for black and white children alike, our observation proves that it is not done. The county superintendent and Mr. Claughton, school trustee, exerted themselves greatly to induce our people to give up their schoolhouse for a public school, and pledged their word that the colored children should have equal justice and share the public money with the white children. We were present and heard the promise. Heathsville, the county-seat and residence of the county superintendent, four miles from us, had that same year an appropriation of public money—$500. The number of colored and white children was about the same. The white children received $450 for their schools, and only $50 was used for the colored children. There are four towns in this county. Through our friends, the [Freedman's] Bureau has aided to establish two other schools besides ours—that is, in three of the four towns there were schools. The crying want of the fourth town, which had a larger proportion of colored children than the others, had not received one cent for its colored children at the last account I had, while hundreds of dollars (for which the colored men were taxed) were used to maintain the white schools in that town—Wicomico Church. The colored schools are not heartily supported, and are purposely of as little real benefit as possible. All our hundred Lottsburgh colored voters are taxed every year $150 each for the support of schools, and pay it. To show how determined the school officers have ever been to break up our schools, let me remind you that all our colored voters but two signed a petition three years ago to have me made the public-school teacher, that they might have the benefit of the school-money for which they were taxed. Their petition was denied solely because ours is a Republican school."

It is but right to add that the above extracts are made from a private letter, addressed by Miss Putnam to a lady in New York, who with others has aided her with money and otherwise in carrying on her work, and was not written with a view to publication, or with any idea of affecting public opinion in any way. It will be seen, too, that our quotations contain little or nothing in the way of inference or vague imputation, but relate to matters of fact which Mr. Ruffner can have no difficulty in examining.—Ed. *Nation*.

76 The Decision to Uproot

At the end of the 1870s thousands of freedmen and their families decided to move away from the South and resettle in what they hoped would be a more congenial environment. While the wind and cold of Kansas would prove to be a thorough challenge, anything often seemed better than what they left behind. The following affidavits and testimony collected by a special Congressional committee investigating this exodus from the South reveal the specific grievances felt by these people in their Southern experiences, their aspirations, and their reception by other blacks. Of life in the South they complained bitterly and frequently, and more specifically of the share-cropping and crop-lien systems, of the high interest rates, of the chain-gang systems and of a general persecution that they commonly likened unto slavery. In their hopes for the new land they were careful to express less than generous expectations. While the nature of the movement caused many observers to compare it to the exodus of the Israelites from the persecution of the Pharaoh as they went to the promised land of Canaan, the blacks who were moving to Kansas seem to have had no delusions about their future homes. All they wanted, they said, was a home where they could settle under the terms of the homestead law and become fee-simple owners. Put another way, all they wanted was independence, the very quality denied systematically by the agricultural and social systems of the South. Moreover, as the testimony of John H. Johnson of St. Louis indicates, they were often received cheerfully and sympathetically and aided on their way by the black communities they passed through. This aspect reflects the penchant for self-help and racial identity among blacks as does also the formation of black communities and colonies once they arrived in Kansas.

Source: Report and Testimony of the Select Committee of the United States Senate to Investigate the Causes of the Removal of the Negroes from the Southern States to the Northern States. 46th Congress, 2d Session, U.S. Senate Report No. 693 (Washington, 1880), Part 2, 211-14, 288-93; Part 3, 413-18.

DE SOTO PARISH,
State of Louisiana:

My name is Anthony Witch. I live in DeSoto Parish. I had to pay this year, 1874, twelve dollars tax, and I only had one horse and one cow and calf. Do not own any land, nor never owned any land, and a large number of us have been made to pay that much on three horses and cows; and if we do not pay the money right away they take our stock, and then make us pay a great deal more as taxes. We have all been prosecuted about taxes again this year, but we don't know what the amount will be, as we have only a few horses & cows.

his

ANTHONY X WITCH.

mark

* * *

CADDO PARISH,
State of Louisiana:

We, George Underwood and Bellun Harris and Isaiah Fuller, make this statement: We live in the parish of Caddo, and worked, or contracted to work and make a crop on shares, on Mr. McCrowning's place, for one third we make or made, and McCrowning to furnish provisions or rations. But, in July, when we were working along in the field, Mr. Mack Morring and Mr. Mack Borrington came to us and said, "Well, boys, you all got to get away from here, for we have been going as far as we can, and you all must sign agreements, or you all must take what follows." They then went and got their sticks and guns and told us we must sign the papers, and we told them we would not sign it, because we did not want to give up our crops for nothing. They told us we had better sign, or we would not get anything. They said they only wanted justice; so we told them we would get judges to judge the crops, and to say what it is worth. But they told us no judges should come to see the crops, and we did not want to sign the paper. But they beat me (Isaiah), and then we got afraid and we signed the paper. We had about thirty acres in cotton, and it was the best cotton crop in that part of the parish, and we had about twenty-nine acres in corn. The corn was ripe and the fodder was ready to pull, and our cotton laid by. They then run us from the place, and told us not to come back any more. We owed Mr. Mack Morring one hundred and eighty dollars altogether. They then told us if they ever heard from us again they would fix us. During the time we was working and living on the place they did not half feed us, and we had to pay for half of our rations, or whatever we eat. We worked just as hard as if we were slaves, and in return was treated like dogs.

his
GEORGE X UNDERWOOD
mark
his
BELLUN X HARRISS
mark
his
ISAIAH X FULLER
mark

* * *

DE SOTO PARISH,
> State of Louisiana:

My name is Hiram Smith; I lived on Joe William's place, about two miles southeast of Keachie. I asked Mr. Williams to pay me what he owed me on my cotton; also seventy-five dollars he had taken away from me, what another man had paid me. He jumped on me and beat me so badly I fear I cannot live. He made me crawl on my knees and call them my God, my master, the God of all power. They then drew revolvers on me; all because I had asked for a settlement. This was done on the 16th day of March, 1876.

HIRAM SMITH

* * *

BOSSIER PARISH,
> State of Louisiana:

My name is Simon Dickson; I worked for Miss Lizzie Dickson, on her place, about sixteen or seventeen miles from Shreveport, north, on the bank of Old River, in the year 1873. I was due her the sum of twenty dollars. I made six bales of cotton and each bale weighed about six hundred pounds. I was to give her one hundred pounds to the acre, but she took all I made that year for the amount I owed her, twenty dollars. In 1874 I made eight and a half bales of cotton, weighing an average about five hundred and twenty-five pounds to the bale. I was to give her one-half of what I made. But she again took all, and would not let me have any. I then owed her about forty dollars. She said I owed her about one hundred and fifteen dollars, so she taken all of my crop every year, for what she claimed I owed her, yet she would never tell me what anything cost. In 1875 I asked her to tell me what such and such things cost, but she refused to tell me. I asked her for the account sales of my cotton, but she would never give them to me, nor to any of us on her place, though she has about two hundred and fifty hands working on her place, and out of them all there are but three she will give anything like justice. She even takes our cotton seed.

She furnishes us a mule to plant with. This place is near Benton, La., and belongs to Miss Lizzie Dickson.

his
SIMON + DICKSON
mark

* * *

JOHN H. JOHNSON (colored) sworn and examined as follows:
  By Mr. WINDOM:
  Question. Mr. Johnson, where do you reside? — Answer. Saint Louis is my place of residence.
  Q. How long have you lived there? — A. I was born and raised there.
  Q. How old are you? — A. I am thirty-four years of age.
  Q. What is your business? — A. By profession I am an attorney at law, but at present I am clerk to the disbursing agent of the new custom house at Saint Louis.
  Q. Have you given special attention to the arrival of colored people at Saint Louis on their way to Kansas or elsewhere? — A. I have.
  Q. Have you been connected with any committee looking after these emigrants? — A. I belong to the colored refugee board of Saint Louis. I have been secretary of it from the day of its organization.
  Q. State if you had any conversation with these people? — A. I have had frequent conversations with them, after their arrival in our city.
  Q. How many times did you converse with them? — A. At almost every arrival of them I have had conversations with them.
  Q. When was the first arrival? — A. I think in the latter part of February, 1879.
  Q. Where did they come from? — A. They came from Mississippi.
  Q. Do you remember from what part of the State and what number of them there were? — A. I do not remember what part of Mississippi they came from, but I think there were seventy-five or one hundred emigrants.
  Q. How did they come after that? — A. After that they came in parties of twenty-five and fifty, and on up to two hundred and fifty and three hundred.
  Q. From what period did they come? — A. From the first of March up to almost the time that I left the city to come and answer your subpoena.
  Q. Is the exodus continuing? — A. Yes, sir.
  Q. In what parties are they coming now? — A. They are coming in small and large parties both, principally five and ten at a time.
  Q. What time did your relief board organize? — A. The latter part of March or the first of April.
  Q. In 1879? — A. Yes, sir.
  Q. What was the object and purpose of that board? — A. Ours was a work of humanity, to relieve distress.
  Q. Was there anything political in its object? — A. No, sir; nothing whatever. It was a work of humanity, for they arrived there almost destitute. The first

arrival came when it was dry, cold weather. They arrived in one of the packet boats and camped on the levee. Information came that a number of these people had arrived from down South, and several of us got together and went down there and saw them. We went around among the people, white and black, and raised some money and went down there and gave it to the emigrants.

Q. Where were they destined to go? — A. To Kansas. The Sunday following there came a shipment of two hundred and fifty. That Saturday there was a heavy fall of snow and it was sleeting. It was a regular winterish day, and several citizens went down there and found them in their destitute and helpless condition. They took them and marched them up in procession and distributed them in the churches.

Q. That first arrival you sent off? — A. Yes, sir.

Q. What did you do with the second? — A. We distributed them in the churches and took care of them the best that we could.

By the CHAIRMAN:

Q. What time was that? — A. That was some time in the month of March. We raised what funds and provisions we could, and then made an arrangement, I think, with the Northern Star Company to take these people to the nearest point to Kansas, up the Missouri River. We kept them one or two weeks in the churches and we shipped a second cargo; then another shipment came, and most of those from Mississippi, and they were sent on, and subsequently others came from Louisiana.

Q. About how many have arrived there altogether? — A. There must have been of those who passed through the hands of the board between fifteen and twenty thousand, men, women, and children.

By Mr. WINDOM:

Q. You say they were destitute. Now will you give us an idea of how they were clothed and their condition generally? — A. Their clothes were very poor, indeed; some of them had nothing but rags and some had on old clothes very much worn; they were very poor for the commencement of the fall down South, let alone the winter in Saint Louis. Some of them had clothes, and had three or four pair of pants and coats on at the same time.

Q. They had to put that many on in order to keep warm? — A. Yes, sir; some of them had on nothing but rags and the women had on calico dresses, and their condition was such as to excite the sympathy of any person who saw them.

Q. Did any of them have any money? — A. Some of them had some money and others had none.

Q. Had they paid their fare to Saint Louis? — A. Yes, sir; some of them said they had sold their crops for little or nothing and sold all their goods, and some had sold a portion of their clothes in order to get to Kansas, which was their objective point.

Q. Was that the destination of all of them? — A. Yes, sir.

Q. They had nothing to live on and were dependent upon the charity of the people? — A. Yes, sir. Our own people there in Saint Louis collected food for them.

Q. Whom do you mean by our own people? — A. I mean the Saint Louis colored people. Some of the commission merchants helped us and sent us beans and pork, bread and crackers, and we raised also donations of clothes and money.

Q. What was the arrangement between that boat line and your board? — A. It was that they would take these people for from two dollars and a half to three dollars a head to their point of destination, either Topeka or Kansas City.

Q. Will you tell the committee what reasons they gave for coming under these adverse circumstances? — A. Well, sir, their arrival there in that condition and at that season of the year was a thing that we could not understand.

Q. Did they come on you suddenly? — A. Yes, very suddenly; and we naturally desired to know why they were making for Kansas at such a time, and we asked one and another of them, and they stated that it was owing to the treatment they received down South. They stated that they had no security for life, limb, or property; that they worked year in and year out, and, notwithstanding they raised good crops, they were at the end of the year in debt; that they were charged exorbitant prices for provisions, and all these things kept them down and in debt. The high prices charged them for lands and the denial of their rights as citizens induced them to leave there and seek a genial spot where they could have an opportunity to build up themselves and their families. Some of them stated that they had been on plantations alongside of theirs where men were shot down for political purposes, and the women stated all the impositions practiced on colored women in the South.

Q. What were they? — A. One old lady stated to me, when I saw her at the levee, that she was from Louisiana, and that while she and another colored woman were on their way to the boat to come to Kansas some white people met them and asked them if they were going to Kansas; they said that they were, and this white man said, "God damn it, you will get there some time or other." One of the women was seven months gone in a family way, and she said she was going to join her husband, when the white man pulled out his revolver and shot her; and the child came to life there and he took it and mashed its brains out. There were other cases of the same kind which were stated to me by various parties.

Q. If you know of any others please state them. — A. Some of them stated that they were not allowed the freedom of voting as they pleased; that men commanded them to vote, and being Democrats, compelled them to vote the Democratic ticket and they had to do it or lose their employment; others stated that they had brothers who were shot for political offenses or else offenses in the shape of a quarrel with a white man.

Q. What did they say as to the expense of making a living in the South? — A. They stated that they endeavored to live as economically as possible, and notwithstanding the fact that they did that and raised good crops, at the end of the season they would have nothing left except probably five, ten, or fifteen dollars.

Q. Did they state anything as to the charges made against them for provisions at the stores? — A. Yes, sir; I jotted down some of their statements on that point. Some of them stated that they were charged for tobacco 50 and 60 cents per plug for ordinary chewing and smoking tobacco.

Q. Can you give us some of the prices charged in Saint Louis? — A. Yes, sir; in our place I should say that 15 to 20 cents per plug would be the price.

By Mr. VANCE:

Q. Did you see what kind of tobacco they had? — A. Yes; it was black Navy tobacco, I think they call it. For flour they were charged per barrel—and small sized ones, fourth grade flour—eight to ten dollars per barrel, the same flour which could be bought in our city for three and four dollars a barrel. For corn meal they paid five and six dollars a barrel, which could be bought in our place for two dollars and a half or three dollars. Ordinary bacon was 30 and 40 cents per pound; in our place, 8 or 9 cents, while in larger quantities it is cheaper. Molasses was a dollar and twenty five cents to a dollar and a half per gallon; in our place it is 50 to 60 or 75 cents. Whisky, the ordinary farm whisky of the commonest kind, was from 75 cents to a dollar a pint; up in our place it is 25 cents or cheaper. Coffee was 50 or 75 cents a pound; only 12 or 15 in our place. Sugar was twenty-five to fifty cents, while in our place it is eight to twelve. For the rent of land they would pay from seven to nine and ten dollars per acre. I do not know the value of the land, as I have never been south of Mason and Dixon's line.

Q. Where were these people from? — A. Some were from along the river and some back in the back counties.

Q. Did they state what they paid for transportation? — A. They told us from Vicksburg to Saint Louis they paid three to four dollars a head for deck passage.

Q. I mean, did they say to you what they paid for the transportation of flour and meal? — A. They charged from 75 cents to a dollar per barrel from our town to Vicksburg.

Q. That is the point to which provisions for these people would have to be taken? — A. Yes, sir.

Q. About how many of these people do you think you talked to? — A. Well, sir, at very nearly every arrival I have had conversations with persons among them. In our board rooms, at the office, we talk with them in the presence of several members of the board, and also in the presence of the vice-president and corresponding secretary. Generally I would go down to the river and correspond for them and act with the committee on transportation and arrival. I questioned them with a view to finding out the causes of their leaving their homes in the South.

Q. How many have you talked with? — A. I should say between six hundred and a thousand.

Q. Please state if there were any discrepancies in their statements to you. — A. Their statements were singularly unanimous, bearing to the same point, and notwithstanding their coming from different sections of the South, in Louisiana and Mississippi, it was always a repetition of the same statement.

Q. When they were suffering on the wharf from cold and hunger, did they express any desire to go back to the South? — A. No, sir. In our capacity as a board of relief we had received letters from different places in the South asking us if we could supply farmers with hands, as they were scarce. We tried to get some of them to return, and consulted with them on the subject, and they said they would rather go into the open prairie and starve there than go back to the South to stand the impositions that were put on them down there; and every member of them went through, with some few exceptions. I do not think there were two hundred of them who went back South.

Q. Efforts were made, however, to get them to go back? — A. Yes; there were. There were several firms there dealing in the cotton brokerage business, and several members were active in trying to get them to go back; but they did not succeed very well. At the meetings held in the churches when we were trying to raise contributions, they came and made speeches, endeavoring to advise these people to return to the South, but they could make no impression upon them.

Q. Were there any efforts made to help them return? — A. Yes, sir; they offered to pay their fare if they would return South.

Q. What was the answer given to such offers? — A. They would not go. They said they were in a land of freedom and were going to stay there.

Q. And the cold and hunger had no effect to change their minds? — A. No, sir; they were not considered anything in comparison with the injustice they suffered in the South.

Q. Did you talk to any of them who were returning home? — A. There was a statement that some of them were returning. They were stated to be going on the James Howard, and I went on the boat, but did not see any of them there. I did learn, though, that several families had passed on their return down South, but I did not meet any of them.

Q. I understood you to say that your committee had tried to induce them to go back to some points in the South? — A. You understood me correctly. We did. We said that we could refer them to certain business men who would pay their transportation to any point in the South, in Mississippi and Louisiana, where they wanted to go. In fact we wanted to test their sincerity. Seeing their condition, and that they were enduring the same hardships that the fathers of this country endured in discovering and settling this country, we desired to test the honesty of their statements, and the real truth of their determination.

Q. What was their answer to your endeavors? — A. They said whoever wanted to go could go; but one of them said he was about to bounce me for suggesting it to him; but I laughed it off, and gave him a quarter. He said to me that he would not return South under any consideration. He said, they were suffering, it was true, but not more than they did in the South. I

should say from their experience at the time of their arrival in our city, and
what they endured in Kansas, it led me to believe that whatever suffering
they might encounter in getting away from Louisiana and Mississippi, they
were fully prepared to meet it.

Q. Did they say anything about political motives involved in their moving? —
A. No, sir; there was no political movement in it. We understood that the
press had circulated things in the South trying to show that it was political;
also circulars were distributed in the South saying if they would go to Kansas
they would find themselves in possession of forty acres of land, a mule,
and farm utensils. Out of the number that I talked to they all said that
nothing of the kind was said to them, but on account of the injustice and
political wrongs they were subject to, they had decided to leave. That was
their unanimous statement.

77 Toward a New Community

The prospects of the migrants were bleak. While the openness of the wide prairies and the unstilled wind and the huge sky all signalled a freedom vastly different from the closely settled and slave-heritage-bound land of the South, it was nonetheless often a stark and brutal land. The new all-black communities that emerged did not spring up overnight but came slowly through suffering and work. That they emerged at all, though, was the mark of success. The sense of cooperation in the colonizing effort is perhaps a chief legacy of the experience. But another legacy came in the South; there the efforts to move were often met with intimidation and violence which proved counterproductive, spurring others to relocate. When this happened, those proponents of the market identified normally as the "best" citizens and leaders of communities in the South began sometimes to take a stand against such violence. Because this violence drove black people from the South, it tightened the market in labor and presented a real, material threat to planters and businessmen. This development, a division in Southern society, was not new, but it was becoming more accentuated. The "friend," at least in terms of seeing that the black stayed in the South and was subjected to less brutal treatment, was more apt to be the commercially alert businessman than the white farmer who had shared similar experiences. This made sense given the market conception of freedom harbored by the businessmen and the leaders of the "New South" and their sensitivity to the dollar rather than to heritage or color and also given the preference demonstrated by those businessmen for cheaper black labor that could be bossed and exploited with less outward friction than the white cropper or tenant. It may be that the black cropper was coming to be seen as a competitor in a market society thus leading to friction between poor white and black. Or, it may be more accurate to suggest that the poor white, victimized by the new market society and averse to the organization and values of such a market orientation, attempted to restore a paternalistic society or at least a society governed more by heredity and color in the allocation of work and rewards than an ethereal and illusory market.

Source: "The Colored Exodus," Harper's Weekly, 23 (July 5, 1879), 533-34.

Past experience shows that the emigration of Southern negroes toward the West has not resulted unfavorably. Whatever cause for alarm there may be in the vast proportions assumed by the present exodus, there can be no doubt that small bands have profited by their removal from the scene of their late bondage. One or two instances will show that as Western pioneers and colonists the negroes have proved themselves possessed of energy, endurance, and ability to provide for their own maintenance. Thirty miles northwest of Kinsley, and twenty-five miles north of Dodge City, on the Atcheson, Topeka, and Santa Fe Railroad, is a flourishing negro settlement. The location is 280 miles from the east line of the State of Kansas, and 120 miles from the western border. It is far out upon the great plains, which until lately were supposed to be uninhabitable. This colony was formed near Lexington and Harrodsburg, Kentucky. Its location was selected in 1877, by a committee of their own number sent out for the purpose.

The colony arrived at Kinsley March 24, 1878, 107 in number, and immediately commenced their settlement. Additions have since been made to the number of about fifty. About fifty homesteads have been taken, besides a few timber claims, and all have been improved. But one has been abandoned—that in the case of a young man who left and came to Topeka. Their houses are chiefly of sod and dug-outs. There are one stone house and two frame houses. Some of the colonists have teams, and such ploughed and planted last spring, raising a little corn and considerable of garden vegetables—potatoes, beans, onions, melons, etc. Sorghum and millet were raised for feed for stock. A large proportion of these colonists, as they came with little or no means, have had to earn their own living at the same time that they were making their homestead improvements. Being clear out on the frontier, this has been difficult. They have had to go to the railroad towns, or near them—in some instances fifty miles or more away—for work. In the wheat harvest they found the best time for employment. But work has been scarce, as much time having been spent in searching for employment as was given to labor when obtained. Wages have ranged from seventy-five cents to $1.50 per day, the latter price being paid only in harvest. The people have, however, been healthy, two deaths only having occurred. They make no complaint of the climate, enduring all the hardships that fall to their share bravely.

In Graham County, Kansas, is located a negro colony called Nicodemus. It consists of about 125 families, comprising about 700 souls, scattered over an area twelve miles in length by six in breadth. Nicodemus has its post-office, store, hotel, land-office, etc., and, like nearly all new towns, aspires to the possession of the county seat. The colony had its first start in August of 1877, a few families locating at that time. In October and November of the same year large accessions were made by the arrival of new immigrants, who, with the usual want of forethought of the race, pushed out to the then extreme frontier at the commencement of winter, in almost utter lack of the means to shelter, feed, or clothe themselves during the winter. With the opening of the spring of 1878 more came. They were mainly from the farming regions of Kentucky and Tennessee. In the beginning the colonists, as a rule, were nearly destitute of means, a few only bringing either teams or money. They located on government homesteads, and set about to provide themselves with shelter, which was easily and cheaply secured by building dug-outs and sod houses, roofed with poles and brush, with a covering of earth sufficient to keep out the rain. As board floors were regarded as an unnecessary luxury, all the lumber required was for a door and its frame and one window. A fireplace at one end in most cases takes the place of a stove, and serves the double purpose of heating and cooking. Coming as most of them did in the autumn, but one resource was open to them in order to support life during the winter, and that was an appeal to the charity of the people of the State. This was resorted to, and agents of the colony, duly authenticated, canvassed the older-settled portions of the State for aid which was freely given in provisions, seed grain, clothing, etc., the Kansas Pacific Railroad generously transporting all such contributions without charge. Many of the men and women sought and obtained work in the towns along the line of the railroad and in the settled counties east, and by their labor aided to carry the colony through the winter. With the spring of 1878 every effort was made to put all the ground possible under cultivation; but the great practical difficulty was that they had but few teams, and these not in good serviceable condition, for want of proper feed during the winter. But every body went to work. Those who had teams broke for themselves and others. Some were able to get a little breaking done for them by outside parties. Those who could do no better went to work digging up the ground with the spade and grub-hoe, determined to make a crop in some way; and some families (the women helping) got two or three acres in crop by this slow and laborious process. At the present time the land under cultivation will average about six or seven acres to every family. The solicitation for aid has continued all along to some extent, but recently a public meeting was called, and after full consideration of the subject it was decided to discontinue the colony organization. A series of resolutions was passed thanking the people of the State for the aid that had been so freely given, and stating that henceforth no further aid would be solicited, as it was believed that from that time the colony, with proper effort and industry, could be self-supporting.

One of the most important features of the movement of the negroes toward Kansas, and the proofs given that they have found a suitable asylum for their wretchedness in that hospitable State, is the effect had upon the agricultural interests of the South. A thorough feeling of alarm has taken possession of the white population. In many cases, it is said, the planters have declined to make arrangements for raising crops during the ensuing season on account of the uncertainties that attend the situation, and the doubts whether there will be laborers enough to take care of the harvest. In certain sections public sentiment is actually aroused against the modern amusement of "bulldozing," and mass-meetings have been held denouncing it as an unworthy practice. At Caseyville,

Mississippi, a gathering of the citizens to consider the difficulties of the present situation resulted in the following resolutions, which forcibly suggest the sudden reformation of a culprit who finds that his next meal depends upon his good behavior:

"*Whereas*, That for two years or more certain citizens of this and adjoining counties have been committing acts of lawlessness disgraceful to the civilization of this age; and whereas, this community, hitherto peaceful, has been thrown into the utmost consternation by an act of certain lawless characters acting in the night-time, and unknown to the good citizens of this community, to wit, the burning of Mr. Thomas Erwin's gin, to his great damage: and *whereas*, within a short time after the committal of said act, this community was shocked by a greater act of violence (seeming in retaliation of said act), to wit, the whipping and otherwise ill treating certain colored citizens, and the assassination of another at the dead hour of night—the assassin's chosen hour; and whereas, divers burning, whipping, and ordering of colored citizens in various parts of this county to leave their homes and crops have occurred, to the great injury of the country at large; and *whereas*, it is the sense of this meeting that those lawless characters are citizens of adjoining counties who invade this county at night, and commit these lawless acts, and return to their homes before daylight, leaving the stigma of their acts to rest on the good citizens of this county; and *whereas*, we admit these citizens (styled bulldozers) may have had some cause for acts hitherto committed, by being deprived of their homes by a system of extortion under the lien laws of this State, which are erroneous and bad as class legislation, favoring one class of citizens and utterly ruining another greatly in the majority, yet this is no justification for acts of punishing and assassinating unoffending colored citizens; and *whereas*, we have waited patiently for the courts to bring to condign punishment those lawless characters, and having been sadly deceived by seeing them, instead of being visited by swift justice, turned loose on straw bonds or no bonds at all, at great expense to the county, already nearly bankrupt; therefore, be it

"*Resolved*, 1. That it is the sense of this meeting that such acts must be stopped.

"2. That we look with indignation on all lawless acts by any and all citizens who have not the fear of the law before their eyes.

"3. That it is the sense of this meeting that all such lawless persons be requested to desist from such lawless acts in the future.

"4. That it is the sense of this meeting that we look with contempt on the party or parties who wrote the notice posted at this place, near Caseyville, warning the good citizens of this community from doing their duty."

Action of this kind on the part of the citizens of Caseyville or other communities unfortunately comes too late to stop the progress of the negroes toward their land of promise. Threats and arguments are without efficacy, and the exodus goes steadily on. Even the Southern newspapers, which have been doing their best to induce people to believe that the tide of emigration is stayed, have finally concluded to abandon their policy of profitless mendacity. The New Orleans *Times* says:

"Our newspapers all through the lower valley, our Washington, St. Louis, and Kansas correspondents, for a month past have been repeating that the exodus has ceased; that the negroes are miserable in Kansas, and are coming home; that every body now admits the movement was induced by land speculators, and such twaddle and nonsense. The truth is that the threatened departure of the great body of the colored laborers from several portions of the State is still impending. The truth is that there were more who left this city last week than have returned to the entire South from Kansas. Why in the world can we not be honest and truthful to ourselves about this matter? Why not recognize the evil, acknowledge its causes, appreciate its seriousness, understand the necessity of averting and checking the movement which threatens to impoverish the fairest portions of the State?"

At the same time, while the Southern planters are uttering their wail, and the Southern newspapers alternately denying and acknowledging the fact that their industrial population is rapidly passing away from them, Kansas is holding out her hospitable arms, and making the best arrangements she can for the reception of the poor fugitives who launch themselves upon her in such overwhelming numbers. A certain amount of alarm is naturally felt at the approach of such a vast horde of suffering and impoverished human beings; but as yet the opposition to their coming has taken no decided shape, and Senator Ingalls undoubtedly expressed the sentiments of the people of his State when he said: "I do not think there is any class prejudice or any feeling of hostility to the colored people that would prevent their being cordially welcomed as an element of our population. We have an area of about 81,000 square miles, comprising 55,000,000 of acres of arable land, not more than one-tenth of which has been reduced to cultivation. The remainder is open to settlement under the Homestead Act, requiring five years' residence before title can be secured, and I am inclined to think we could absorb 100,000 of these people without serious injury or inconvenience."

78 A Foreboding Prophecy

Although the market seemed to generate greater problems in race relations, it could also present a hope for equality, albeit an equality loaded with the assumptions of the marketplace. In the following excerpt from his 1889 book *The Prosperity of the South Dependent Upon the Elevation of the Negro*, Lewis H. Blair argued that the South needed to develop the institutions and habits of the market in order to escape from poverty. A central theme in this transformation was the acceptance of an individual according to his merit, as evidenced by his productivity, rather than according to his race. In so arguing Blair made explicit the attack on what he termed a caste society and the defense of a market society. And it was exactly this posture that enraged many Southerners whose commitment to a system designed exclusively to generate greater profits and to a society dominated by economics fell considerably short of the gospel of the New South that Blair, Henry Grady, and others espoused. And Blair made no pretense of placing the welfare of blacks in the first priority. The first and main goal throughout was economic growth, and as he put it, an elevated black man could be more useful to whites. He made the choice plain: acceptance of the market or oppression of the black man. If one were to resist the market and oppose, for whatever reason, the competitive and profit-oriented features of the system, Blair suggested the only alternative was to oppress blacks. That this choice had also been so narrowed by the elite is significant for its own implications in its time. Yet there is a further significance. In 1963 C. Vann Woodward edited a new printing of Blair's book, calling it *A Southern Prophecy*. He saw Blair's argument as an attack on "injustice of any kind" and dedicated the edition to President Lyndon Johnson, thereby demonstrating the incredible persistence of the market conception of freedom.

In the portion of Blair's argument printed below several particular points can be discerned. First, Blair's prefatory emphasis on the economic imperative for the elevation of the Negro reveals a sys-tematic assumption about the nature of man (indeed, as opposed to the nature of woman); according to Blair, man is an economic animal driven by material desires even in his receptivity to moral arguments. Second, that assumption is undermined by Blair's own logic. He notes that blacks are too idle, that other values than economic benefit dominate them, such as their "political and religious gatherings," and that they consequently need the discipline of education. Indeed, in the scheme of progress and civilization that he presents it appears increasingly that the economic drives are less and less natural to man but must come through an education and efficient organization centering on the gospel of wealth. Moreover he develops a critique of caste society based on its inherent tendency to inhibit hopes of material improvement by denying a market in labor. In this he sug-gests not only that such hope is a necessary incentive to efficient labor but that if the black man is not more productive, "and thus an instrument of our own prosperity, he will continue as he is, a depredator upon others' industry and a consumer of wealth." Since Blair had gone to great lengths to associate various psychological and social qualities with the market—pride, self-esteem, and inde-pendence—the significance of this observation, or fear, is enormous. By the logic of the market those people who operate within it, seeking however modest or grand a reward, seeking survival or riches, could well nurture a growing antagonism toward those whose culture and circumstances place them outside the market and thus even in an apparently privileged situation. On the other hand, as Blair again suggests, to reject the market system could mean for whites the further degradation of the blacks.

Source: Lewis H. Blair, *The Prosperity of the South Dependent Upon the Elevation of the Negro* (Richmond, 1889), pp. 27-28, 48-51, 75-78.

Although justice—and we should always bear in mind that justice is a stern virtue that will sooner or later avenge herself upon her violators, though at the same time she never fails to honor and reward those who respect her require-ments—although justice demands that the whites elevate the Negroes, for in the light of morality we stand responsible for their welfare, their elevation will not be advocated on any such ground, nor on the ground of religion either, but simply on economic grounds, on the ground of advantage to the whites. Just as we would urge the South to improve its animals, tools, methods of planting, etc., so that it may derive the more good from their labor and capital, so we urge the elevation of the Negroes, because the better men and citizens they are the more we, the whites, can in the end make out of them.

That is a very hard doctrine, perhaps, but we must remember that facts themselves are hard things, and that they never think of accommodating them-selves to either our desires or our fancies. We would like a more "comforting" (as the women would say) doctrine, did not reading, observation and experience show that morality and even religion are very poor advocates, unless they can show to their listeners that material benefit is on their side. Convinced, therefore, as I must be that benefit is the only safe and sound ground to base an argument upon (for if a thing does not benefit or afford us pleasure in some way, how can it interest us?) I shall address all my arguments to prove not only that the prosperity of the South will be increased by, but that it is dependent upon, the elevation of the Negro, and if it is not so shown, then this effort will be in vain, and if it cannot be so shown, then all effort to elevate the Negro will be in vain. If the Southern people cannot be shown that his elevation is for their interest, then the Negro must forever grovel, but if it is demonstrated as we go along that his elevation is essential to our welfare, then as sensible people we should throw aside the thickly encrusted prepossessions or prejudices of centuries and hasten the day when we shall have made the Negro a free man (for as long as he labors under any but natural disabilities he is little better than a serf), and therefore a worthy and competent co-worker in the race for prosperity, which we have long seen through a glass darkly, but which, like an *ignis fatuus*, has eluded our grasp, and which will continue to as long as the Negro is degraded and without hope of rising above his present status—a status of perpetual inferiority and subordination.

* * *

But the question will be very generally asked, Why elevate the Negro at all? Is he not now good enough to obey us obsequiously, and to make our corn, our cotton, our tobacco, our rice, and our sugar? What more do we want of him? The reply is that if the Negro is forever to remain simply the instrument for doing our menial and manual work, for plowing and sowing, for driving mules, for worming tobacco and picking cotton, he is already too elevated, and he should be still further humbled and degraded. In his present condition he has some of the ideas and aspirations of a freeman, some desires for education, and he has almost entire control of his personal movements. He works when it suits him, but then he may idle at the crisis of a crop; but as we cannot compel him with the lash to work, he is on the whole not a profitable laborer either for himself or for any employer. To make him efficient, and to make him work the crop at the proper time, in spite of the attractions of political and religious gatherings, the overseer with the lash must be ever before his eyes. To allow the Negro to remain as he is, is for him a still "lower deep" in the social scale, and in his descent he drags us down with him.

But if the Negro is to become an intelligent voter, is to be a citizen capable of taking a sensible part in the affairs of his community, and to be a valuable co-worker in adding to the wealth of the State, then we have a vast deal to do in order to elevate him. To make him our assistant in the production of wealth, the Negro must be made to work, or he must be induced by ambition, by the hope of enjoying in full the fruits of his labors, to work steadily and intelligently. If we are not willing to elevate him, we should set to work resolutely and deliberately to manacle both his mind and limbs, and to cow him, so that a little white child shall control a thousand. We will then at least get enough out of him to supply his few physical wants and to enable us to live in idleness and comparative comfort, which is not now the case. But if there is no hope of our ever being able to do this, what is the next best thing for us to do for our own good? Make a man of him. But this can be done only by means of education and other fostering influences, by cultivating his self-respect, by inspiring his hope, by letting him see that the land of his birth is as much his country as it is that of the wealthiest and haughtiest white. Now he is not only an alien, but an inferior—in reality a serf, in the land of his nativity.

We must trample, or we must elevate; to maintain the *status quo* is impossible. To trample is to perpetuate and intensify the poverty and stagnation under which we groan; to elevate is to make the South rich, happy and strong.

* * *

The South ... is a veritable land of caste, and its chains hang heavily upon those of the lowest caste. In the palmy days of slavery, when one man held in his hand the lives of a thousand, there were several castes; but now, though there are still many social and other gradations, there are primarily only two castes.

Then there was first in rank and influence the caste of educated and wealthy planters, who assumed the airs and imitated the manners of the most exclusive aristocracy of England and France, whence their families had immigrated. In Virginia, Louisiana and South Carolina, but especially in the last state, many were highly cultivated and intellectual, were polished and refined to a high degree, the men being elegant and chivalric, and the women charming and beautiful. In them we beheld all that was noble and attractive in the system of caste. Next came an intermediate caste of planters. They were frequently men of wealth, but without education and of little refinement, and though they met the first caste on nearly equal but yet deferential terms on the hustings and court green, the families of the two castes never thought of visiting socially. Then came the overseer caste. This caste, usually hard and heartless, was composed mainly of men who had been overseers, but who had acquired a few slaves, and had set up for themselves. Although the men mingled on semi-equal terms with those next above them, they were generally looked down upon, if not despised; and their families, as a rule, never thought of visiting socially the families of those above them. Finally came the "poor white" caste, possessed of no Negroes, but of a few acres, and despised alike by whites and blacks.

The Negroes, of course, were lower still, but they were hardly considered as human beings. They were regarded pretty much like horses and cattle, simply as instruments like them, to enable the other castes to live, some in elegance, some in ease, but all in comfort without thought and without toil. They were treated, too, pretty much as cattle; many, when the masters were kind, treated mildly and their physical necessities carefully provided for; and many, when the masters were harsh and brutal, treated with cruelty and sometimes worked or beaten to death, it being a maxim with some cotton planters that it was cheaper to work a Negro to death and buy another than to work him reasonably and prolong his life.

But now, in the new order of things, all these castes have become amalgamated into one, and a new caste has been formed of those who were formerly considered too low to form a caste at all, and Southern society is now virtually divided into two castes. In the first caste are merged indiscriminately gentleman, farmer, oveseer, poor white, and each and every one of these, regardless of education, worth, refinement, decency or morality, belongs to this class simply by reason of a white skin. The second caste is composed promiscuously of all who have a black skin and all related to them, however remotely; and all who are thus marked, however cultured and refined they may be, however able and however excellent, are confined as by fate to this caste, and are not permitted to throw off its galling chains; and society, by its inexorable verdict, decrees that the meanest, lowest, and most degraded of the first caste are, *ipso facto*, the irreversible and perpetual superiors of the best, highest and ablest of the second caste.

Hope cannot exist, certainly cannot flourish, under such a weight. If he is to remain forever a "nigger," an object of undisguised contempt, even to the lowest whites, the Negro will naturally say to himself, Why strive, why labor, why practice painful self-denial in order to rise, if I am to derive no good from my effort? On the contrary, he will not exert himself, but will sink into despondency, and instead of becoming a net producer, and thus an instrument of our own prosperity, he will continue as he is, a depredator upon others' industry and a consumer of wealth. The South can never become prosperous, with its laboring population bereft of hope. Without hope the proudest Anglo-Saxon sinks into despair—much more the helpless Negro, who is little more than a child.

79 A Slave Line Rather Than a Color Line

That there was indeed another option available besides racial equality through competition and market relations or besides racial suppression through acceptance of market values and resentment toward those who seemed to resist, was evident in the following letters from workers, black and white, to the *United Mine Workers' Journal* in 1892 and 1893. These letters are important for their common theme, the possibility and often necessity of interracial cooperation to address common problems, and also for the diversity in which that position is developed. The perspectives range from the common heritage of blacks and whites as serfs or slaves to the practical necessity of cooperation against the same enemy and system of corporate greed. They provide examples of interracial brotherhood as well as lectures on the need to overcome prejudice. The recurring point so often, however, is simply that a divided community of workers benefits neither whites nor blacks but only the owners and that racial prejudice and competition serve only the interests of a system that exploits both. Whether the workers found hope in the United Mine Workers or the Knights of Labor or simply in the actions of their fellows in the cause, their affirmation of relations properly conceived as brotherhood and cooperation indicates a rejection of the market system itself.

Source: United Mine Workers' Journal, dates of publication noted with each selection.

[April 14, 1892]
... I am an Afro-American myself, and have lived all my life in the South but the last eight months, and if the Afro-Americans are union men for principle, as I believe they are, then it is more than the most of the whites were when it

became necessary to remove a colored mine foreman and checkweigher, as all of the power that the president and secretary-treasurer of District 19 could not avoid it. You are right, no true union man will stop reading the JOURNAL, but what we want is to test them and get the tried and true ones. My object in speaking of the Memphis and all other such outrages was to call organized labor's attention to them as both parties have said by their ways, that they cannot bring the violators to justice, while if it was for the benefit of Mammon, and to oppress labor all the detectives of the county and the State militia to assist them would be brought out as at this time in Tennessee, and as to the votes that they get don't deserve them by one-half. Brother W. R., would the United Mine Workers or the Knights of Labor be guilty of passing a law as is being done in Kentucky and in force in Tennessee that will not let an Afro-American ride in the same car as a white person, even though one is President and the other Secretary-Treasurer of District 19? I am sure it would not and you are welcome to write all you can and I shall take pleasure to read it. I am also proud that you can fill the position you have, also one that is higher than the pick or shovel either. As to the declaration of independence it is so in theory only and I trust that you will read the Knights of Labor platform before you act critic, as I stand upon Section 1 and then all that is just. Now what is needed most is principle and discipline and in conclusion, brothers, buy and read a few Afro-American papers, to see just what the negro has to fight, as I believe that brothers are so far behind they don't know how to start to catch up from the resolution that was tabled at Columbus.

Willing Hands.

* * *

[May 5, 1892]

... I will make this statement, that there is no color line at all, but simply the slave line; and, to sustain my assertion, I will say that I have known men and women of other nationalities who were nearly as black, a great deal more ignorant, and four-fold more degraded than the very meanest "nigger" I ever saw, yet they never had that infernal curse of slavery upon them, and they were received by some of the kickers against the black man with open arms as their social equals. "Oh, consistency thou art a jewel." Now, the fallacy of such things is really sickening to a person of any thought, no matter whether he be black or white.

Just to illustrate the matter I will suppose that a citizen (white or colored) of the United States should go to Africa and happen to be nabbed as was the colored man and become a slave for years and should then escape and get back to his native heath, would he be received as one below the general order of humanity or as a hero? A hero by all means. Well, why is not the colored man as much a hero who escaped the tyranny of slavery in this country? Now I will make another assertion, viz., that some of the smartest men we have in this country are men whose skins are black, whether so by nature or by climatic influences for centuries I will not discuss, but I say that a few days ago I heard a colored man illustrate the cause of his condition in a manner that for simplicity of understanding and correctness of detail was ahead of any definition of the cause I ever head. He said: "I was a bound slave, my master controlled me and my wages, he was a smart man and they could not fool him. Now I am a free slave, I am ignorant and at the mercy of the rich man and cannot help myself; they made me so on purpose to rob me." But, he said, "through organization I know I can better my condition," although, he continued, "no man can be a true Knight of Labor man and be either a Democrat or Republican." Now I would like to know which is the best and smartest man, this poor old slave or the white gentlemen who on election day will carry around a body full of whiskey and hurrah for some low-down drunken ward politician? If I was not afraid of getting on dangerous ground I would say that in a great many places the worst line that is drawn is the political line. When men who are white do not like to sit in the same assembly with the colored man, yet are glad to welcome him into the political club room just before election day and pat him on the back and call him a good fellow and then after the election; my Lord! why they just can't stand a nigger. Another thing let me tell you, but I want you to remember not to say anything about it, the party that is in the majority or minority is the one that is most likely to do this. The K. of L. declares that it abolishes races, creeds and colors and the man who can't stand that kind of doctrine, let him just get up and git. Now, I will say in conclusion that I would like for some one to tell me the difference between a negro who has seven-eighths of white blood in him and a white man with one-eighth of negro blood? " 'Tis place not blood that makes the man," and if we could have a few transpositions of souls or at least the cultivated brain of James G. Blaine placed in the being of a colored man who had been blacklegging and vice versa, what would be the consequences? Why you would have a colored man with capabilities to be secretary of state and a white man who would blackleg. So I can say let politics go to thunder, stick to the principles of the K. of L., do all we can for one another, irrespective of race, creed or color. If we do this when we come to the jumping off place we will most likely go to a country where in reality there is no color line, if they do think there is one here.

Wm. Camack.

* * *

[June 9, 1892]
When visiting this community previously I found a compact, well-united and disciplined body of workingmen enjoying the privileges and conditions incident to well organized communities; contented and happy enjoying equal advantages, a means at hand to rectify any disadvantages or inequalities existing, no trouble with the free click, no favorites to whom the boon of free click must be granted and their word had no charm nor portent in them days, for the law of common rights, equal privileges and the brotherhood of miners, was the rule by which miners measured their conduct to each other, and man scorned any advantages secured at a disadvantage to his fellow-man: "Then man to man was true," then was a prosperous community, all were happy, all basking in the sunshine of prosperity, all made an attempt to better their condition. Every man's ambition was to better his condition socially and financially, and with that end in view land lots were purchased by the hundreds, homes were built, the people ex-

pected to make of the community their permanent dwelling place so long as life lasted. It was their ambition to labor for the means to make themselves homes, while, if not imposing and grand should at least be comfortable. They had a right to expect this. Had not men who counted their wealth by the millions, men who were honored by the fellow-men and who were trusted and looked up to as the very personification of business rectitude and commercial honesty invested a considerable portion of their wealth there? Had they not issued manifesto after manifesto drawing attention to the superior advantage offered by them to investors? Had they not proclaimed how comparatively easy it was for an industrious community to build up a very Eden of comfort and enjoyment under the beneficial and munificent plans adopted by them? Hundreds of our fellow craftsmen under the promise of good and steady work invested their all, little dreaming that the unwritten law concerning the conditions under which all the promised blessings and prosperity was to be secured was the deprivation of every privilege as a man, that any independence on his part was to be the sign for dismissal from his employment or an introduction of a system of espionage so tyrannical on his action that his further continuing in their employment was an impossibility. And to further assist in the work of destruction, men who were willing to lend themselves to the schemes of employers were selected as the recipients of free-click and these vampires readily caught at the opportunity to injure their fellowman, and, like Judas of old, "these fellows whose every true interest lay in being true to their fellow-miners, forgot every obligation, obliterated every consideration, save the fact that they were the recipients of the favors of the employers, not because they were loved better than others, but because they were less manly than others and could be used for a purpose that no true man could be used for, namely, the disruption and destruction of the miners hopes, their methods and plans lay in creating factions among them that would prevent that degree of unification that could successfully cope with the needs of the mining community. Well, do these people understand that a house divided against itself cannot stand! When will the miners and mine workers realize the fact that factional fights of all kinds must cease and the house united so that it may offer effective resistance to unjust encroachment from any quarter offered, whether it be from the free-click quarter or whether it be from national and religious prejudices, which it is evident is being done in this community. Under our American constitution there is no room for such prejudices to exist, there should be no room in our craft affairs for such prejudices, and where they do or might exist they can only do so at the expense of the craft, and he who would stir them up whether employer or employee must be regarded as the worst enemy of our craft, and dealt with accordingly. I am reminded when such tales are told me of the man who having been caught with a chicken on his person which he had undoubtedly purloined, upon giving his explanation of how it got on his person said that the man who put it there was no friend of his, and my fellow-craftsmen the recipients of free-click at the expense of your more manly brother miner, the man who given it to you is not your friend any more than he is your friend when stirring up your national or religious prejudices. Twenty to one he don't care a fig what your national pride or religious prejudices are and in his sleeve is laughing at your silly, senseless action in allowing yourselves to be betrayed unto factions, which gives him all the advantages and you all the disadvantages. Cease giving him gratification by creating factions among you. Close up your ranks as of old; direct your efforts against a common enemy. Let there be no Irishman, no Welshman, no Scotchman, no Italian, no German, no Bohemian and no Polander; no Catholic, no Presbyterian, no Baptist and no Methodist with their peculiar prejudices, but let there be one brotherhood of miners under a fatherhood of God, who made all men equal in their privileges, no matter what is our individual preference as to methods of worship. Let the glad anthem of unification be sung by a united craftsmen all over the mining communities of this country and if the reign of peace and the millenium is to be established when each man can sit under his own vine and fig tree it will be when the factions cease from troubling and the disrupter and designer is laid at rest under the contempt and ridicule of the regenerated craftsmen, secured by the unification of the whole and let the miners of Spring Valley and every other valley, as well as mountain top and plain, come unto the chariot of organization and it will carry you to the Mecca of success without doing violence to any of our national religions and denominational prejudices. Then will the bright sun of prosperity cast its beneficient rays upon us, filling all our homes with comforts and blessing. So may it be.

Thomas W. Davis.

* * *

[June 9, 1892]
. . . a word about the traveling accommodations in this part of the country for one of my race. I will say that had it not been for Brother E. E. Page, traveling salesman of the West Virginia Cut and Dry Tobacco Co., of Wheeling, and Brother Moran, this boy would have seen a hard time of it on last Saturday and Sunday, on my way from Pocahontas to the New river regions. I will try to give your many readers a short description of it: We left Pocahontas at 3:30 p.m. on Saturday, May 28, and arrived at Peterstown at about six o'clock, in time for supper. After washing and getting ready for eating as I thought, the colored man who worked there came to me and told me that he would show me my room, and just to think taking me to my bed before eating my supper. Well, I went with him, and where do you suppose he took me? Away, away from the main building, out in the wood yard, to an old dilapidated log cabin. I looked in and saw the bed. I turned to the man and asked him was it intended that I should sleep there? He said yes, that he slept there. I told him that he might sleep there but I wouldn't, that I would walk to Lowell, 30 miles away, that night first. About that time Brother Page came and took an observation of my bedchamber. He went away and held a consultation with the proprietor, which resulted in my getting about the best bed in the house and I would not be afraid to bet that I am the first negro to eat at the table in that man's dining room. Well, the next morning we started for Lowell across the mountains in a hack, we got to Red Sulphur Springs about 10 o'clock and stopped for dinner, but I was told that I could not eat in that house. My dinner was prepared outside. I lost my appetite and told him no, I didn't want anything to eat. We started from there a little after two o'clock and arrived at Lowell at about 6 o'clock. Brother Moran asked the proprietor, could I get supper there, and his answer was, oh,

yes, but lo, when the bell rang and I was about to enter the dining-room, he caught me by the shoulder and told me to wait awhile. Brother Page turned around to him and told him that I was with them. He looked as though he was thunderstruck and of course I got my supper, but had it not been for those two white brothers I don't know but that I would have been by this time behind the bars, for I would have got tired had I been by myself and I don't know what the consequences would have been, for I felt like cursing and I would have used cuss words had I been by myself.

R. L. Davis

* * *

[May 25, 1893]

The race problem, or what aught or should be done with the negro, is a question that has seemingly been troubling the minds of a great number of the American people. It seems, however, plainly evident that he is a citizen of this country and should be treated as such. This, in my mind, is the only solution to the supposedly knotty problem. Less than thirty years ago he was given his freedom, and turned loose to the cold charities of the world without a dollar or an acre of land. Turned loose as he was is there any nation of people who has made such rapid progress as the Negro has made? No. Search all history and we find them not. During all these years in a said-to-be Christian and civilized country, notwithstanding the rapid strides he has made, he has been looked down upon by both the church and party politics, both of which should have been his best friends. Being poor and used to it he had to obey the divine injunction, viz.: To earn his bread by the sweat of his brow. In so doing we find him a great competitor with the American white labor. It is at this period that we find that the labor organizations or rather some of them, did that which no other organization had done, the church not even excepted, threw open their doors and admitted him as a full member with the same rights and privileges as his white brother. This, in our opinion, was the first or initiative step toward the equality of mankind, and we are sorry to say that until the present day the labor organizations are the only ones that recognize the Negro as an equal and as a man. Recognizing this to be true it is also true that some of our people have not yet gained enough confidence in his white brother as to trust him very far. And yet, is this very strange? When we notice the fact that right in our midst we have some as bitter enemies as anywhere else.

While we admit that our labor organizations are our best friends, it would be well to teach some of our white brothers that a man is a man no matter what the color of his skin may be. We have nothing but the best of words to say for labor organizations, and hope they may continue in the same line of actions, and we are confident that they will not only better the conditions of the working classes, but will also wipe out all class and race distinctions, and in the meantime the Negro will be found as loyal to labor organization as his white brother. It has been said that the Negro as a union man was a failure, but we are inclined to think that those words were uttered more from a prejudiced mind than as a truthful statement. Let us hope for better days for organized labor with the Negro in the ranks doing his share in the way of emancipating labor.

Confidence in each other is the thing lacking. This we can readily gain if we will but try. Believing as we do that all the reform needed must and will come through the medium of organized labor, it should be our proudest aim to do all that we can for the upholding of our organizations. Let us make them grand and perfect, and in so doing we will have accomplished a noble work, and by following this line of action we will solve the race problem, better the condition of the toiling millions and also make our country what it should be, a government of the people, for the people and by the people.

R. L. Davis.

80 The Other Side of the Lien

By the end of the nineteenth century the crop-lien system had marked the countryside in a seemingly permanent way. The contours of the change remained the same as those noted earlier (Documents 68 and 69) but not intensified or accelerated with one major exception. The whites were leaving the land in large numbers, forced out by low cotton prices, the foreclosure of their mortgages, inadequate educational facilities, or fear of blacks. The merchant's and landlord's dependence on black farm labor increased enormously. It was this ironic change in importance of the black labor supply that possibly accounts for the sensitivity of the merchant and the landlord each to the demands of the other. In this development the black again became the loser.

The following two letters indicate some of the contours of the evolution of the agricultural system in the South from the 1880s up to 1912. In 1912 Robert Preston Brooks, a professor at the University of Georgia, conducted a survey of agriculture in the state in which he was especially concerned with the crop-lien system. One of his respondents wrote Brooks his own observations as a merchant in Columbus, Georgia, since 1882. Apparently in response to an additional inquiry by Brooks the merchant supplied him further information in a second letter.

Source: R. Preston Brooks, "Inquiries Concerning Georgia Farms Since 1865," Vol. 1, Robert Preston Brooks Papers, Box no. 28, Rare Books and Manuscripts Department, University of Georgia Libraries.

POU BROTHERS COMPANY
WHOLESALE GROCERS
COLUMBUS, GEORGIA

1045-47 Broad Street

February 15, 1912.

Mr. R. P. Brooks,
  395 Lakeside St.
  Madison, Wis.

Dear Sir:

I am in receipt of the enclosed communication which I am returning to you, and which I suppose will be of no service to you in view of my inability to answer your questions. However, I have been an observer and a student to some extent, of the labor situation, and I am going to write you a letter that I would not write if you were not a southern man, as otherwise, it would be abscribed to prejudice.

I began clerking in the mercantile business nearly thirty years ago, and at that time there were but few negro tenants, so far as I know, and if they existed at that time, the goods which they consumed during the year were bought by the landlords and furnished to them. For the past fifteen or twenty years, the negro has been trading direct with the merchants and the custom has grown until it has almost become universal. The negro became first a cropper on shares as a step towards what you term in your inquiry, "a more independent position." Also largely due to the fact that if he hired himself out for wages, he alone drew wages and his family such pay for day work as they might secure on the farm. By running the crop himself, he could put his wife and children in his own crop.

The negro would rather be his own master on scant rations than to have a white man supervise him on full rations. Of course, I am not speaking of individuals, but as a class. In their effort to gain still "more independent position," they began demanding rent privileges where they could enforce it.

I will state parenthetically, that I do not rent to them, but they work crops on shares on my land under my agent's supervision.

The negro as a labor proposition from the white man's point of view, has been growing worse for fifteen years, and in the last five years, it has grown worse at a more rapid rate. The negro is a peculiar race unto himself. Any other race that I know of, will work a day for a dollar but they will work harder for $1.50 and they are willing to do night work to make it $2.00 or $2.50; but as a general thing, the negro worked six days in the week when wages were 40¢ a day. But if you give him a dollar a day, he will work about three days in the week.

The renter acquires a horse and buggy at the first opportunity and rides in the road until grass has grown almost as tall as his small crops, before he thinks it is necessary to begin to kill the grass. He is absolutely unreliable as regards a contract unless he is bound so that you can force him to his contract.

It may be entirely foreign to the subject matter of your inquiry, but in my judgment, and in which I am concurred in by all intelligent thinking white people, the negro lodge and the negro preacher is a great curse to the negro labor.

Two reasons have run the white people from the country. One was the extreme low price at which cotton ranged for years prior to the last two or three years, and the inability of the white people in the country to find opportunities to send their children to school, coupled with the fear that overhung all white men who had women and especially young girls in their families.

I wish I was in a position to give you the information asked for, instead of expressing these opinions on a different line which may be of no interest to you.

Yours truly,
/s/ Jno Dozier Pou

* * *

POU BROTHERS COMPANY
WHOLESALE GROCERS
COLUMBUS, GA

1045-47 Broad Street

March 1st, 1912.

Mr. R. P. Brooks
   395 Lakeside St.,
   Madison, Wis.

Dear Sir:

I am in receipt of your favor of February 26th. I never knew of any law existing which gave merchants any liens upon farmers' crops, even though they furnished the farmer provisions etc. to make that crop. Ever since I have known anything of such things, merchants have had the right to take mortgages upon growing crops, and the states differ somewhat in that law. A mortgage given on the first day of January for a crop in the state of Alabama is valid, but a mortgage given on a crop in Georgia before the seed have been placed in the ground is void. The condition results in the Georgia farmer being forced to pay two record fees. When he begins to buy his goods in the early part of the year, the merchant usually takes a mortgage upon his live stock which is duly recorded, and on or about the first of May, he takes a mortgage on his crop as further collateral on the original paper.

In Georgia the landlord has a statutory lien upon everything that a tenant raises on the place, and it is not necessary for him to take any kind of paper from his tenant, and if the tenant removes any part of the crop without the landlord's consent before he has settled with the landlord, then he is guilty of a misdemeanor.

I have never known of any law which protected merchants from taking mortgages upon the renter's crops, but regardless of any statement made by the tenant, and regardless of any kind of paper which he might give, the landlord's statutory lien is paramount to the merchants lien so the merchant in taking his mortgage on a tenant's crop knows that his paper is subject to any debts which the tenant may owe his landlord and it behoves the merchant to find out to what extent the tenant will become indebted to his landlord before he allows him to get to heavily in debt. Very few landlords, in fact I do not know of one, who will become security to the merchants on a renters debt, though they do sometimes where a tenant is a cropper working on shares under the direct supervision of his landlord or his agent.

Trusting I have answered fully the questions you have asked, and assuring you it is a pleasure to do so, I am,

Yours very truly,
/s/ Jno Dozier Pou

81 And the World Passed On

The situation of blacks in 1900 offered little hope; indeed things seemed only to get worse. While Lewis H. Blair could preach the benefits of the market, that market ground down black and white people alike. While the prospects of interracial cooperation for black and white workers and farmers surfaced occasionally, the forces operating to effect a fragmentation or division of the work force by lines of race, job, and locale proved more powerful. While both merchant and landlord depended upon black labor to a substantial degree and competed for the fruits of his labor, ultimately the black man paid. The plethora of forces at work in the demoralizing and debilitating process of social change came together in the concrete reality described by Du Bois in his journey through Dougherty County, Georgia.

Source: W.E.B. Du Bois, *The Souls of Black Folk* (Chicago, 1903), pp. 126-34.

It is a beautiful land, this Dougherty, west of Flint. The forests are wonderful, the solemn pines have disappeared, and this is the "Oakey Woods," with its wealth of hickories, beeches, oaks and palmettos. But a pall of debt hangs over the beautiful land; the merchants are in debt to the wholesalers, the planters are in debt to the merchants, the tenants owe the planters, and laborers bow and bend beneath the burden of it all. Here and there a man has raised his head above these murky waters. We passed one fenced stock-farm with grass and grazing cattle, that looked very homelike after endless corn and cotton. Here and there are black freeholders: there is the gaunt dull-black Jackson, with his hundred acres. "I says, 'Look up! If you don't look up you can't get up,' " remarks Jackson, philosophically. And he's gotten up. Dark Carter's neat barns would do credit to New England. His master helped him to get a start, but when the black man died last fall the master's sons immediately laid claim to the estate. "And them white folks will get it, too," said my yellow gossip.

I turn from these well-tended acres with a comfortable feeling that the Negro is rising. Even then, however, the fields, as we proceed, begin to redden and the trees disappear. Rows of old cabins appear filled with renters and laborers,— cheerless, bare, and dirty, for the most part, although here and there the very age and decay makes the scene picturesque. A young black fellow greets us. He is twenty-two, and just married. Until last year he had good luck renting; then cotton fell, and the sheriff seized and sold all he had. So he moved here, where the rent is higher, the land poorer, and the owner inflexible; he rents a forty-dollar mule for twenty dollars a year. Poor lad!—a slave at twenty-two. This plantation, owned now by a foreigner, was a part of the famous Bolten estate. After the war it was for many years worked by gangs of Negro convicts,— and black convicts then were even more plentiful than now; it was a way of making Negroes work, and the question of guilt was a minor one. Hard tales of cruelty and mistreatment of the chained freemen are told, but the county authorities were deaf until the free-labor market was nearly ruined by wholesale migration. Then they took the convicts from the plantations, but not until one of the fairest regions of the "Oakey Woods" had been ruined and ravished into a red waste, out of which only a Yankee or an immigrant could squeeze more blood from debt-cursed tenants.

No wonder that Luke Black, slow, dull, and discouraged, shuffles to our carriage and talks hopelessly. Why should he strive? Every year finds him deeper in debt. How strange that Georgia, the world-heralded refuge of poor debtors, should bind her own to sloth and misfortune as ruthlessly as ever England did! The poor land groans with its birthpains, and brings forth scarcely a hundred pounds of cotton to the acre, where fifty years ago it yielded eight times as much. Of this meagre yield the tenant pays from a quarter to a third in rent, and most of the rest in interest on food and supplies bought on credit. Twenty years yonder sunken-cheeked, old black man has labored under that system, and now, turned day-laborer, is supporting his wife and boarding himself on his wages of a dollar and a half a week, received only part of the year.

The Bolton convict farm formerly included the neighboring plantation. Here it was that the convicts were lodged in the great log prison still standing. A dismal place it still remains, with rows of ugly huts filled with surly ignorant tenants. "What rents do you pay here?" I inquired. "I don't know,—what is it, Sam?" "All we make," answered Sam. It is a depressing place,—bare, unshaded, with no charm of past association, only a memory of forced human toil,—now, then, and before the war. They are not happy, these black men whom we meet throughout this region. There is little of the joyous abandon and playfulness which we are wont to associate with the plantation Negro. At best, the natural good-nature is edged with complaint or has changed into sullenness and gloom. And now and then it blazes forth in veiled but hot anger. I remember one big red-eyed black whom we met by the roadside. Forty-five years he had labored on this farm, beginning with nothing, and still having nothing. To be sure, he had given four children a common-school training, and perhaps if the new fence-law had not allowed unfenced crops in West Dougherty he might have raised a little stock and kept ahead. As it is, he is hopelessly in debt, disappointed, and embittered. He stopped us to inquire after the black boy in Albany, whom it was said a policeman had shot and killed for loud talking on the sidewalk. And then he said slowly: "Let a white man touch me, and he dies; I don't boast this,—I don't say it around loud, or before the children,—but I mean it. I've seen them whip my father and my old mother in them cotton-rows till the blood ran; by—" and we passed on.

Now Sears, whom we met next lolling under the chubby oak-trees, was of quite different fibre. Happy?—Well, yes; he laughed and flipped pebbles, and thought the world was as it was. He had worked here twelve years and had nothing but a mortgaged mule. Children? Yes, seven; but they hadn't been to school this year,—couldn't afford books and clothes, and couldn't spare their work. There go part of them to the fields now,—three big boys astride mules, and a strapping girl with bare brown legs. Careless ignorance and laziness here, fierce hate and vindictiveness there;—these are the extremes of the Negro problem which we met that day, and we scarce knew which we preferred.

Here and there we meet distinct characters quite out of the ordinary. One came out of a piece of newly cleared ground, making a wide detour to avoid the snakes. He was an old, hollow-cheeked man, with a drawn and characterful brown face. He had a sort of self-contained quaintness and rough humor impossible to describe; a certain cynical earnestness that puzzled one. "The niggers were jealous of me over on the other place," he said, "and so me and the old woman begged this piece of woods, and I cleared it up myself. Made nothing for two years, but I reckon I've got a crop now." The cotton looked tall and rich, and we praised it. He curtsied low, and then bowed almost to the ground, with an imperturbable gravity that seemed almost suspicious. Then he continued, "My mule died last week,"—a calamity in this land equal to a devastating fire in town,—"but a white man loaned me another." Then he added, eyeing us, "Oh, I gets along with white folks." We turned the conversation. "Bears? deer?" he answered, "well, I should say there were," and he let fly a string of brave oaths, as he told hunting-tales of the swamp. We left him standing still in the middle of the road looking after us, and yet apparently not noticing us.

The Whistle place, which includes his bit of land, was bought soon after the war by an English syndicate, the "Dixie Cotton and Corn Company." A marvellous deal of style their factor put on, with his servants and coach-and-six; so much so that the concern soon landed in inextricable bankruptcy. Nobody lives in the old house now, but a man comes each winter out of the North and collects his high rents. I know not which are the more touching,—such old empty houses, or the homes of the masters' sons. Sad and bitter tales lie hidden back of those white doors,—tales of poverty, of struggle, of disappointment. A revolution such as that of '63 is a terrible thing; they that rose rich in the morning often slept in paupers' beds. Beggars and vulgar speculators rose to rule over them, and their children went astray. See yonder sad-colored house, with its cabins and fences and glad crops! It is not glad within; last month the prodigal son of the struggling father wrote home from the city for money. Money! Where was it to come from? And so the son rose in the night and killed his baby, and killed his wife, and shot himself dead. And the world passed on.

I remember wheeling around a bend in the road beside a graceful bit of forest and a singing brook. A long low house faced us, with porch and flying pillars, great oaken door, and a broad lawn shining in the evening sun. But the window-panes were gone, the pillars were worm-eaten, and the mossgrown roof was falling in. Half curiously I peered through the unhinged door, and saw where, on the wall across the hall, was written in once gay letters a faded "Welcome."

Quite a contrast to the southwestern part of Dougherty County is the north-west. Soberly timbered in oak and pine, it has none of that half-tropical luxu-riance of the southwest. Then, too, there are fewer signs of a romantic past, and more of systematic modern land-grabbing and money-getting. White people are more in evidence here, and farmer and hired labor replace to some extent the absentee landlord and rack-rented tenant. The crops have neither the lux-uriance of the richer land nor the signs of neglect so often seen, and there were fences and meadows here and there. Most of this land was poor, and beneath the notice of the slave-baron, before the war. Since then his poor relations and foreign immigrants have seized it. The returns of the farmer are too small to allow much for wages, and yet he will not sell off small farms. There is the Negro Sanford; he has worked fourteen years as overseer on the Ladson place, and "paid out enough for fertilizers to have bought a farm," but the owner will not sell off a few acres.

Two children—a boy and a girl—are hoeing sturdily in the fields on the farm where Corliss works. He is smooth-faced and brown, and is fencing up his pigs. He used to run a successful cotton-gin, but the Cotton Seed Oil Trust has forced the price of ginning so low that he says it hardly pays him. He points out a stately old house over the way as the home of "Pa Willis." We eagerly ride over, for "Pa Willis" was the tall and powerful black Moses who led the Negroes for a generation, and led them well. He was a Baptist preacher, and when he died, two thousand black people followed him to the grave; and now they preach his funeral sermon each year. His widow lives here,—a weazened, sharp-featured little woman, who curtsied quaintly as we greeted her. Further on lives Jack Delson, the most prosperous Negro farmer in the county. It is a joy to meet him,—a great broad-shouldered, handsome black man, intelligent and jovial. Six hundred and fifty acres he owns, and has eleven black tenants. A neat and tidy home nestled in a flower-garden, and a little store stands beside it.

We pass the Munson place, where a plucky white widow is renting and struggling; and the eleven hundred acres of the Sennet plantation, with its Negro overseer. Then the character of the farms begins to change. Nearly all the lands belong to Russian Jews; the overseers are white, and the cabins are bare board-houses scattered here and there. The rents are high, and day-laborers and "con-tract" hands abound. It is a keen, hard struggle for living here, and few have time to talk. Tired with the long ride, we gladly drive into Gillonsville. It is a silent cluster of farm-houses standing on the crossroads, with one of its stores closed and the other kept by a Negro preacher. They tell great tales of busy times at Gillonsville before all the railroads came to Albany; now it is chiefly a memory. Riding down the street, we stop at the preacher's and seat ourselves before the door. It was one of those scenes one cannot soon forget:—a wide, low, little house, whose motherly roof reached over and sheltered a snug little porch. There we sat, after the long hot drive, drinking cool water,—the talkative little storekeeper who is my daily companion; the silent old black woman patching pantaloons and saying never a word; the ragged picture of helpless misfortune who called in just to see the preacher; and finally the neat matronly preacher's wife, plump, yellow, and intelligent. "Own land?" said the wife; "well, only this house." Then she added quietly, "We did buy seven hundred acres up yonder, and paid for it; but they cheated us out of it. Sells was the owner." "Sells!" echoed the ragged misfortune, who was leaning against the balustrade and listening, "he's a regular cheat. I worked for him thirty-seven days this spring, and he paid me in cardboard checks which were to be cashed at the end of the month. But he never cashed them,—kept putting me off. Then the sheriff came and took my mule and corn and furniture—" "Furniture?" I asked; "but furniture is exempt from seizure by law." "Well, he took it just the same," said the hardfaced man.

82 The Servant Question and a Restless Spirit

From the circumstances in the countryside generated by the new system of agriculture and the accompanying despair, one hopeful sign was the migration to a place where presumably labor might be in greater demand. Although many would no doubt experience the frustrations that led to the migrant son's request for money from his already depressed father in Du Bois' account (Document 81), the hope for many would not be dimmed so easily. And such hopes fueled a steadily increasing drive to the North where, it was believed, the demand for servants or more optimistically, industrial workers, would provide a better life. This feature, combined with the passing of the generations accustomed to the obsequiousness required during slavery, created for prosperous white families in the South what was known as the servant problem. The available servants, the lament predictably ran, expected too much and gave too little. Orra Langhorne, who wrote regularly her "Southern Sketches" for the Hampton Institute's *Southern Workman*, addressed this problem in a way that revealed not only her own racial views and her own social biases favoring the market as a solution to the problem it appears that the market created, but also the complete domination of the South's elite and white "friends" of the Negro by the values and institutions of the market. The market had created a situation of potential advantage to whites who inculcate the notions of self-reliance in their children and of potential advantage to blacks by providing "the best opportunity ever offered poor and struggling people for employment," but somehow the gains of the system remained obscure. Moreover, that the industrial schools should teach the necessary skills of the servant and thereby be as Langhorne termed them "the best hope at present," appears a dubious solution if the goal is that of servitude modeled along ante-bellum patterns or cultivation of the race's "natural" gift of amiable qualities and manners.

Source: Orra Langhorne, "Southern Sketches," *Southern Workman,* 19 (October 1890), 102.

Many complaints are made of the rude and boisterous manners of the servants, particularly of the young generation. Most of the older colored people, who grew up in slavery, were carefully trained by their owners, and are noted for their pleasant and respectful manners.

The ex-slaveholders are probably more exacting, especially on the point of manners, and feel the discomfort of rude and irregular service more than any other people on earth would do, because under the former dispensation, to which the white southron will always look back as "the good old times," such things as changing servants, except in case of death or pecuniary disaster, were almost unknown.

The slaves of a well-ordered household were apt to be slow, as neither they nor their owners, felt the need of hurry, which is the prevailing idea in modern life; but they were well trained and efficient in their several departments, and almost universally well mannered.

One of the indispensable things in the old system was to require obsequious respect from the slave to his owner, from every Negro to every white man. In these days of transition, "we have changed all that."

The average Negro seems to feel that he cannot fully realize his freedom unless he has reversed all the habits of slavery. It is quite natural that people recently released from bondage should throw off the obsequiousness of the slave, but it is unfortunate for all concerned that they should go to the other extreme. The Negro is endowed by nature with amiable qualities and the "gift and grace of manners," and it will prove a great loss to the race if they do not cultivate this gift.

It was once thought that the local attachments of the Negro were so strong that one could not be persuaded to leave his birthplace, but in these latter days a spirit of unrest seems to pervade the colored people. The children of slave parents who were, perhaps, never out of sight of the plantation where they first saw the light, wander from place to place as if compelled to follow the policeman's injunctions to "poor Jo" or "move on."

One of my friends has recently had in her service the daughter of an old slave who has lived in Washington, Pittsburgh, and sundry other cities North and West. She came back to Virginia last winter, as she stated, on account of her health, though her appearance is very robust. Since her return she has lived in various families of her native village, then went to the Springs, and will probably continue her perigrinations in the fall, carrying comfort in her services and discomfort in her methods wherever she goes.

With all these disturbances in domestic relations, it is natural that great changes should gradually be taking place in Southern society. The tendency with the colored people is to go North or West, or if they stay in the South, to collect in the towns.

In my native county of Rockingham there were, in 1860, 4,000 slaves and a large number of free Negroes. Now, in some of the country districts, the colored people have almost disappeared. At one point, where a few years ago Lucy Simms, a Hampton graduate taught a colored school, only one or two Negroes can be found within a radius of several miles. A Presbyterian minister accustomed to colored servants, who received a call to a church in this district recently, was advised by a friend to decline the call on account of the impossibility of procuring servants in the neighborhood.

The change is not without advantages for the white people, as the children are learning self-reliance and usefulness to a degree that would have seemed incomprehensible to the parents in ante-bellum days.

While at Dr. Ruffner's house I asked his opinion, as I have asked that of many other wise and thoughtful people, in regard to the "servant question" of to-day. The doctor thinks, as many other people do, that the whole system now in vogue must be changed before a satisfactory adjustment of the subject is reached. In the almost universal complaint of white people about colored servants, it was pleasant to hear the doctor speak of a Negro man who has been constantly employed on his place for twenty-five years, and has always proved himself honest, faithful and reliable.

As I have given some of the grievances of white employers, justice requires me to say, that I think the colored women who go into service, often have grievances on their side to complain of. Wages are very low in the South in comparison with the North and West, and it's not only natural and right that people who work for small pay should want to go where they can earn more. This accounts a great extent for the restlessness of the Negroes. A colored girl who was brisk, cheerful and efficient was employed in a family near me last Winter at $4 per month. Her sister in Philadelphia was earning $4 a week. The latter sent money to pay her youngest sister's fare North, having engaged service for her in a nice family. This had quite an unsettling effect upon servants here, and as such cases are constantly occurring there is a steady drain of colored people from Virginia, which must soon count perceptibly in raising wages. It will doubtless result also in many families who cannot pay high wages, learning to do without servants, and the advent of the "char-woman" of English life, may confidently be expected.

The hours which household servants are expected to devote to their employers are very long, often from five or six o'clock a.m. until ten o'clock, or even later, at night. A great many Southern housekeepers, particularly in the towns, make no arrangements for their servants to sleep under the roof where they labor. Many young girls go to their working places at dawn, and long after dark are wending their way to the house which they call home. This home is but too often a den, where Negroes of both sexes and all ages crowd together, and it is impossible to foster delicacy and preserve morality.

Everybody in the South is ready to talk about the terrible morals of Negro women, but how many Southern mistresses trouble themselves to see that the girls who toil for them have proper protection outside of the employer's house?

I heard a lady here say not long since, "Bad as the Negroes are, I prefer them always to white servants. Why, if I were to employ a white cook, I should have to give her a nice a room to sleep in as the rest of the family have. We should have to alter all our arrangements to suit her. I dare say she would expect an 'evening out' once a week, as the Yankee help do." I could but think that if a colored woman were treated with this sort of consideration, there might be a great advance among them in the direction of virtue.

This question of immorality among the colored women is a very serious one indeed, involving important changes in the laws of the State, as well as in the habits of the family life.

That the discomforts and difficulties of householders, who depend on colored servants are very great at this time cannot be denied, but I believe very great improvements could be made by concerted and patient efforts from all interested. Under our old system the Negroes were the best servants in the world, and strong affection, with the constant exercise of mutual kindness, existed between white and colored people. With a proper disposition to adapt themselves to the great change which has transformed the slave into a citizen, there is no reason that the efficiency of colored servants and mutual kindly relations should not be again the order of the day.

The best hope at present seems to be in the training schools for cooking, etc., which are fast growing in popularity in other parts of the country. If the old adage of the demand creating the supply be true, they must soon be introduced here. Lynchburgh is an excellent place for such a school. Half the population of the town is colored, and while there are many thrifty and prosperous Negroes, there is a large proportion who are extremely poor, and when the tobacco factories are not working, they often suffer greatly. In this class are many young girls, who, with proper training, would no doubt make excellent household servants. I have often wished that some of the Hand fund could be obtained for the establishment of a school here, where these young girls could be trained to efficiency as cooks, laundresses, etc.

I believe many benefits would be derived by both employers and employees, if a regular contract were made when a colored girl enters service.

In such a contract the employer should be required to pay reasonable wages, at the time they are due, and not keep the servant employed beyond a reasonable hour at night, should furnish a comfortable sleeping apartment, etc.

The employee should give faithful service, be held responsible for all household articles in her hands and should consent to have the amount deducted from her wages if she fails to work during the hours contracted for by her employer. Each party should be required to give due notice if they wish to part.

* * *

Southern housekeepers have at their doors abundant material to make efficient and faithful servants. The colored people have the best opportunity ever offered poor and struggling people for employment, which, if justice is done on both sides, can be made mutually helpful. It is to be hoped that both classes will see the advantages to be gained by kindness and patient effort.

83 Disfranchising Via the Law

At the end of the nineteenth century the process of disfranchisement assumed a different shape as a variety of legal techniques became available for restricting the vote to white people. These included the white primary, the poll tax, and the literacy test. In the following selection the individual given the responsibility of registering voters recounts his role in that process in his own district of North Carolina. The vehicle for achieving disfranchisement there was the literacy test. As he makes clear, this was merely a pretense since actual literacy counted for virtually nothing in the determination of the right to vote. Of course, as a saving measure for the illiterate whites of the area, they could vote since their grandfathers had been able to vote. The disfranchisement would last through much of the twentieth century. In 1932 when this registrar spoke, he boasted that only two blacks voted in his district. Their grandfathers had been free before the Civil War.

Source: Tom E. Terrill and Jerrold Hirsch, eds., *Such as Us: Southern Voices of the Thirties* (Chapel Hill, 1978), pp. 262-63. Copyright 1978 The University of North Carolina Press.

I can say this: this township has never gone against a candidate I supported! We have about 340 voters, with 700 in the whole township. For over thirty years I've conducted elections in the township, startin' back yonder in 1902. In 1900 I was a Red Shirt; that was what they called us, though we didn't actually wear red shirts as they did in some sections. But the legislature had fixed it so we could disfranchise the nigger, and we aimed to tote our part in gettin' it done. Judge Farmer organized the county; they was about thirty-five of us around here that called ourselves Red Shirts. Up to 1900 the niggers had rushed in to register whether or no, and with control of the vote they had put in nigger officeholders all over the county. They wa'n't but one white family in the county that could get a office under the nigger rule of the time, and that was Dr. Hughes's. Dr. Hughes was so good to all the pore folks, goin' when they sent for him and not chargin' 'em a cent, that they'd give him anything he asked for. When the registration book was opened in 1900, the Red Shirts was ordered to get their rifles and shotguns and protect the registration from the niggers. When the word come to me, I remember I was in the field plowin'. I got my gun and hurried out to where the rest of the Red Shirts was assembled with shotguns.

Word come that the federal authorities was comin' to protect the nigger vote; if they had, it would o' meant war. We wa'n't totin' shotguns just for show. Well, the upshot was not a nigger come nigh the registration book that day, from sunrise to sunset. Nigger rule was over!

Two years after, when I first took hold o' registerin' voters, a right smart o' niggers come to register at first, claimin' they could meet the requirements. Some wrote the Constitution, I reckon, as good as a lot o' white men, but I'd find somethin' unsatisfactory, maybe an i not dotted or a t not crossed, enough for me to disqualify 'em. The law said 'satisfactory to the registrar.' A few could get by the grandfather clause, for they was some free niggers before the Civil War, but they couldn't get by an undotted i or a uncrossed t. They wa'n't no Republicans in the South before the Civil War; the free niggers always voted like their old masters told 'em to—and 'twa'n't Republican! That's what the war was fought over, politics; they didn't care so much about freein' the slaves as they did the Republican party.

A few years after we disfranchised the nigger, they was a great excitement down Butler Road slam to Allport. The niggers commenced to hold meetin's in the woods, and the report got out that they was fixin' to rise. You couldn't hardly travel the roads for niggers afoot, in carts, and on wagons, goin' to the woods. We found out about the meetin's through two white niggers who went to the woods along with the crowd—a nigger'll join anything, you know—and was voted out o' the meetin'. The leader, a colored feller by the name o' Henley from Allport, said these two was too white, that they didn't want no white blood in their organization. So the white niggers come to me and told me to warn the white folks to be on the lookout, for somethin' was up 'mongst the niggers; they also got their colored preacher to try to calm down his folks and persuade 'em out o' their plot to try to get back the vote. White folks down our way was mighty upset. Some gathered in neighbors' houses for protection. Henry Tyler and his boys set on their front porch all night long with their guns on their laps. It ruint Lambeth, it scared him so bad that for two years he was crazy. If you talk to him long enough now, you'll find out he ain't right. Me? I never lost a minute's sleep!

Henley was arrested, but they couldn't seem to get enough evidence to convict him. The judge twisted the law around some way so Henley could be convicted of tryin' to interfere with the law, and he got five years in the pen. I never heard no more o' Henley round here. We found out it was a white scalawag that stirred the niggers up.

84 The Darkness and the Horror of the Present Situation

Whether conceived as a frontier system of justice to take the place of established authority or as the outgrowth of "mob-psychology," the lynching of blacks left a particular mark on the South. The meaning of that mark, beyond the gory trail of blood, however, is difficult to establish. Clearly, as the following account suggests, justice—in the sense of punishment (not to mention rehabilitation) of the offender—was not a major consideration. For here, even when the crowd knew that it had the wrong persons it went ahead with its deadly plan. The crowd even knew that the real culprit would go unidentified and unpunished because of its determination for immediate blood. The retribution was simply an action that emphasized caste and race more than individual merits or deserts. Indeed, throughout the discussion and course of events individual distinctions mattered little. The division over the fate of the victims, whether to let the processes of the law take their course or to let the crowd have its way immediately, appears to have been based on social and political prominence, with those identified with the establishment favoring the legal routes while the crowd seems to have consisted mainly of more reckless young farmers with only a few of the "maturer and more conservative" citizens among their number. The lack of an individualistic set of perceptions can be seen also in the justification developed by even the critics of lynching; when the allegation involved an affront to or rape of a white woman lynching appears to have been nearly universally approved. No matter which woman, no matter which black, no matter what the circumstances or evidence, a black would have to die. To do otherwise would have the white women of the South, it was said, "at the mercy of the lustful brutes." As it was, the women would be only at the mercy of the white men, whether conceived as protection or subjugation. It may be that in this the real basis and origin of lynching can be detected. As Levell indicated, "Lynching is resorted to not merely to wreak vengeance but to terrorize the Negro." It was first and foremost an important and powerful element of a system of social control. The target of the lynching was not the unfortunate victim of the crowd but all blacks. They were put on warning that their race made them vulnerable to serious reprisal at the whim of the white community. So too was it a warning to whites, especially white women, that their friendly actions or gestures toward blacks could spell doom for the blacks. Thus the lynching served to generate a fear among blacks and unity among whites. But two other points made by Levell in his article suggest that it also generated unity among blacks in a counterproductive way. Criminality among blacks, he noted, made individual heroes in the black community and the black man pursued, regardless of his offense, could find sanctuary among others of his race, "even the best of them." It was not simply that the system of laws and established justice did not work; they worked, rather, to opposite ends, to individualizing the situation when popular attitudes focused upon caste and collectivity and to allowing the possibility of freedom for an innocent black man (or, as in this case, a black woman and her daughter and son). That possibility could not be permitted without completely undermining social attitudes and structures built up over long generations. Indeed, it is entirely a possibility that lynching emerged, with these characteristics, precisely in response to the forces of market, law, and polity which were undermining that caste society in which white men and white women and black men and black women occupied distinctive and separate realms by virtue of their genes alone.

Source: William Hayne Levell, "On Lynching in the South," *The Outlook*, 69 (November 16, 1901), 731-33.

Last summer I happened to be spending my vacation at "Cotesworth," the old country home of the late United States Senator George, about two miles from the town of Carrollton, Miss. During the time I was there I heard one day that on the night previous two defenseless old people had been done to death in a most foul and brutal fashion, and that because of it the people of the county were coming into town, and there was like to be a lynching of several negroes who were suspected of the crime. Never before having been in the immediate neighborhood of a lynching, and wishing to learn something of the character of these repeated outbreaks, I rode into town to study the situation close at hand, hoping that something might occur which would make it possible to prevent any violence. I found that three negroes, a mother with her son and daughter, tenants of the murdered couple, had been arrested on suspicion of having committed the murder or having guilty knowledge of the facts, and were at that time confined in the county jail. I found present on the streets of the town many young farmers from the county who were carrying rifles, shotguns, or pistols, and mixed with them a few of the maturer and more conservative citizens of the county, to whom the young fellows seemed to look for direction. All of them had a serious and determined look upon their faces.

I found also that a committee of prominent men, among them the State Senator from that district, the District Attorney, and a lawyer who had several times represented the county in the Legislature, had been formed and at the hour of my arrival were at the jail examining the negroes. The committee was earnestly solicitous to prevent a lynching. It satisfied itself that those three negroes did not personally commit the crime, but knew who did, and were as yet not willing to reveal their guilty secret. Several times, both individually and as a committee, these gentlemen addressed the mob, trying to dissuade it from violence, and pleading, in the name of humanity and for the good name of the county, to let the law take its course, the more particularly because the only apparent hope of learning who were the real murderers was involved in keeping these three negroes alive. The mob was not to be dissuaded. As the authorities offered practically no resistance, the mob took the negroes, hanged them just outside of town, and riddled their bodies with bullets.

Realizing that it would be regarded as an impertinent intrusion for me to offer any suggestion, since I was an outsider, and knowing that there was no chance for me to do what well-known gentlemen who had the confidence of their neighbors there failed to do, I rode away home some time before the lynching took place.

From what I learned of the whole matter, of the circumstances leading up to the crime, it seemed to be a case particularly demanding that the law should be permitted to take its course. It was not a question of the rape of a white woman by a negro brute. It was the assassination of the aged parents of a young white man who had previously shot to death the son of the negro mother for attempted poison. The young man was out on bail awaiting the action of the Grand Jury. But there was only one way to prevent that lynching. That way was by superior force, and the constituted authorities did not offer it.

In connection with my experience and observation on the day of the lynching, I took care afterwards to discuss the case itself and the whole matter of lynching, as it obtains in the South, with some of the best and maturer and more conservative citizens of that part of the State of Mississippi, to learn whether and how far they approved of lynching for crime. Of course I found some extreme men, who are good citizens in their way, who are yet very nervous over the whole question of the negro and his preponderance in their part of the State, and who assert that for any considerable crime, of whatever nature, committed against a white person by a negro, they would take the law in their own hands and shoot him down as they would a dog. These are extremists.

The greater part of the educated, conservative, thoughtful, and, in ordinary situations, more influential citizens approve of lynching for the rape of a white woman, but deplore the seeming necessity for it, and are groping helplessly in the dark for some way to make lynching unnecessary. They see that it is gradually undermining their civilization, destroying all respect for law, and, with reference to all sorts of offenses, is substituting mob law for the ancient forms which have safeguarded the liberties of the English-speaking peoples for centuries. They contemplate the future with something akin to terror, and confess themselves tied hand and foot to a situation from which it seems impossible to break away without hastening the very thing they fear. They believe that to turn over to the law a black fiend who has raped a defenseless white woman and made over her whole life into a living hell would inevitably tend to multiply rapes and practically put all our women at the mercy of the lustful brutes.

Their explanation of the situation as it is now found in the South may not be entirely satisfactory to the denizens of the cities and the dwellers amidst a predominant white population, but I will try to give it as it was given to me by some of the most conservative, most thoughtful, and most wise citizens of the South.

1. The natural barbarism of our human nature, whose first impulse is to wreak vengeance for an outrage, is to be always considered, for, as a matter of fact, neither individuals nor communities ever get far away from nature—and that is human nature.

2. From the earliest times in the South seduction has always resulted in either what is known as a "military wedding" or a homicide. The community has always supported the family of the seduced woman for killing the seducer if he would not redeem the situation as far as possible by marriage. If that was the result where there was "consent," how much more certainly would homicide be the result where there was force used to accomplish the ruin of a woman— where there was rape? A white man would no more escape than a negro. If the white man must pay with his life for rape, how much more certainly a negro for the rape of a white woman, where in addition the revolt of all the instincts of race was involved?

3. In many if not most rural communities in the South the white population is very small compared with the negro population. The whites are really at the mercy of the blacks, if the latter but once should get the notion that there is a reasonable hope of escape. For there are always enough vicious negroes in every community ready to commit the crimes of lust if they can do so and yet escape justice or vengeance. Lynching is resorted to not merely to wreak vengeance but to terrorize the negro.

4. Every one who handles large bodies of negro laborers—every one with whom I talked—believes that the average negro fears nothing so much as force. The whites believe that the moment the negro ceases to fear the power of the white man crimes will rapidly increase—crimes of the most revolting character. Among the negroes, criminals, when the crime is committed against a white man, attain to a certain heroic character, and are the objects of a certain sort of admiration which they crave and rejoice in. The conviction is general that terror is the only restraining influence with the average negro.

5. The negroes, even the best of them, will ordinarily conceal a fleeing negro, assist him in his flight, and whenever practicable, protect him; and this without regard to the requirements of justice or the character of his offense.

6. The famously slow processes of the law and the frequent miscarriages of justice. In New Orleans a few months ago a negro insulted a refined white woman, was arrested and put upon his trial. The woman put aside her modesty and went on the witness-stand and testified to the facts. The facts were outrageous and cruel. The lawyer for the defense succeeded in deferring the case some months upon a technicality, and later the brute upon conviction got only a three months' sentence. One such case as that does away with the confidence

in the law engendered by a hundred cases where justice is accomplished, and the mind of the people turns to lynching as the only certain remedy.

If you call their attention to the fact that lynching does not stop rape, their answer is, No, but it prevents it more than any other process would do.

The thinking men of the South realize the horror of their situation; they see that mob law is coming to be the law for all sorts of crimes, that it is beginning to be used even in private quarrels and against the whites themselves. They think it is a cruelty to serve them with condemnation, when they need the sympathy and assistance of that portion of our people who live securely amid a predominant white population. It is easy to prescribe practically impossible premises, but you can by such means get no satisfactory or adequate result.

It will need the best wisdom and the best conscience and the best heart of our whole people, of the North and of the South, to lead us out of the darkness and the horror of the present situation.

85 A Savage Ritual

The course of an individual lynching provides some insight into the forces shaping race relations in a particular situation. The collective pattern of lynchings also suggests ways of understanding race relations. In either form of inquiry several components are especially revealing.

First, the frequency of lynchings indicates beyond doubt that the killing of black people was neither isolated nor occasional. Those murders, instead, were systematic and common. Even excluding consideration of the gross homicide evident in actual race riots in major cities in the period, more than 2,500 black people were murdered by groups of white people between 1889 and 1918. Between 1891 and 1895 an average of 127 black people were killed each year, or an average of one homicide or more at least every third day for five years. In 1892 alone 155 black people were put to death, a lynching almost every other day. This was indeed an environment of terror, not just occasional, individualized cases.

Second, while even the detractors of lynching would support the practice when it involved an affront to white women, and while that oft-assumed justification in many circles provided the pretense of legitimacy to the practice, it appears to have been a carefully constructed myth. Less than a third of the *allegations* (not proven charges) involved either rape or insulting a white woman. In a Congressional report inquiring into a proposed anti-lynching bill in 1920, the following charges resulting in lynchings in 1919 alone added up to more than the number of deaths resulting from assault on a white woman: member of Non-Partisan League, talking of Chicago riot, not turning out of road for white boy in auto, leader among Negroes, circulating incendiary literature, misleading mob, intimacy with a white woman, expressing himself too freely re lynching of Negro, causes unknown, and abetting riot. The lynchings were not massive efforts to protect white womanhood. Indeed, in many of the instances the "crime" appears to have been most obscure or something as highly subjective as appearing to a white man as neglecting the required standards of obsequious behavior and deference, or simply being black.

Third, it is again worthy of note that in most instances offenses were simply charged and not proven. Moreover, the system of justice prevalent in the South makes even "convictions" suspect regarding fair trial and sufficient evidence. The notorious lack of indictments and prosecutions of whites involved in lynchings only confirms the heavy bias in the system of justice. Again, the fact that the victim of the lynching was patently innocent of a crime mattered little in numerous instances. In the following accounts a number of blacks lost their lives not in the name of any kind of "justice" but in a frenzy of blood-lust directed at any available black.

It is this savagery that marks the fourth revealing element of the pattern of lynchings. Often revealed below, in accounts selected from a large number compiled by the NAACP, is a level of brutality and sadism that compounds the seriousness of the practice by giving it a pathological character. The burnings of live people attracted crowds not noted for solemnity but marked by a holiday spirit, even accompanied by dancing and singing on occasion. Such a grisly scene should make it clear that such murders are not the exclusive subject for analysis in the framework of due process. The ceremonies were more than vaguely reminiscent of witch burnings of previous centuries. Indeed, the functions may have been remarkably similar. The burning of the witch had served not only justice, in the eyes of the perpetrators, but was the only effective redress against a problem which they were powerless to counter otherwise. Or, in a slightly different vein, Kai Erikson's analysis of the Salem witch prosecutions two centuries earlier indicated that they served to set the behavioral and spiritual limits of the community at a time when older notions of purpose were being undermined by major social changes. Both of these understandings appear relevant to the understanding of lynchings as ceremonies that took on an almost ritualistic complexion. They would normally start with a supposed or believed infraction—the violation by a black of some sacrosanct part of the code of caste obligations—and then move to the quest for a person to be sacrificed, an offering, to redress the grievance. Often it would become that much more virulent if some force or individual happened to frustrate, even slightly or temporarily, the search for a sacrifice. The frustration might come in the form of the law or of the successful escape of the assumed culprit or even the mistake of the crowd itself.

That the "crime" was the violation of the unwritten code of caste suggests further the appropriateness of a larger social analysis. In the years in which lynching was most frequent the pressures upon the social structure of the South were enormous. Whether in the concrete forms of social changes generated by the spread of markets and new relationships generated by the growth of "the New South" or in the more threatening but less tangible promises of people like Lewis Harvie Blair who saw in market relations the possible rise of blacks in a competitive society, the strains on an older pre-market system intensified. It would not be misleading, moreover, to find some of the most intensive pressures exactly within those years 1891-1895 when lynchings were most abundant. In 1892 the Southern white power structure based on a single party received a significant challenge from a third political party that caused a number of whites, though embittered by an unresponsive government, to recoil at the racial implications of the third party and to support the government of their oppressors. Moreover, in those years the severity of the structural changes in society were accentuated by a nationwide depression of unprecedented magnitude. The problem was the transformation of society by overwhelming forces; the solution, all too often, was not to counter those forces of change (which may even have required an acceptance of some of their elements) but to intensify efforts to maintain or to revive the caste system with a deepening commitment exhibited in the barbarous sacrifice of blacks. Such unforgettable experiences could not help but be reminders to blacks of their limitations, but much more to the crowds of white witnesses of the omnipotence of the whites. The irony, therefore, is that whites were not omnipotent. Rather they were victims of social change and market expansion and a colonial system within that market. The South and its farmers, and its poor farmers especially, were in a colonial situation where their power had vanished or was fading in an industrial society and their way of life was being altered to conform to the habits and disciplines of modern society. J. Glenn Gray speaks directly of this phenomenon in his essay, "Understanding Violence Philosophically," when he observes that the frustration of the power of the individual, and possibly of the collective entity as well, to act in a meaningful way and indeed the situation where he can only be acted upon and rendered unfree, gives violence a special appeal. In a very different but equally relevant context, Frantz Fanon, in The Wretched of the Earth, argues that in a colonial situation tribal feuds (of which this may be an example) serve an important function: "by throwing himself with all his force into the vendetta, the [colonialized] native tries to persuade himself that colonialism does not exist, that everything is going on as before, that history continues." In other instances Fanon notes that: "At the level of individuals, violence is a cleansing force. It frees the native from his inferiority complex and from his despair and inaction; it makes him fearless and restores his self-respect." As Fanon wrote in defense of black revolution against white power, the logic in understanding lynchings should not be mistaken for a defense of them. The lynchings were frequent and brutal. The allegations were often trivial. Many victims were never proven guilty. The tragedy was, however, that even when the crowd lynched a person who may have been guilty of a crime, the attack was misdirected; they killed the wrong person—not the one who generated social problems but the one who was conveniently at hand.

Source: National Association for the Advancement of Colored People, *Thirty Years of Lynching in the United States, 1889-1918* (New York, 1919), pp. 12-16, 18-24, 26-27.

Georgia, 1899

Sam Hose, a Negro farm laborer, was accused of murdering his employer in a quarrel over wages. He escaped. Several days later, while he was being hunted unsuccessfully, the charge was added that he raped his employer's wife. He confessed the murder, but refused, even under duress, to confess the other crime.

The following account of the lynching is taken from the New York *Tribune* for April 24, 1899:

"In the presence of nearly 2,000 people, who sent aloft yells of defiance and shouts of joy, Sam Hose (a Negro who committed two of the basest acts known to crime) was burned at the stake in a public road, one and a half miles from here. Before the torch was applied to the pyre, the Negro was deprived of his ears, fingers and other portions of his body with surprising fortitude. Before the body was cool, it was cut to pieces, the bones were crushed into small bits and even the tree upon which the wretch met his fate was torn up and disposed of as souvenirs.

"The Negro's heart was cut in several pieces, as was also his liver. Those unable to obtain the ghastly relics directly, paid more fortunate possessors extravagant sums for them. Small pieces of bone went for 25 cents and a bit of the liver, crisply cooked, for 10 cents."

No indictments were ever found against any of the lynchers.

Louisiana, 1899

A peculiarly horrible affair occurred two days ago at Lindsay, near Jackson, La. Mitchell Curry, hearing that someone was in his cornfield, took two Negroes and went to drive away the intruder. There had been an attempted assault on a white woman by a Negro, Val Bages, and by some unexplained course of reasoning, Mitchell Curry, on seeing a large Negro in the field, became convinced that the man was the criminal.

The fellow took fright, was followed, and finally climbed a magnolia tree. The tree was surrounded and the Negro ordered to remain where he was while one of the pursuers was sent for rope to hang him. Presently, however, the man deliberately slid down out of the tree, and halfway down he was shot to death. On examination of the body the man's clothing marked No. 43, was found to be that worn at the State Insane Asylum in the neighboring town of Jackson. On investigation it was learned that the insane occupant had escaped a few days before and the helpless fellow, wandering at large, had suffered death for a crime he had not committed.

Tennessee, 1901

Ballie Crutchfield, a colored woman, was lynched by a mob at Rome, Tennessee, because her brother stole a purse.

The mob took Crutchfield from the custody of the sheriff, and started with him for the place of execution, when he broke from them and escaped.

"This," says the despatch, "so enraged the mob, that they suspected Crutchfield's sister of being implicated in the theft and last night's work was the culmination of that suspicion."

The Coroner's jury found the ususal verdict that the woman came to her death at the hands of parties unknown.

* * *

Louisiana, 1901

Louis Thomas, at Girard, La., a Negro, broke into a local store and stole six bottles of soda-pop. He was later found by a white man named Brown, disposing of its contents, and on being accused of theft, struck his accuser. Brown procured a rifle and shot the Negro twice through the body, but as neither wound proved fatal, a mob of white men took the Negro from the house where he lay wounded and strung him up.

* * *

Georgia, 1904

For the brutal murder of a white family (the Hodges family) at Statesboro', Georgia, two Negroes, Paul Reed and Will Cato, were burned alive in the presence of a large crowd. They had been duly convicted and sentenced, when the mob broke into the courtroom and carried them away, in spite of the plea of a brother of the murdered man, who was present in the court, that the law be allowed to take its course. None of the lynchers were ever indicted.

* * *

Georgia, 1904

Because of the race prejudice growing out of the Hodges murder by Reed and Cato and their lynching, Albert Roger and his son were lynched at Statesboro', Ga., August 17, for being Negroes. A number of other Negroes were whipped for no other offense.

* * *

Georgia, 1904

On account of the race riots which grew out of the above murder (Hodges) and lynching, McBride, a respectable Negro of Portal, Ga., was beaten, kicked and shot to death for trying to defend his wife, who was confined with a baby, three days old, from a whipping at the hands of a crowd of white men.

* * *

West Virginia, 1912

In Bluefield, W. Va., September 4, 1912, Robert Johnson was lynched for attempted rape. When he was accused he gave an alibi and proved every statement that he made. He was taken before the girl who had been attacked and she failed to identify him. She had previously described very minutely the clothes her assailant wore. When she failed to identify Johnson in the clothes he had, the Bluefield police dressed him to fit the description and again took him before her. This time she screamed on seeing him, "That's the man." Her father had also failed to identify him but now he declared himself positive that he recognized Johnson as the guilty man. Thereupon Johnson was dragged out by a mob, protesting his innocence, and after being severely abused, was hung to a telegraph pole. Later his innocence was conclusively established.

* * *

Texas, 1912

Dan Davis, a Negro, was burned at the stake at Tyler, Texas, for the crime of attempted rape, May 25, 1912.

There was some disappointment in the crowd and criticism of those who had bossed the arrangements, because the fire was so slow in reaching the Negro. It was really only ten minutes after the fire was started that smoking shoe soles and twitching of the Negro's feet indicated that his lower extremities were burning, but the time seemed much longer. The spectators had waited so long to see him tortured that they begrudged the ten minutes before his suffering really began.

The Negro had uttered but few words. When he was led to where he was to be burned he said quite calmly, "I wish some of you gentlemen would be Christian enough to cut my throat," but nobody responded. When the fire started, he screamed "Lord, have mercy on my soul," and that was the last word he spoke, though he was conscious for fully twenty minutes after that. His exhibition of nerve aroused the admiration even of his torturers.

A slight hitch in the proceedings occurred when the Negro was about half burned. His clothing had been stripped off and burned to ashes by the flames and his black body hung nude in the gray dawn light. The flesh had been burned from his legs as high as the knees when it was seen that the wood supply was running short. None of the men or boys were willing to miss an incident of the torture. All feared something of more than usual interest might happen, and it would be embarrassing to admit later on not having seen it on account of being absent after more wood.

Something had to be done, however, and a few men from the edge of the crowd, ran after more dry-goods boxes, and by reason of this "public service" gained standing room in the inner circle after having delivered the fuel. Meanwhile the crowd jeered the dying man and uttered shocking comments suggestive of a cannibalistic spirit. Some danced and sang to testify to their enjoyment of the occasion.

* * *

Oklahoma, 1914

Marie Scott of Wagoner County, a seventeen-year-old Negro girl, was lynched by a mob of white men because her brother killed one of two white men who had assaulted her. She was alone in the house when the men entered, but her screams brought her brother to the rescue. In the fight that ensued one of the white men was killed. The next day the mob came to lynch her brother, but as he had escaped, lynched the girl instead. No one has ever been indicted for this crime.

Index

About the Author
MICHAEL J. CASSITY is a Professor of History at the University of
Wyoming at Casper. He taught previously at the University of Missouri-
Columbia, the University of Kansas, and the University of Georgia. In
1981 he served as Director of the Wyoming Historical Survey at the
University of Wyoming. He is the author of *Chains of Fear: American Race
Relations Since Reconstruction* (Greenwood Press, 1984) and of articles on
American social history that have appeared in the *Journal of American
History*, the *Southwest Review*, *South Atlantic Quarterly*, and a variety of
other journals and magazines.